JIM BLINN'S CORNER
DIRTY PIXELS

The Morgan Kaufmann Series
in Computer Graphics and Geometric Modeling

SERIES EDITOR, BRIAN A. BARSKY

Jim Blinn's Corner: Dirty Pixels
Jim Blinn

Rendering with Radiance: The Art and Science of Lighting Visualization
Greg Ward Larson and Rob Shakespeare

Introduction to Implicit Surfaces
Edited by Jules Bloomenthal

Wavelets for Computer Graphics: Theory and Applications
Eric J. Stollnitz, Tony D. DeRose, and David H. Salesin

Jim Blinn's Corner: A Trip Down the Graphics Pipeline
Jim Blinn

Interactive Curves and Surfaces: A Multimedia Tutorial on CAGD
Alyn Rockwood and Peter Chambers

Principles of Digital Image Synthesis
Andrew S. Glassner

Radiosity & Global Illumination
François X. Sillion and Claude Puech

Knotty: A B-Spline Visualization Program
Jonathan Yen

User Interface Management Systems: Models and Algorithms
Dan R. Olsen, Jr.

Making Them Move: Mechanics, Control, and Animation of Articulated Figures
Edited by Norman I. Badler, Brian A. Barsky, and David Zeltzer

Geometric and Solid Modeling: An Introduction
Christoph M. Hoffmann

An Introduction to Splines for Use in Computer Graphics and Geometric Modeling
Richard H. Bartels, John C. Beatty, and Brian A. Barsky

Jim Blinn's Corner
Dirty Pixels

Jim Blinn
Microsoft Research

MORGAN KAUFMANN PUBLISHERS, INC.
San Francisco, California

Sponsoring Editor *Michael B. Morgan*
Director of Production and Manufacturing *Yonie Overton*
Assistant Production Manager *Julie Pabst*
Assistant Editor *Marilyn Uffner Alan*
Copyeditor *Jennifer McClain*
Text Design *Studio Arno*
Illustration *Windfall Software*
Composition *Technology 'N Typography*
Color Insert Preparation *Side by Side Studios*
Indexer *Ty Koontz*
Cover Design *Ross Carron Design*
Cover Photograph *Christine Alicino*
Printer *Courier Corporation*

Morgan Kaufmann Publishers, Inc.
Editorial and Sales Office
340 Pine Street, Sixth Floor
San Francisco, CA 94104-3205
USA

Telephone 415/392-2665
Facsimile 415/982-2665
Email *mkp@mkp.com*
WWW *http://www.mkp.com*
Order toll free 800/745-7323

Library of Congress Cataloging-in-Publication Data
Blinn, Jim.
        Jim Blinn's corner : dirty pixels / Jim Blinn.
            p.   cm.
        Includes index.
        ISBN 1-55860-455-3 (pbk.)
        1. Computer graphics.   2. Image processing—Digital techniques.
        I. Title.
T385.B586   1998
006.6—dc21   97-44811

Contents

Preface

You hold in your hands the second compilation of articles from my semi-regular column in the *IEEE Computer Graphics and Applications* journal. When Mike Morgan first approached me about collecting these columns into book form, I had accumulated over 40 articles, about two books' worth. I could have just split up the backlog chronologically, but in looking them over I found that the articles fell roughly into two groups, based largely on the connectivity tree of the cross-references between them. I felt that it was better to use this grouping to select which columns went into which book since it makes most of the cross-references between the chapters stay within one volume. The first volume (*A Trip Down the Graphics Pipeline*), then, dealt mostly with geometry and the graphics pipeline. This volume deals mostly with image processing and pixel arithmetic. It contains some of the articles that I am most proud of.

Within both books I have ordered the chapters chronologically. This intermixes the topics somewhat, so here's a grouping of the chapters in *Dirty Pixels* by categories of topics.

Miscellaneous geometric algorithms
- Chapter 1: The World's Largest Easter Egg and What Came Out of It
- Chapter 7: Triage Tables

Signal processing tutorials
- Chapter 2: What We Need Around Here Is More Aliasing
- Chapter 3: Return of the Jaggy
- Chapter 14: What's the Deal with the DCT?

Cubic curve catalog
- Chapter 4: How Many Different Cubic Curves Are There?
- Chapter 6: Cubic Curve Update

Tensor notation and manipulation tools
- Chapter 9: Uppers and Downers, Part I
- Chapter 10: Uppers and Downers, Part II

Implications of fixed-point arithmetic on pixels
- Chapter 5: Dirty Pixels
- Chapter 15: Quantization Error and Dithering
- Chapter 19: Three Wrongs Make a Right

The alpha channel
- Chapter 16: Compositing—Theory
- Chapter 17: "Composting"—Practice
- Chapter 20: Fun with Premultiplied Alpha

Video
- Chapter 8: The Wonderful World of Video
- Chapter 11: The World of Digital Video
- Chapter 13: NTSC: Nice Technology, Super Color

Fun
- Chapter 12: How I Spent My Summer Vacation, 1976
- Chapter 18: How to Attend a SIGGRAPH Conference

Finally, writing this column is a learning experience. Sometimes I learn something before I write about it, and sometimes I learn something while I'm writing about it. And sometimes I learn or discover something new after I've written about it. While gathering together these articles I have had occasion to go over the unanswered questions from past columns and I find that I now have answers to a few of them, as well as other ideas and thoughts. I have woven many of these into the text, but I have supplied others as explicit addenda to a few of the chapters. I believe, therefore, that the term "revised and expanded for book form" can therefore be applied to this collection. Even so, I feel that I have only scratched the surface of the potential of some of the ideas presented here.

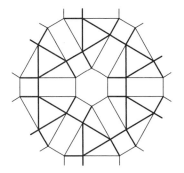

CHAPTER ONE

The World's Largest Easter Egg and What Came Out of It

Since it's almost Easter, I thought I would take this opportunity to write about the world's largest Easter egg. The egg was designed, fabricated, and erected by Ron Resch with the assistance of his student Robert McDermott at the University of Utah. I became involved for a time near the end of the project and learned several interesting lessons in geometric modeling and numerical analysis, which I will pass on here. I will also point out some as-yet-unsolved problems concerning the geometry of some of Resch's dome structures.[1]

The Problem

Why an Easter egg, you might ask? Well, it seems there's a town in Alberta, Canada, just east of Edmonton, named Vegreville, which has a large Ukrainian population. The town fathers wanted to build a monu-

---

1 More details can be found in McDermott's thesis, *Geometric Modeling in Computer Aided Design*, University of Utah Computer Science Department, March 1980 (available from University Microfilms, 300 N. Zeeb Road, Ann Arbor, MI 48106).

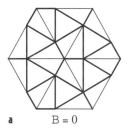

a   B = 0

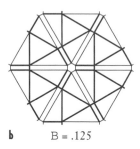

b   B = .125

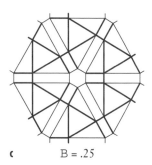

c   B = .25

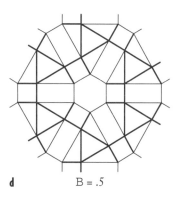

d   B = .5

Figure 1.1 *Basic cell of paper folding pattern*

ment in the local park that would symbolize their culture and bring recognition to the town. The Ukrainians are well known for their very elaborate decoration of Easter eggs, so what better way to commemorate their cultural heritage than to build a permanent, three-story-high, monumental sculpture of an Easter egg! Now, egg builders are not easy to find; yet after months of looking, the town council ultimately became connected with Resch (then a professor at Utah and now an independent consultant), who had been working on novel dome structures.

The problem was how to build not an ellipsoid but an actual replica of a chicken egg on a grand scale—and to do this accurately, decoratively, and (hardest of all) inexpensively. Resch chose not to use a typical longitude and latitude method for defining the geometry, as this method would produce a large number of non-identical parts that would drive up the cost.

Any number of triangulation schemes could be employed to approximate the egg surface, yet these would not preserve modularity. Fortunately, Resch had already been creating and experimenting with the modular tiling of general surfaces in three dimensions with a view toward architectural applications. So he wondered if some of his domes could be adapted to build a complete egg shape. Resch chose to build the egg out of flat aluminum plates. The question then was how to design a pattern of triangles that could be fabricated and connected together to achieve the egg's shape, decorative pattern, and structure while still preserving the constraint of modular tiling.

Paper Folding

The basis for the triangulation method came from Resch's early work in paper folding. In the early sixties, he discovered a set of remarkable ways to fold paper into interesting three-dimensional patterns. The idea was to start with a flat sheet of paper, make only straight-line folds, and make them in a pattern that could be generated by symmetry operations on some simple seed pattern.

The simplest such seed pattern is the hexagonal shape shown in Figure 1.1a. Imagine this pattern repeated over and over again in a bathroom tile sort of arrangement. Then make "mountain folds" on the thick lines and "valley folds" on the thin lines. The resultant sculptural form makes a textured sheet that can be bent around to follow various curved surfaces. Figure 1.2 (Color Plates) shows the sort of thing you might get, bulging up into a kind of dome shape. For reference, the equilateral triangles are colored yellow, and the indented three-pointed star patterns (which Resch, borrowing from architectural nomenclature, called "coffers") are brown. This particular figure was made using six-fold symmetry operating on a unit cell that is a 60-degree pie slice. Using notation for transformations that I defined in *A Trip Down the Graphics Pipeline* (and reprinted in the Appendix), the complete surface is

```
DEF SURFAC
DRAW SURF3
DRAW SURF3, ROT, 120,3
DRAW SURF3, ROT,-120,3
----

DEF SURF3
DRAW SLICE
DRAW SLICE, SCAL,1,-1,1
----
```

I generated the triangles for the primary slice manually for purposes of this illustration, but Resch and Hank Christiansen have written a program to do this automatically.[2]

In the more general case, each triangle edge can fold at a different angle, so you can get many more arbitrary shapes. There are therefore a lot of free variables that control the shape, but it must still essentially be made out of a collection of rigid plates hinged together at their edges. Simulating the general surface might be a good application for the constraint-satisfying sorts of modeling systems coming into vogue nowadays. If anyone out there tries this, let me know the results.

This pattern is a special case of a more interesting class of folding patterns that Resch worked out, illustrated in the rest of Figure 1.1. Each of these seed patterns can be generated by starting with the four-line primitive UNIT shown in Figure 1.3 and drawing it with the above two DEFs and the following:

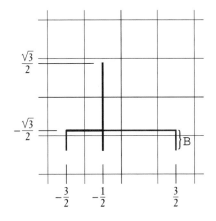

Figure 1.3 *Primitive* UNIT *used to make* SLICE

2   R. D. Resch and H. N. Christiansen, The design and analysis of kinematic folded plate systems, *Proceedings of the Symposium for Folded Plate Structures*, International Association for Shell Structures, Vienna, Austria, October, 1970.

```
DEF SLICE
PUSH
TRAN B*1.73205, B, 0,
TRAN 1.5, .866025, 0,
DRAW UNIT ,
ROT 120, 3,
DRAW UNIT ,
ROT 120, 3,
DRAW UNIT ,
POP
----
```

The parameter B selects the pattern within the range. Again, replicate this pattern over and over in a hexagonal grid, fold down on thick lines and up on thin lines. Resch made physical models of these, but to my knowledge no one has done computer simulations. Someone out there might like to try these also.[3] In fact, there may be other, totally different, types of patterns that, when replicated, make interesting folded structures. Another challenge for you.

Trying to Lay an Egg

The program of Resch and Christiansen just specified some variables for the folding, and simulated whatever surface resulted from the rigid polygon mesh. For a particular set of variables, the vertices of the equilateral triangles will follow some curved surface in three dimensions. As the input variables vary, the sheet flexes, and this surface moves through some class of surfaces. There might be some way of categorizing the set of such surfaces, but this problem also has not as yet been solved.

In order to triangulate an egg with Resch's scheme, you have to solve essentially the reverse problem; i.e., rather than inputting the angles and seeing what surface they generate, try to match the folded plates to approximate an already defined surface. Take a target surface (like an egg) and try to sculpt the folded surface so that the vertices of each equilateral triangle lie on it. Resch and Christiansen expended six months of effort on this, but the sheet just wouldn't conform to the egg shape. This may have been because the egg surface wasn't in the set of surfaces that could be generated by the sheet geometry, or maybe not. It just didn't seem to want to happen.

---

3 More pictures of these shapes and a discussion of their properties appears in Resch's The topological design of sculptural and architectural systems, *Proceedings of the 1973 National Computer Conference*, Volume 42, AFIPS, Reston, Va., pages 643–650.

Ultimately, a modification of the design was chosen to free up the geometry a bit. The coffers were removed, leaving just the equilateral triangles. Then you have to find the locations of only the equilateral triangles and cap the holes off with three-pointed stars made of four triangles each. No new vertices would be created by this; in fact, one (at the bottom of the coffer) would not be needed. Since the coffer region doesn't have to be folded out of a flat sheet, it gives greater flexibility to the positioning of the equilateral triangles.

Now the problem is how to find the locations of the equilateral triangles algorithmically. First, the end of the egg was defined to have the same six-fold symmetry as above, so only one 60-degree slice was necessary. Let us start out by solving the problem in 2D and then work up to 3D.

You can think of the equilateral triangles as hinged together at their common corners. The trick is to play with the hinge angles to make them spread out nicely across the surface. The topological connectivity of the equilateral triangles is shown in Figure 1.4. It is broken into consecutive belts of triangles with the vertices numbered as shown. The bottom point of belt m is point number $2m^2 - m + 1$.

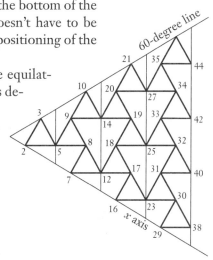

Figure 1.4 *Triangle numbering scheme for egg end caps*

The location of certain key points serves as input to the algorithm, i.e., the ones on the x axis (2, 7, 16, . . .). Then, whenever you have the location of any two points on an equilateral triangle, you have enough information to find the third point. The algorithm below will assume a routine called FIND(I,J,R,K), which takes the coordinates of points I and J, finds the point a distance R from both of them, and stores the result in point K. Now, fixing the locations of the other points is a sort of game of Chinese checkers. Follow along on Figure 1.4 to see how this goes. (Note that's the x axis along the bottom edge, even though it is rotated down by 30 degrees to emphasize the symmetry.) The edge of an equilateral triangle has length R.

Belt 1 (one triangle) goes like this:

1. Input the x coordinate of point 2.
2. Find the location of point 3 as being distance R from point 2 and the fact that it lies on the 60-degree symmetry line. This can be done by mirroring point 2 about the symmetry line and using FIND on 2 and the mirrored 2.
3. Find point 5 from points 2 and 3.

Belt 2 (three triangles) works as follows:

1. Input the x coordinate of point 7.
2. Find 8 from 5 and 7.
3. Find 12 from 8 and 7.
4. Find 9 from 5 and 8.
5. Find 10 from 9 and the symmetry line (i.e., from 9 and mirrored 9).
6. Find 14 from 10 and 9.

Translating all this indexing into pseudo-code gives the following program. We assume the existence of a routine `MIRROR60(I,J)` that mirrors point `I` about the 60-degree line and puts the result in point `J`. Also, since we don't use point 1 for the final shape, it is used as a scratch area in mirroring operations.

```
for M = 1...N
     ILEFT = 2*M*M -3*M+ 3
     IMIDL = 2*M*M - M + 1
     IRITE = 2*M*M + M + 2
     input location of point IMIDL
     repeat M-1 times
         FIND(ILEFT   ,IMIDL   ,R, IMIDL+1)
         FIND(IMIDL+1,IMIDL   ,R, IRITE  )
         FIND(ILEFT   ,IMIDL+1,R, IMIDL+2)
         ILEFT+=2;    IMIDL+=2; IRITE+=2
     MIRROR60 (IMIDL, 1)
     FIND(1        ,IMIDL,R, IMIDL+1)
     FIND(IMIDL+1,IMIDL,R, IRITE  )
```

The locations of the input points were actually given in terms of how far they were from a previous nearby point; for example, the location of 7 is defined in terms of its distance from point 5 and the fact that it is on the x axis. This can be solved using the same mirroring technique as above. Replace

```
input location of point IMIDL
```

with

```
input distance Q between ILEFT and IMIDL
MIRROR0(ILEFT,1 )
FIND(ILEFT,1 , Q, IMIDL)
```

The actual inputs are then the x coordinate of point 2 and a set of distances between points (5, 7), (12, 16), (23, 29), ... Resch spent many days adjusting these numbers interactively to get the nicest looking coverage of the surface.

Now, how do we implement FIND? (See how nice and top down we are being?) Look at Figure 1.5. The desired point is found as follows: Find the distance d between points i and j and find the point midway between them. Start there and move perpendicularly to the i,j line by the distance p where

$$p = \sqrt{(d/2)^2 - R^2}$$

Pseudo-code for this function is

```
FIND(I,J,R,K)
      DX = X(J) - X(I)
      DY = Y(J) - Y(I)
      D2 = DX*DX + DY*DY
      D  = SQRT(D2)
      if D/2 > R   no solution
      P = SQRT(D2/4 - R*R)
      X(K) = (X(I) + X(J))/2 - P*DY/D
      Y(K) = (Y(I) + Y(J))/2 + P*DX/D
```

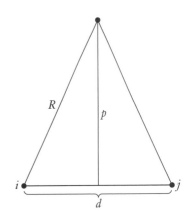

Figure 1.5　*Finding a point a distance R from points i and j*

Since there are two solutions (the positive and negative square root), a convention was made to return the leftmost one as seen looking from point i to point j. Thus the order of the first two parameters to FIND is important. Also note that if the two points are greater than $2R$ apart, there is no solution.

Now let's play with this a bit. It'll soften the blow when we go to three dimensions. Another way to look at this problem is that we are finding the intersections of two circles of radius R centered at the points in question. That means that we are solving the two simultaneous equations

$$(x - x_i)^2 + (y - y_i)^2 = R^2$$
$$(x - x_j)^2 + (y - y_j)^2 = R^2$$

Subtracting these equations gives a linear equation

$$x[2(x_j - x_i)] + y[2(y_j - y_i)] + [x_i^2 + y_i^2 - x_j^2 - y_j^2] = 0$$

This is the equation of the line that is the perpendicular bisector of the i, j line. Remember this; we'll use it later.

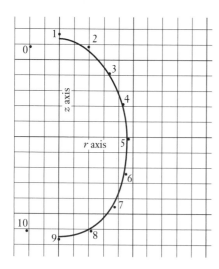

Figure 1.6 *B-spline curve defining the egg shape*

Moving into Three Dimensions

To do this in three dimensions, we just need to generalize the FIND routine to find the x, y, z coordinates that lie on some given surface rather than the flat ($z = 0$) plane we have used so far. ("Just," he says, neatly summarizing six months of arduous toil.) Locating a point in three dimensions requires the intersection of three surfaces. These are the egg itself and two spheres of radius R centered at points i and j.

The egg is defined as a surface of revolution about the z axis. Its cross section is the B-spline curve shown in Figure 1.6 with the control point coordinates shown in Table 1.1.

These control points define two piecewise cubic functions that we will simply call $r(u)$ and $z(u)$, with the parameter u going from 0 to 8 (for the 8 pieces). The entire surface can then be parameterized as

$$x(u, \theta) = r(u)\cos \theta$$
$$u(u, \theta) = r(u)\sin \theta$$
$$z(u, \theta) = z(u)$$

We now have one surface defined parametrically (the egg) and two surfaces defined implicitly (the spheres). This is the ideal situation. Simply plug the parametric equations into the implicit equations

$$(r(u)\cos \theta - x_i)^2 + (r(u)\sin \theta - y_i)^2 + (z(u) - z_i)^2 = R^2$$
$$(r(u)\cos \theta - x_j)^2 + (r(u)\sin \theta - y_j)^2 + (z(u) - z_j)^2 = R^2$$

and merely solve for the (u, θ) values that simultaneously satisfy both equations.

Well (ahem), these are nonlinear equations, so it's probably easier to solve them numerically. Let's use bivariate Newton iteration. This is a very useful generalization of the more familiar univariate Newton iteration, where an approximation to a zero of $f(x)$ is repeatedly improved by the iteration

$$x \leftarrow x - \frac{f(x)}{f'(x)}$$

The bivariate version works like this: You are given two bivariate functions to find the common zeros of, i.e., find a common solution to

Table 1.1 *The control point coordinates of the egg's B-spline curve*

Point number	r	z
0	−3.91176	11.67764
1	0.00000	13.32470
2	3.91176	11.67764
3	6.72824	8.21882
4	8.54330	4.24940
5	9.35694	−0.26352
6	8.98140	−4.80940
7	7.49494	−9.09176
8	4.31858	−12.23764
9	0.00000	−13.32470
10	−4.31858	−12.23764

$$F(u, \theta) = 0$$
$$G(u, \theta) = 0$$

This is done by starting with an initial guess (u_0, θ_0) and improving it by approximating each function by the linear expansion

$$F(u, \theta) \approx F(u_0, \theta_0) + (u - u_0)F_u(u_0, \theta_0) + (\theta - \theta_0)F_\theta(u_0, \theta_0)$$
$$G(u, \theta) \approx G(u_0, \theta_0) + (u - u_0)G_u(u_0, \theta_0) + (\theta - \theta_0)G_\theta(u_0, \theta_0)$$

where the notation F_u denotes the partial derivative of F with respect to u, etc. One step of the iteration then consists of setting these two approximations to zero and solving for u and θ. Working it all out gives the iteration

$$u \leftarrow u - \frac{FG_\theta - F_\theta G}{F_u G_\theta - F_\theta G_u}$$
$$\theta \leftarrow \theta - \frac{F_u G - FG_u}{F_u G_\theta - F_\theta G_u}$$

This all sounded very mystical to me until I came up with a graphical way of thinking of it. We are approximating the F function by a linear function. Imagine this as a plane tangent to the actual function at (u_0, θ_0). This plane intersects the (u, θ) plane in a line. A similar line is generated by the $G = 0$ approximation. We are just finding the intersection of these lines.

It remains only to define F and G. One obvious choice comes from the equations of the spheres

$$F(u, \theta) = (r(u)\cos\theta - x_i)^2 + (r(u)\sin\theta - y_i)^2 + (z(u) - z_i)^2 - R^2$$
$$G(u, \theta) = (r(u)\cos\theta - x_j)^2 + (r(u)\sin\theta - y_j)^2 + (z(u) - z_j)^2 - R^2$$

These would probably work, but actually we did it in a more roundabout way. (What's historical accuracy compared to some post facto cleanups?) Our way was as follows: First, find the three-dimensional locus of all points a given distance from points i and j. It's a circle of radius p, perpendicular to the i,j line, centered at the midpoint between i and j. The radius is the same p we calculated above (but now using the three-dimensional distance d between the points). The plane of the circle has the four-element column vector

$$\begin{bmatrix} 2(x_j - x_i) \\ 2(y_j - y_i) \\ 2(z_j - z_i) \\ x_i^2 + y_i^2 + z_i^2 - x_j^2 - y_j^2 - z_j^2 \end{bmatrix} = \begin{bmatrix} a \\ b \\ c \\ d \end{bmatrix}$$

This is the generalization of the perpendicular bisector we got in the 2D case. So one function we used is the condition that the solution lie on this plane:

$$\tilde{F}(u, \theta) = ar(u)\cos\theta + br(u)\sin\theta + cz(u) + d$$

And the other function measures the difference between the distance to the midpoint and the desired value p:

$$\tilde{G}(u, \theta) = (r(u)\cos\theta - x_{mid})^2 + (r(u)\sin\theta - y_{mid})^2 + (z(u) - z_{mid})^2 - p^2$$

The values and partial derivatives of both these functions can be calculated easily (but carefully, as seen below).

What do we learn from this? When intersecting two functionally defined curved surfaces, the desired intersection will also lie on any surface that is a linear combination of the original functions. For example, with some algebraic fiddling, you can show that

$$\tilde{F} = F - G$$
$$\tilde{G} = F + G$$

In general, by picking the right linear combination, you can usually find a lower-order (linear, in this case) function as one of the two you must intersect. It behooves you to do this if you're evaluating the functions frequently, though in our case the savings were probably not substantial.

Anyway, back to the iteration: To do iteration, you need an initial guess. Anything reasonably close will work as long as it "chooses" the desired one of the two possible solutions. In our case we interpreted the (u_i, θ_i) and (u_j, θ_j) of the two input points as polar coordinates. We converted these to rectangular coordinates, solved the resultant 2D problem, and converted back to polar to get (u_0, θ_0).

Implementation showed an interesting property of this numerical technique—it converged very slowly. After a lot of hacking I finally realized why. We were using a "convenient" version of the SIN and COS routines, ones that accepted arguments in terms of degrees instead of radians. Then, for the derivatives, we were just using COS and -SIN. Sounds reasonable—but wait a minute! The derivative of the sine of an angle *measured in degrees* is *not* the cosine; it's $(360 / 2\pi)$ times the cosine. The iteration was slow because it was taking teeny-weeny steps toward the solution. Fixing this problem made it converge 57 times faster. So we have another fundamental principle:

> *Newton iteration converges fast or not at all. If it seems to be converging slowly, you did something wrong* (except in very perverse cases).

Getting It Together

The entire egg was generated as three pieces of continuous triangulation, the two end caps and a middle barrel section. Compared to the end caps, generating the barrel was simplicity itself. The barrel was composed of "staves" that covered a 10-degree extent in θ. The points were numbered as shown in Figure 1.7. The input to the algorithm was the location of point 1. Then the Chinese checkers game went like this:

1. Find 2 from 1 and symmetry with $\theta = 0$.
2. Find 3 from 1 and 2.
3. Find 4 from 3 and symmetry with $\theta = 0$.
4. Find 5 from 4 and 3.
5. And so on.

Or, in pseudo-code (using point j as a scratch area),

```
for I = 1 to N by 4
    MIRROR0(I,j)
    FIND(I, j, R, I+1)
    FIND(I, I+1, R, I+2)
    MIRROR10(I+2, j)
    FIND(j, I+2, R, I+3)
    FIND(I+3, I+2, R, I+4)
```

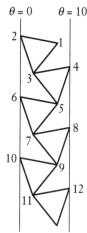

Figure 1.7 *Triangle numbering scheme for barrel staves*

The result was mirrored about $\theta = 0$ to give a 20-degree slice, and then this was replicated 18 times to give the whole barrel.

The whole egg is illustrated in Figure 1.8 (Color Plates). Note the fake shadow (see Chapter 6 in *A Trip Down the Graphics Pipeline*). The gaps between the end caps and the barrel were filled in with some irregular triangles (shown in white) that used vertex points from the two adjacent regions.

Then there was the fabrication. I think it was one of Resch's most impressive achievements of the project that he was able to convince the University Computing Center to let him use their flatbed plotter to fabricate the pieces. He removed the plotter pen and replaced it with a motorized milling tool and replaced the paper with sheets of aluminum. The plotter then carved out the triangles. Each four-triangle star plug was made in one piece with tabs sticking out to fasten to the equilateral triangles. The egg was made at a scale so that an edge of an equilateral triangle was one foot long, making the whole thing almost 30 feet tall.

The actual coloring pattern was designed by Resch and a local artist from Vegreville. It appears in Figure 1.9 (Color Plates). The triangles were anodized in the three colors shown and bolted together. Carving out 3512 pieces of theoretically correct triangles, flying to Canada with them, and just bolting them together took guts, but it worked. A picture of the actual egg sculpture appears in Figure 1.10 (Color Plates).

Unsolved Questions

We have stated above some still unsolved questions.

1. How do you automatically generate the distances so that triangles are "nicely arranged" on an arbitrary surface?
2. How can you characterize the continuum of surfaces achievable by one continuous folding of one of the original flat-plate folding patterns?
3. Is it possible to sculpt such a sheet to any desired surface?
4. How do you, in the general case, simulate the three-dimensional result of a specific two-dimensional folding pattern?
5. Are there any more symmetric folding patterns, perhaps using different symmetry operations than the ones Resch has already found?

This should give you something to chew on until next time. Happy Easter.

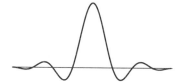

CHAPTER TWO

What We Need Around Here Is More Aliasing

J A N U A R Y   1 9 8 9

Isn't it weird that when you apply for something, you can either "fill in a form" or "fill out a form"? If a chicken is "boned," what about one that's "deboned"? If "flammable" means that something can catch fire, what does "inflammable" mean? If you want to create something out of sheet metal you can "stamp it out." If you want to destroy something, you also "stamp it out." (And some people want to program computers in English!)

Why do I bring this up? I recently attended a product demo of a display system where the demonstrator promised, "We can get rid of the jagged edges by using aliasing." (He was probably in the marketing department.)

I think he meant "antialiasing." I suppose the mere mention of the word in either a positive or negative sense means you are aware of the problem and are doing something about it. Anyway, I thought this would be a good time to give a brief tutorial on what aliasing means, show plots of some relevant functions, describe some of the conventional wisdom about aliasing, and tell why that wisdom may not be so wise.

Some Basic Knowledge

To understand aliasing, you need to start with three basic mathematical concepts: the Fourier transform, convolution, and the convolution theorem.

I want to try to do this in an intuitive way, so I will mostly state results without proving them, and I'll explain things mostly with pictures rather than equations. (Much as I love algebra, this is an area where the algebra seems to make things look more complicated than they really are.) You can get more information from any book on signal processing.[1]

The Fourier Transform

Loosely speaking, the Fourier transform (FT) is a way of representing a function as the sum of a bunch of sine waves of various frequencies. It's as though there were a Twilight Zone version of each function. Normal functions exist in the "spatial domain," while the FT doppelgangers exist in the "frequency domain."

There are actually two numbers to specify each frequency component: an amplitude and a phase offset (or horizontal position). These two are usually encoded as a single complex number. A complete FT plot would then require three dimensions (real and imaginary axes versus frequency) and be a bit confusing, so I will just plot the magnitudes (amplitudes).

If an input picture happens to be symmetric about the origin, the imaginary part of the FT is zero. In this case I will plot the real part of the FT, which may have negative values, instead of the magnitude.

Remember, there's no new information in a Fourier transform; it's just a different way of looking at an existing function.

Convolution

A convolution takes two input functions and generates a third. It is a sort of sliding weighted average of the first function, with the second function providing the weights. Glossing over a few details, it is formed as follows: Multiply the two functions together and integrate the result. Plot this number at 0. Slide the weighting function to the right by x. Multiply and integrate again; plot this number at x. Repeat this for every x you want to plot. Look at the convolutions of Figure 2.1 to get a feel for this.

---

1 My favorite is D. E. Pearson's *Transmission and Display of Pictorial Information* (New York: Halsted Press, 1975).

The Convolution Theorem

Convolutions are interesting because of how they interact with Fourier transforms. Suppose you multiply two functions together to get a new function. What do their FTs look like? It turns out that if you convolve the FTs of the original functions, you get the FT of the new function. Symmetrically, if you convolve two functions to get a third, you can multiply their FTs to get the FT of the third. Multiplication in the spatial domain becomes convolution in the frequency domain and vice versa. It's sort of like logarithms, where multiplication of normal numbers becomes addition in the "logarithm domain." (You remember what logarithms are, don't you? They're what they use to make slide rules.)

What Does This Have to Do with Pictures?

Let's look at the image-making process in just one dimension, along a single 16-pixel scan line. I'll present the story in parallel, with spatial functions in Figure 2.1 and with the FT of these functions in Figure 2.2. The horizontal scales of the FTs are in units of cycles/pixel. The little boxes down the center show how the functions are combined: "×" for multiplication and "C" for convolution.

First, a few things about the production of the pictures. In order to get an approximately continuous plot, I supersampled the functions by 8 times, giving a total of 128 subsamples. This is not an awful lot, so functions that are supposed to be impulses appear as tall, skinny triangular pulses. Also, a straight FT of 128 samples generates amplitudes that are 8 times too big. They have, therefore, all been scaled by one-eighth.

Getting back to the pictures, we start with some continuous intensity as a function of the x position, PICT. It has a sharp edge, some smooth area, and some highly detailed area. Its FT has a spike at frequency 0 (this represents the average intensity over the whole line) and trails off with lower amplitudes for the higher frequencies. Notice the bump in the FT at about 1.6 cycles/pixel that comes from the high-detail region of the original image.

Next, sample the intensity at the center of each pixel. That's tantamount to multiplying PICT by the function COMB, giving SPICT. Remember, multiplying spatial functions implies convolving frequency functions. The FT of COMB happens to be another comb with teeth spaced at 1 cycle/pixel. So, looking at the sampling process in the frequency domain, what we have done is convolve the original FT with a comb function. That's the same as adding together a whole lot of copies of the FT all shifted 1 cycle/pixel apart. Since the original frequency function stretches

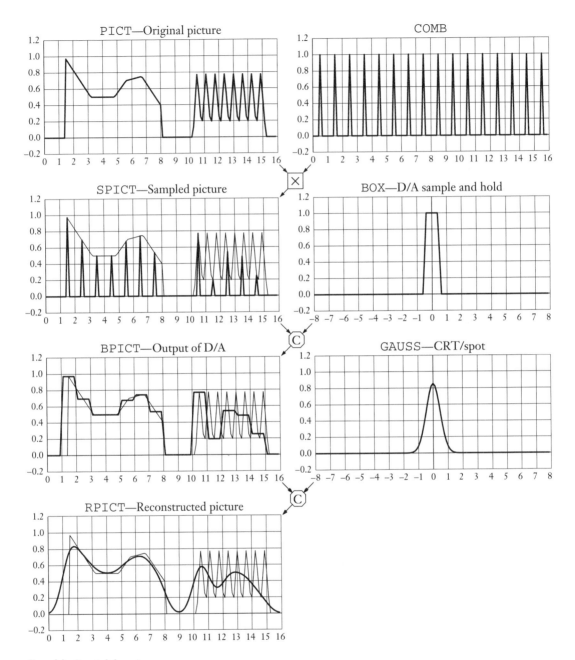

Figure 2.1 *Spatial domain*

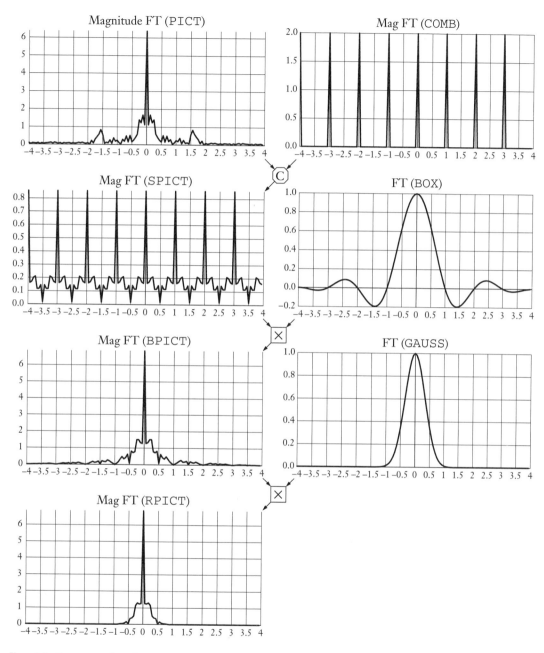

Figure 2.2 *Frequency domain*

quite far in the plus and minus direction, the copies will overlap. This is where "aliasing" comes from. The high frequencies of a shifted copy overlap onto the low frequencies of the central copy. This shows up with the 1.6 cycles/pixel bump producing the little spikes in the FT of SPICT at frequencies of .6, −.4, etc., and the −1.6 bump making spikes at −.6, +.4, etc. Once these have been added in, there is no way to tell them apart from the original amplitudes at .4 and .6. Sampling, then, is essentially an information-destroying process. We started out with unique frequencies across the whole spectrum. Now we have only the region between −.5 and +.5 and several identical copies of it.

Next, we try to display the scan line on a CRT. This process is called *reconstruction*. We pass each pixel value through a D/A converter for the duration of 1 pixel time. This turns the sampled function from a train of spikes into a stairstep function. This can be represented functionally as a convolution of the sampled picture with a box one pixel wide, BOX. (I have plotted the stairsteps centered at the pixels to make it easier to compare with the original picture. Really they should be shifted half a pixel to the right.) The frequency domain interpretation of this is to multiply the sampled FT with the FT of BOX. This shrinks down the extra copies of the spectrum, but there is still a bit of them left. Remember that all the stuff above .5 cycles/pixel and below −.5 cycles/pixel looks like information but isn't. It's just mathematical debris left over from the frequency-replicating sampling process. The frequency .5 is called the Nyquist frequency.

Finally, the spot on the CRT itself has an approximately Gaussian intensity distribution. Stroking across the screen, the electron beam convolves itself with the output of the D/A converter. In the frequency domain, this means multiplication by the FT of the Gaussian (another Gaussian, as it happens).

You can see what damage is done to the picture both in the spatial domain and in the frequency domain by comparing the bottom plot on each side with the top plot. The sharp edges are smoothed over. The high-frequency ripple region has turned into something completely bogus. In the FT the high frequencies have been removed, and there are some extra spikes in the low frequency caused by aliasing.

The Signal Processing Solution

The world of signal processing tells us what to do about aliasing: kill it before it multiplies. Follow along in Figure 2.3 (the spatial domain) and Figure 2.4 (the frequency domain).

Since we can't represent high frequencies accurately, and since they will return to haunt us disguised as low frequencies, we have to get rid of them before sampling. It's obvious how to do this in the frequency domain. Just multiply the FT of the picture by zero for frequencies beyond ±.5 cycles/pixel. What does this translate into in the spatial domain? Convolve the original picture with the inverse FT of a box function—the function $\sin \pi x / \pi x$. This is interesting; we would not have thought of this particular function off the top of our heads. The result is a blurred image whose FT has no frequencies greater than .5 cycles/pixel.

The sampling process then operates as before, but now when we convolve the FT with a comb, we have the happy consequence that the FTs do not overlap. No aliasing occurs because there are no high frequencies to alias.

Actually, the filtering and sampling can be combined into one operation. Since we know we only need the samples at pixel centers, don't bother convolving the LFILT continuously through the picture. Just calculate a weighted average at each pixel center, using LFILT as the weighting function.

Signal processing theory then goes on to tell us that, to reconstruct our best approximation to the original picture, we must remove the extra copies of the FT by convolving with another low-pass filter. Again, obvious in the frequency domain: multiply by a box function to squash out the extra copies. In the spatial domain, this consists of placing copies of LFILT at each pixel, scaled by the sample value, and adding them up.

So . . . simple. The problem is solved. We can all go home now. Or can we?

What's Wrong with This Picture?

Most signal processing was invented to deal with sound or radar signals. But remember, this is computer graphics—it's not supposed to be this easy. And, as usual, the real world doesn't disappoint us in this regard. We will continue this discussion in Chapter 3.

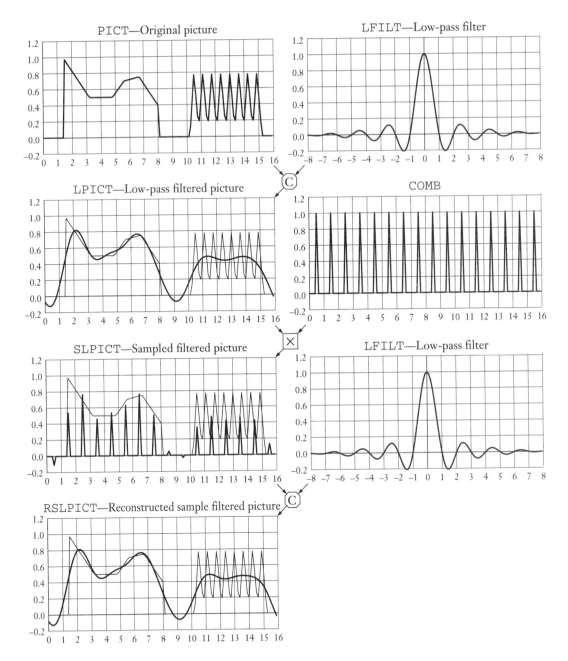

Figure 2.3 *Spatial domain*

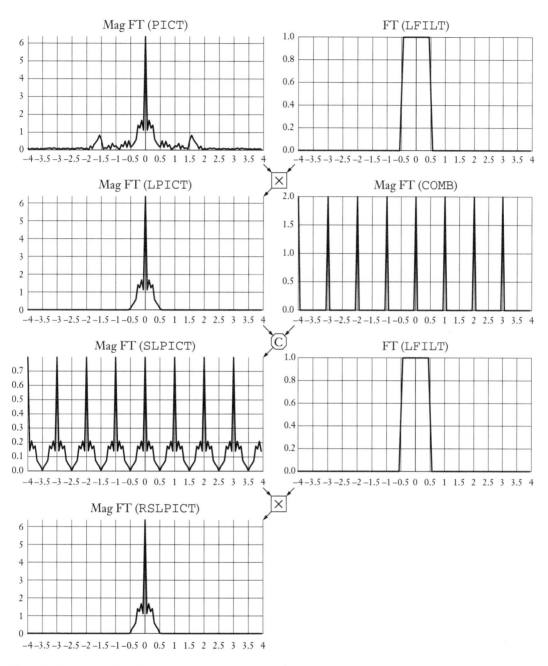

Figure 2.4 *Frequency domain*

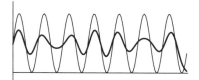

CHAPTER THREE

Return of the Jaggy

In our last episode the evil high frequencies from the Aliasing Empire were sneaking into our image and transforming themselves into deadly Jaggies. Our research labs had come up with a theoretical weapon to defeat the Jaggies. Unfortunately, the purely theoretical solution cannot be used in practice. This time I will discuss why this is so and give some ideas about how close we can come.

To best understand this process, you need some facility for thinking in the frequency domain as well as the spatial domain. So, as with the previous chapter, this chapter will largely be a picture show to help you build your intuition.

Simple Filters

Let's remember the punchline of the theory from Chapter 2.

Before sampling an image you must first filter out the high frequencies. To view (reconstruct) the sampled image, you must interpolate between (i.e., filter) the samples.

Filtering is the same as taking a weighted average of the intensity function. This weighting function is sometimes called an *impulse response* or a *point spread function* (PSF). You center the PSF at a pixel, multiply by the continuous intensity function, and integrate the result. This number becomes the filtered value to display at that pixel.

Let's look at some functions commonly in use and their effects. You can judge the effectiveness of a particular PSF by examining its Fourier transform, so in Figure 3.1 a PSF is on the left and its Fourier transform is on the right. Notice that each PSF is scaled so the total integral under it equals 1. This is done so that filtering a constant-intensity image gives back the same intensity.

The Box Filter

The box filter is the most common function and the easiest to implement; just average the intensities over the area from −.5 to +.5 of the pixel center. When textbooks discuss finding the amount of a pixel covered by an edge, this is the filter they are using. Frank Crow came up with a clever algorithm for implementing this filter.[1] The problem is that the filter is a pretty crummy approximation to what we really want. Its Fourier transform shows that many high frequencies can slip through relatively unscathed. It even hits zero twice as far from the origin as we want (at ±1 instead of ±.5). It also attenuates some nice, friendly frequencies in the range .3 to .5, which produces the visual effect of excessive blurring.

It may be bad (purely coincidentally, it's just the Fourier transform of what we want), but it's better than doing nothing. High frequencies are reduced, low frequencies are kept. I've gotten away with using it for years.

The Triangle or Tent Filter

The triangle or tent filter is the next easiest to implement. Paul Heckbert and Ken Perlin have described clever ways to expand on Crow's technique to implement both this and the following filter.[2,3]

It does introduce a new pragmatic difficulty. Notice that a copy of the PSF centered at one pixel will overlap a copy centered at another. The copy applied to a pixel at the edge of the screen sticks out beyond the screen area. You have to be able to calculate intensities a smidgen outside the screen area to calculate the edge pixels properly.

But how good a filter is it? Use your imagination a bit and you can see that the tent is just the convolution of a box with another box. So, in the frequency domain, the FT is just the square of the FT of the box. (That's why the convolution business is interesting. It allows us to find some nonobvious FT of a function by building it up out of simpler functions.) The FT of the tent is better about getting rid of high frequencies than the box,

1 F. C. Crow, Summed-area tables for texture mapping, *SIGGRAPH '84 Conference Proceedings* (New York: ACM), pages 207–212.

2 P. S. Heckbert, Filtering by repeated integration, *SIGGRAPH '86 Conference Proceedings* (New York: ACM), pages 315–321.

3 K. Perlin, Course notes, in *SIGGRAPH '85 State of the Art in Image Synthesis* (New York: ACM).

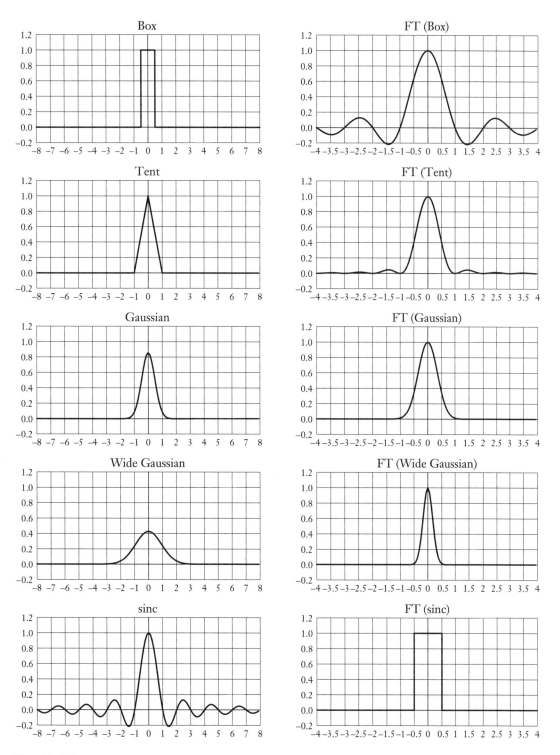

Figure 3.1 *Filters*

but it still hits zero at too high a frequency and attenuates the nice low frequencies.

Gaussian and Similar Shapes

If you convolve a tent with another box, you get a smooth bump made out of three parabolic segments. Convolve with another box and it gets still smoother. Keep doing it and you approximate a Gaussian normal distribution function. How good a filter is it? The FT of a Gaussian is another Gaussian function. The wider the Gaussian for the PSF, the narrower its FT. A pretty wide function gets rid of high frequencies really well, but it also gets rid of nice low ones.

Ideal Filter

The theoretically ideal PSF for both filtering and reconstruction is at the bottom of Figure 3.1. It has the somewhat strange name *sinc* and is defined as

$$\text{sinc } x = \frac{\sin(\pi x)}{\pi x}$$

So why don't we just use this in the first place? Because it's infinitely wide. And you can't just keep the middle part and slam the rest down to zero either. The next section shows why, and what we can do about it.

Building a Nice Filter

For the following, refer to Figure 3.2 (spatial domain) and Figure 3.3 (frequency domain).

Suppose we did just take the middle part out of the sinc function as our PSF. This is the same as multiplying the sinc with a box stretching, say, ±3 pixels around it. In the frequency domain, this implies convolving the ideal box frequency response with $\text{sinc}(3f)$. The middle plot in the left column of Figure 3.3 shows the result. It's all ripply (believe it or not).

To get rid of the ripples in the frequency response, we can do some sort of area averaging (convolution) to the FT. For example, suppose we convolved the ripply FT with a box function that is the width of one cycle of the ripple. This flattens out the ripples fairly nicely. Meanwhile, back in the spatial domain, we have effectively multiplied the original weighting function by $\text{sinc}(x/3)$, giving a nice, usable PSF. This process is called *windowing*. People have used a whole mess of functions for this purpose, with names like Bartlett, Hamming, Hanning, etc. (The one we have used is called a Lanczos window.) They all represent trade-offs between eliminating ripples and rounding off the corners of the desired frequency response.

Our filter keeps low frequencies and rejects high frequencies better than any (achievable) filter we've seen so far. This is largely because of the negative region or *lobe* in the PSF. People who advocate this type of filter are called negative lobists. (Ask people at your next cocktail party whether they are negative lobists and see what happens.)

The FT of this filter is approximately trapezoid shaped, with the sloping sides stretching from frequency $\frac{1}{3}$ to $\frac{2}{3}$. Depending on how paranoid you are about aliasing (see below), you might want to contract it to bring the bottom in to $\frac{1}{2}$. This requires shrinking the FT by $\frac{4}{3}$, which is the same as stretching the impulse response by $\frac{4}{3}$, making it cover 8 pixels. More arithmetic.

Subsampling

It's a real pain to convolve continuous filters with a continuous intensity function. One of the easiest dodges in the antialiasing game is subsampling. You sample the picture at two times or four times the pixel spacing and then average the subsamples together. Our Fourier transform technique lets us see how well this works.

In the top three rows of Figure 3.4, we subsample the picture two times (the calculated samples are half a pixel apart) and take weighted averages. The three weighting functions (also called downsampling filters) are just the box, tent, and NICE filters. The FTs are shown on the right side of the figure. Note that they keep repeating, with a copy of the basic FT at frequencies of 2, 4, 6, 8, etc. This means that, even with the best shape, only about half the alias-producing frequencies are eliminated. But we use a lot less arithmetic than with continuous integration.

There is another trade-off here between the extra arithmetic needed to use the NICE function versus the straight add-and-divide-by-two for the box PSF. Nevertheless, if you are going to go to all the work of calculating subsamples, you may as well make the best use of them by using a nicely shaped downsampling filter.

Now look at the bottom row of Figure 3.4. Here I have plotted the result for a subsampling rate of 4. The effect of higher subsampling rates is to move the copies of the basic FT farther apart. For 4× subsampling they are at 4, 8, 12, etc., cycles per pixel. In general, the shape of the downsampling filter determines the shape of the repeated bumps in the FT. The subsample rate determines the separation distance of the copies.

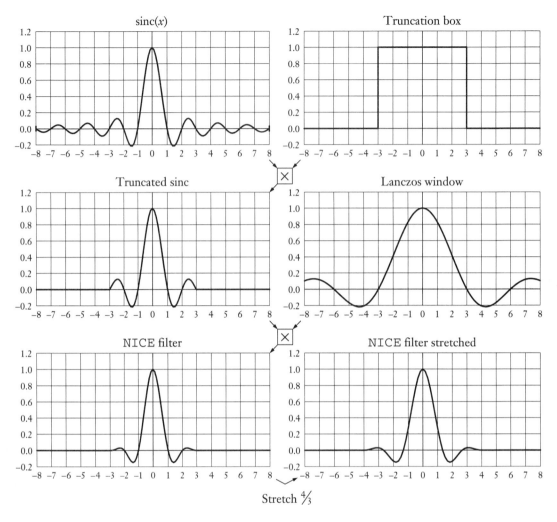

Figure 3.2 *Nice filter (spatial domain)*

The Effect of D/A Converters

Just when we think we have gotten it all figured out, something new comes in to foul things up. Remember what happens when we display our carefully crafted sequence of pixel values. In the theoretical ideal, we convolve the discrete samples with an ideal low-pass filter to turn them back into a continuous signal. You can think of the reconstruction filter as an interpolation technique in this sense.

In the real world we put the samples in a frame buffer, and the hardware sends them to a D/A converter to make the analog signal to send to

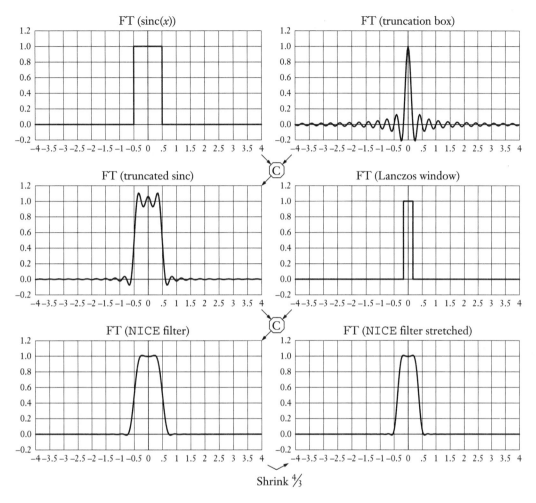

Figure 3.3 *Nice filter (frequency domain)*

the display. The D/A converter holds a particular sample for 1 pixel time and then the next one for 1 pixel time. Thus, it is effectively convolving the samples with a box function. This again is the FT of what we would really like.

As an extreme example of why this causes problems, look at Figures 3.5 and 3.6. We start with a picture of a sine wave of frequency $\frac{7}{16}$ cycles per pixel. This is below the Nyquist rate, so just sampling produces no aliasing. Everything should be fine. But when we reconstruct with the D/A filter, something awful happens. This beat pattern appears out of nowhere. Blurring it with the Gaussian spot helps, but we still get some crud. It's very amusing to put this pattern on your display; in fact, use a frequency of about .49 cycles/pixel to make the effect more obvious.

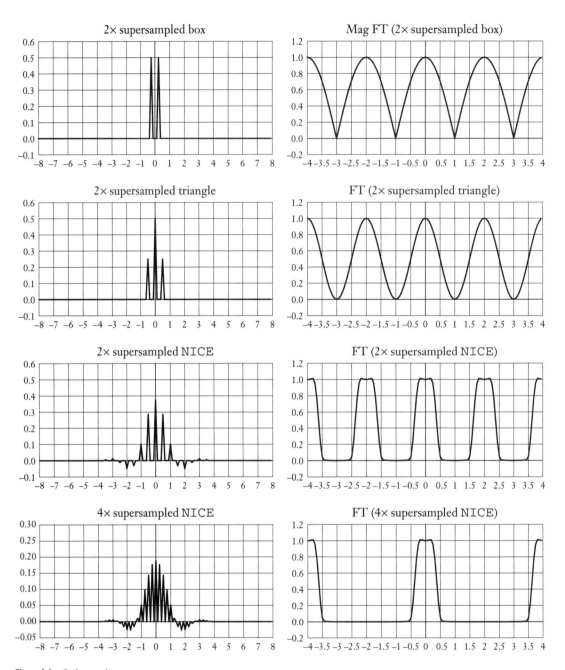

Figure 3.4 *Subsampling*

Why does this happen? Well, the beat pattern comes from the aliases of the $\frac{7}{16}$ cycle-per-pixel frequencies at $\frac{9}{16}$ cycles per pixel. If the reconstruction were perfect (a low-pass filter chopping off at $\frac{8}{16}$ cycles), the $\frac{9}{16}$ cycle portion would be completely eliminated and there would be no problem. With real reconstruction filters, especially Gaussian ones, these too-high frequencies again come back to haunt us.

Here we've gone to all this work to get rid of aliases, and the hardware creates new artifacts out of what we thought were nice, friendly frequencies. One solution is to give up some of the frequencies somewhat below the Nyquist limit by filtering at a somewhat lower frequency than theoretically necessary. (This is another reason for contracting our NICE function by $\frac{1}{3}$.) Then the aliases of the maximum frequencies we keep will be higher and thus farther down the slope of the Gaussian reconstruction filter. Another solution is to modify the display hardware. What should happen (and what does happen on high-quality frame buffers for the broadcast video market) is that a filter contained in the frame buffer corrects for the D/A function. The idea is to design a filter so that the net frequency response of the D/A converter times the filter is close to an ideal low-pass filter. This again means negative lobes. Since computer displays tend to have white, 1-pixel-wide lines on black backgrounds, it might require the production of negative light at some places on the screen.

The Bitter Truth

There is no such thing as full antialiasing. Anyone who tries to tell you differently is trying to sell you something. Any real-world solution to the problem suffers from one or more of the following problems:

- A perfect low-pass filter is not achievable with a finite (or even a reasonably small) PSF.

- The closer you want to come to a perfect low-pass filter (the steeper the sides of the FT), the wider the PSF needs to be and the more arithmetic you have to do.

- There is no such thing as negative light. Any decent approximation to a low-pass filter for either sampling or reconstruction has negative lobes. This might result in a negative pixel value. Clamping them to zero is about all you can do, but it's not ideal.

- Antialiasing requires filtering a continuous function. Subsampling is only a crude approximation to this.

- You have to calculate outside the screen region if the filter PSF is wider than ±.5.

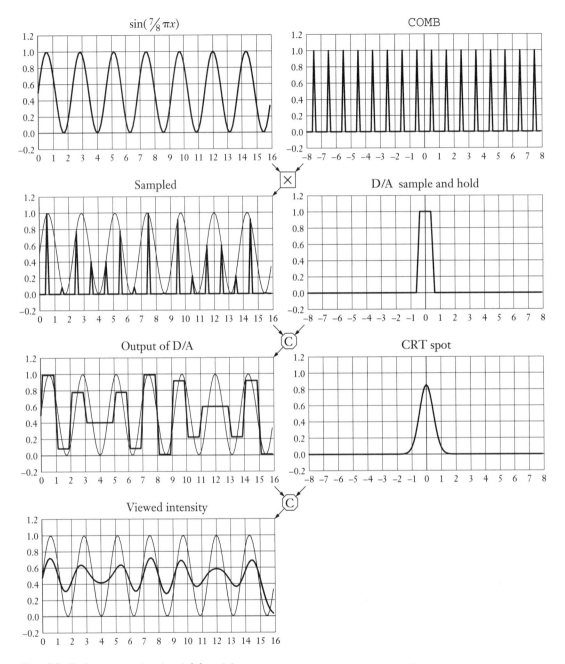

Figure 3.5 *Bad reconstruction (spatial domain)*

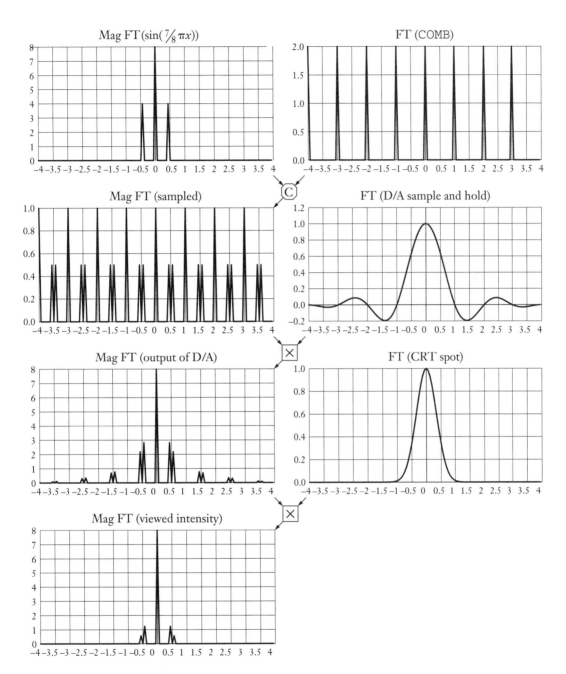

Figure 3.6 *Bad reconstruction (frequency domain)*

- Unless you have a perfect reconstruction filter, your theoretical anti-aliasing efforts cannot achieve their potential. You sometimes must sacrifice some perfectly good, representable frequencies to compensate for imperfect reconstruction, or add special hardware filters to your frame buffer.

- Gamma correction can mess things up too. See Chapter 5 for more on this.

This is a big subject. I haven't even mentioned Cook's stochastic sampling or Kajiya's approximation sampling. Also, I haven't covered the 2D case (complete images) or the 3D case (time).

To build intuition about this, I would recommend that you find or write a program that takes Fourier transforms and play with it. Also, take a look at the *Atlas of Optical Transforms*.[4] This is a whole book of 2D images and their FTs.

---

4 G. Harburn, C. A. Taylor, and T. R. Welberry, *Atlas of Optical Transforms* (Ithaca, N.Y.: Cornell University Press, 1975).

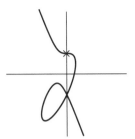

CHAPTER FOUR

How Many Different Cubic Curves Are There?

MAY 1989

Well, I suppose it depends on what you mean by different. In Euclidean geometry, we are used to the idea that all equilateral triangles are the same shape, no matter how they are placed or oriented. Likewise, in projective geometry, an ellipse and a hyperbola are the same shape. In fact, geometry can be described as the study of those properties of a shape that remain unchanged even if it's subjected to some transformation. In this chapter I will deal with two-dimensional homogeneous coordinates, so the transformation is the standard homogeneous projective transformation representable by a 3×3 matrix. Any two shapes that can transform into each other via such a matrix are counted as the same shape. For example, in all the figures in this chapter, the two right-hand curves are the same shape, even though they might not look like it.

As it happens, I haven't found answers to all the questions I have about this subject. Math books don't always seem to answer the questions I am interested in asking. So here's what I have come up with so far, along with a list of questions that I still haven't resolved.

Second-Order Curves

Let's start with something simpler. How many second-order curves are there? It turns out that there are exactly five. Why?

A second-order curve has the equation

$$Ax^2 + 2Bxy + Cy^2$$
$$+ 2Dxw + 2Eyw$$
$$+ Fw^2 = 0$$

All homogeneous points $[x \quad y \quad w]$ that satisfy the equation lie on the curve. The question is, given the universe of possible values of $A...F$, what sorts of different shapes can this equation generate? As you might expect, it can generate conic sections. But all conic sections are really the same shape. Anything else? Remember, two shapes are considered the same if there is some homogeneous transformation (possibly containing perspective) that can change one into another.

To answer the question, I will write the equation as a matrix product

$$[x \ y \ w] \begin{bmatrix} A & B & D \\ B & C & E \\ D & E & F \end{bmatrix} \begin{bmatrix} x \\ y \\ w \end{bmatrix} = 0$$

and invoke several standard results from matrix theory. Let's call the matrix $\mathbf{Q}$. You can transform the curve generated by $\mathbf{Q}$ like this:

$$\mathbf{TQT}^t = \mathbf{Q}'$$

where $\mathbf{T}$ is the inverse of the matrix that transforms points.

Now for the interesting part: it is possible to find a transformation that turns $\mathbf{Q}$ into a diagonal matrix. To convince yourself of this, just consider the eigenvalues and eigenvectors of $\mathbf{Q}$. You remember what those are, don't you? They're values λ_i and vectors V_i such that

$$V_i \mathbf{Q} = \lambda_i V_i$$

Since $\mathbf{Q}$ is symmetric, all the eigenvalues will turn out to be real numbers and all the eigenvectors will be perpendicular to each other. So we can make up the transformation $\mathbf{T}$ by using the eigenvectors scaled to unit length. This will be a pure rotation in 3D, even though we are really thinking of this transformation as a 2D homogeneous transform. Anyway, what we get is

$$\begin{bmatrix} V_1 \\ V_2 \\ V_3 \end{bmatrix} \mathbf{Q} = \begin{bmatrix} \lambda_1 & 0 & 0 \\ 0 & \lambda_2 & 0 \\ 0 & 0 & \lambda_3 \end{bmatrix} \begin{bmatrix} V_1 \\ V_2 \\ V_3 \end{bmatrix}$$

Then just multiply on the right by the inverse of the matrix formed by the column of V's, and you get $\mathbf{Q}$ transformed into a diagonal matrix with the eigenvalues on the diagonal. This is why eigenvectors are so interesting. They allow you to see the essence of a matrix without getting confused by the coordinate system it's in.

We can further simplify this by applying a scaling transformation that will scale the diagonal elements to be +1, −1, or 0. (Notice that you can't change the sign of an eigenvalue even with a mirror transformation, since the transformation is multiplied in twice.) Thus, the only types of second-order curves are those that represent unique combinations of these values on the diagonal. Only one of them generates a true non-degenerate curve; the others are singular and represent such things as the products of two lines. The five possible combinations, along with the eigenvalue signs, are as follows:

+ + −	conic section
+ + +	null curve (no points satisfy equation)
+ + 0	a single point
+ − 0	two intersecting lines
+ 0 0	two coincident lines

Third-Order Curves

Now let's see how we can do this for a cubic equation. The equation for a third-order curve is

$$Ax^3 + 3Bx^2y + 3Cxy^2 + Dy^3$$
$$+ 3Ex^2w + 6Fxyw + 3Gyw^2$$
$$+ 3Hxw^2 + wJyw^2$$
$$x + Kw^3 = 0$$

Given various values for the A's and B's and so forth, what is the zoology of shapes this can generate?

Degenerate Cubics

First of all, let's go through the various degenerate shapes. These are shapes formed when the cubic equation can be factored. This can happen two ways.

First, there are shapes formed if the cubic is factorable into three linear equations. I'll list the possible combinations, along with an example equation for each:

1. three coincident lines; $x^3 = 0$
2. two coincident lines and a third distinct one; $x^2y = 0$

3. three distinct lines that intersect at the same point; $xy(x + y) = 0$
4. three distinct lines that intersect at three distinct points; $xyw = 0$

I won't waste space on pictures of these, use your imagination. Each counts as one shape since it's possible to take any transformed version of the above and transform it into the "standard form" shown. This is not completely trivial but you can figure it out.

Second, there are the shapes formed from a linear term times a second-order term. There are

5. a conic and a line that is disjoint; $(x^2 + y^2 - w^2)(x - \delta w) = 0, \delta > 1$
6. a conic and a line that is tangent to it; $(x^2 + y^2 - w^2)(x - w) = 0$
7. a conic and a line that intersects it; $(x^2 + y^2 - w^2)(x - \delta w), 0 < \delta < 1$
8. a single point and a line that is on the point; $(x^2 + y^2)x = 0$
9. a single point and a line that is not on the point; $(x^2 + y^2)(x - w) = 0$
10. a null curve and a line; $(x^2 + y^2 + w^2)x = 0$

Type 6 is a single shape since we can transform the conic into a unit circle (taking the tangent line with it) and then rotate the tangent line to be, say, $x = 1$. Type 8 is similarly a single shape since we can transform the point to the origin and rotate the line to be vertical. Type 9 is a single shape since we can transform the point to the origin, rotate the line to vertical, and scale the whole thing in x to put it at $x = 1$. Type 10 is a single shape since the line can be transformed anywhere. Types 5 and 7 represent a new regime, however. If we transform the conic to the unit circle and rotate the line to vertical, we will have a continuum of shapes parameterized by the distance from the line to the origin.

Preview

Of course the interesting cubics are the non-degenerate ones. Before we get into these, it will be useful to preview some things that cubics can do that we haven't seen before with lower-order curves.

The most important of these is the inflection point, indicated in Figures 4.1 through 4.5 with an "×". This occurs when the tangent to the curve has the curve lying on both sides of it.

The other interesting thing is the double point, a point of self-intersection, see (Figure 4.5b). We have already sort of seen this in degenerate conics consisting of two intersecting lines.

Some General Formulas

Here are, without justification, some algebraic formulas that apply to any implicitly defined curve.

The line tangent to any curve given by $f(x, y, w) = 0$ is the column vector formed by

$$\begin{bmatrix} f_x \\ f_y \\ f_z \end{bmatrix}$$

where the elements are the partial derivatives of the function f evaluated at the point on the curve where the tangent is desired. If it happens that all three derivatives are zero at a point on the curve, then that point is a double point (e.g., a point of self intersection).

Inflection points can be found by means of an auxiliary curve called the Hessian curve. The equation for this curve is constructed by the determinant

$$\det \begin{bmatrix} f_{xx} & f_{xy} & f_{xw} \\ f_{xy} & f_{yy} & f_{yw} \\ f_{xw} & f_{yw} & f_{ww} \end{bmatrix} = 0$$

where the elements of the matrix are the various second derivatives of the function f. If f is a cubic function, the Hessian will generate another cubic curve. The usefulness of this curve comes from the fact that it intersects the original curve at all double points and at all inflection points.

Thus, we can find double points of f by seeing where all three of the first derivatives are zero, and we can find all inflection points by intersecting the curve with its Hessian and throwing out all the already identified double points. Of course, in a real application this might turn into a lot of algebra, but we will find these equations usable in various special cases.

By the way, if f is a second-order function, the Hessian works out to be a constant, the determinant of the original matrix. If the determinant (Hessian) is zero, it means that the second-order curve is degenerate (lines or a single point).

Standard Position

We can now attempt to find a standard position for a non-degenerate cubic curve that will let us see its geometric properties best. I'm going to be pretty glib about saying what's possible without explicitly telling you how to calculate the transformation. But that's the nature of existence proofs.

First, let's transform the curve so that it passes through the point [0 1 0], the point at infinity on the y axis. Plugging this into the general cubic equation, it means that the coefficient D has to be zero.

Now let's rotate it about that point so that the tangent coincides with the line at infinity, that is, the line $[0\ 0\ 1]^T$. Evaluating the first derivatives at this point, we get

$$\begin{bmatrix} f_x \\ f_y \\ f_w \end{bmatrix} = 3\begin{bmatrix} C \\ D \\ G \end{bmatrix}$$

so we must have $C = 0$ and $G = 0$.

We have to specify that the point we started with was not a double point, or G would be zero. This isn't hard; there are lots of non-double points. But while we're at it, let's arrange it so the point we started with *was* an inflection point. (All non-degenerate cubics have at least one inflection point.) Evaluating the second derivatives at $[0\ 1\ 0]$ and constructing the Hessian gives

$$\det\begin{bmatrix} B & 0 & F \\ 0 & 0 & G \\ F & G & J \end{bmatrix} = -G^2 B$$

so $B = 0$.

What we have said is that *any* non-degenerate cubic can be transformed so that the equation looks like

$$Ax^3$$
$$+\,3Ex^2w + 6Fxyw + 3Gy^2w$$
$$+\,3Hxw^2 + 3Jyw^2$$
$$+\,Kw^3 = 0$$

But we're not done yet. Let's now scale and skew the y coordinate via the transformation

$$y \mapsto -\frac{F}{G}x + y - \frac{J}{2G}w$$

Plug this in, turn the crank, and you will discover that the F and J terms disappear. The result is that all non-degenerate cubics can be transformed into the form

$$y^2w = ax^3 + bx^2w + cxw^2 + dw^3$$

or, in non-homogeneous form (with $X = x/w$ and $Y = y/w$),

$$Y^2 = aX^3 + bX^2 + cX + d$$

That is, the set of possible shapes is constructed by taking the square root of all possible cubic polynomials in X. The parameter a must be non-zero or else we only have a second-order curve.

But this isn't really a four-parameter set of shapes either. We can boil this down still further by translating in x to "center" the cubic polynomial (so that its second derivative is zero at $X = 0$). Then scale in X and Y to make as many terms as possible go away or simplify.

I don't want to wallow in the algebra, so I will briefly outline it and then cut to the chase. The transform is

$$X \mapsto tX - \frac{b}{3a}$$
$$Y \mapsto sY$$

Then pick

$$s = \sqrt{at^3}$$

with the constraint that the sign we will later pick for t is the same as the sign of a. Then our equation becomes

$$Y^2 = X^3 + \left[\frac{3ac - b^2}{3a^2}\right]\frac{1}{t^2}X + \left[\frac{2b^3}{27a^3} - \frac{bc}{3a^2} + \frac{d}{a}\right]\frac{1}{t^3}$$

Now we can break down into some different curves based on what we were given for a, b, c, d.

If it happens that $3ac - b^2 = 0$, the linear term won't be there, and we can pick t to simplify the constant term. There are three cases. The constant term could already be zero. If not, we can pick t to be the cube root of the right-hand thing in square brackets, making the constant term equal 1. But we don't have complete control of t. It has to have the same sign as a. So we might be forced to make t^3 such that the constant term is -1. To summarize, we now have three distinct shapes that have the equations

11. a wiggle; $Y^2 = X^3 + 1$
12. a cusp; $Y^2 = X^3$
13. another wiggle; $Y^2 = X^3 - 1$

These appear in Figures 4.1, 4.2, and 4.3. Note that the three tangents at the three inflection points for type 11 all meet at the same point. The three tangents for type 13 meet at three distinct points.

Some notes about these diagrams and the ones below: The left curve just plots Y^2 for reference. The middle portion plots the curve. Note that the curve only exists for the X extent where Y^2 is positive. But one of the interesting parts of all these curves—an inflection point—is at infinity. For this reason I have also plotted a transformed version of each curve on

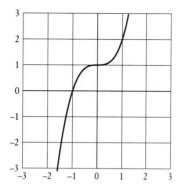

Figure 4.1a $X^3 + 1$

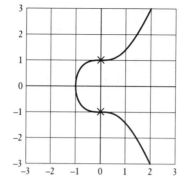

Figure 4.1b $Y^2 = X^3 + 1$

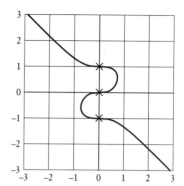

Figure 4.1c $yw^2 = x^3 + y^3$

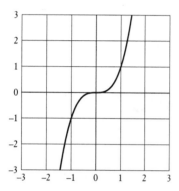

Figure 4.2a $X^3 - 1$

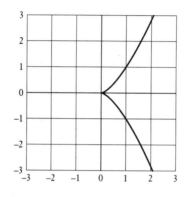

Figure 4.2b $Y^2 = X^3 - 1$

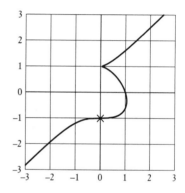

Figure 4.2c $yw^2 = x^3 - y^3$

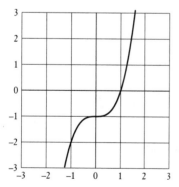

Figure 4.3a X^3

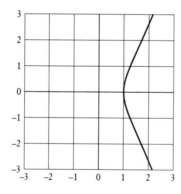

Figure 4.3b $Y^2 = X^3$

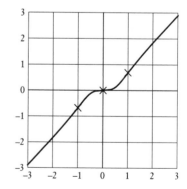

Figure 4.3c $(y - w)^2(y + w) = x^3$

the right. Not all right-hand curves are the same transformation of the original, though. I have selected transformations that keep all interesting points, like inflection points, on the page.

Now let's back up and see what happens if $3ac - b^2 \neq 0$. Then we pick

$$t^2 \left| \frac{3ac - b^2}{3a^2} \right|$$

with the sign of t the same as the sign of a. This makes the linear term's coefficient either $+1$ or -1. The constant term will be some free parameter that we don't have control over. We will call it e. This gives our last two types:

14. a continuum of wiggles; $Y^2 = X^3 + X + e$
15. a whole bunch of weird stuff; $Y^2 = X^3 - X + e$

Type 14 generates a continuum of shapes, parameterized by e. These appear in Figure 4.4, with sample values of e of $+1$, 0, and -1. Type 15 generates a continuum of shapes that can vary radically. The five subcategories (based on ranges of e) are bounded by the critical values $e = \pm 2\sqrt{3}/9 \approx .3849$; I show them graphically in Figure 4.5.

Notice that in all these curves there are two general categories: those with three inflection points, and those with one inflection point and one double point. Also notice that if there are three inflection points, they are always colinear.

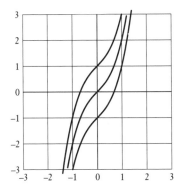

Figure 4.4a $X^3 + X + e$

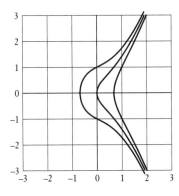

Figure 4.4b $Y^2 = X^3 + X + e$

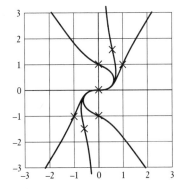

Figure 4.4c $yw^2 = x^3 + xy^2 + ey^3$

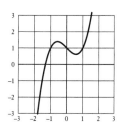

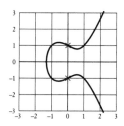

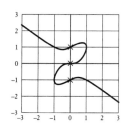

Figure 4.5a $X^3 - X + 1$

$Y^2 = X^3 - X + 1$

$yw^2 = x^3 - xy^2 + y^3$

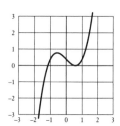

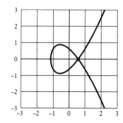

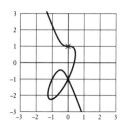

Figure 4.5b $X^3 - X + .3849$

$Y^2 = X^3 - X + .3849$

$(y - w)^2(y + w) = x^3 + x^2(y + w)$

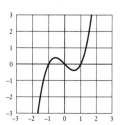

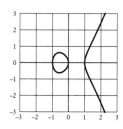

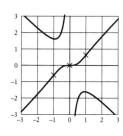

Figure 4.5c $X^3 - X$

$Y^2 = X^3 - X$

$yw^2 = x^3 - xy^2$

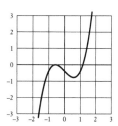

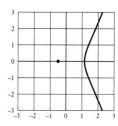

Figure 4.5d $X^3 - X - .3849$

$Y^2 = X^3 - X - .3849$

$(y - w)^2(y + w) = x^3 - x^2(y + w)$

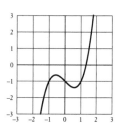

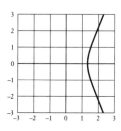

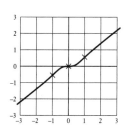

Figure 4.5e $X^3 - X - 1$

$Y^2 = X^3 - X - 1$

$yw^2 = x^3 - xy^2 - y^3$

Nagging Questions

So what still bothers me about this?

1. Is there a foolproof way, given the original coefficients, to find which of these shapes it generates that isn't an algebraic nightmare? Even I have limits on my tolerance for algebra.

2. The form for non-degenerate cubics I have described here is pretty standard, but it has some asymmetries that I am not completely happy with. It doesn't treat all the coordinates in a symmetrical fashion like the one we used for second-order curves. Is there a form that does?

3. It's possible to write the cubic equation as a sort of cubical matrix of coefficients. Sliced up and laid end to end, this would look something like

$$
[x \quad y \quad w] \begin{bmatrix} A & B & E \\ B & C & F \\ E & F & H \end{bmatrix} \begin{bmatrix} x \\ y \\ w \end{bmatrix} x +
$$

$$
[x \quad y \quad w] \begin{bmatrix} B & C & F \\ C & D & G \\ F & G & J \end{bmatrix} \begin{bmatrix} x \\ y \\ w \end{bmatrix} y +
$$

$$
[x \quad y \quad w] \begin{bmatrix} E & F & H \\ F & G & J \\ H & J & K \end{bmatrix} \begin{bmatrix} x \\ y \\ w \end{bmatrix} w = 0
$$

This cube of numbers is really a rank 3 tensor. Is there a theory of eigenvectors for such a beast that would give us the desired symmetric formulation?

4. Some of the curves plotted look suspiciously similar. What geometric property that is preserved under homogeneous perspective transformations makes them different? (Like the thing about the three tangents for types 11 and 13.) I think it has something to do with cross ratios. . . .

Oops

There is a mistake in this chapter. After it was published as a column, the mistake was pointed out by an alert reader. This prompted me to write the column that became Chapter 6 of this book. See if you can figure it out before you get to Chapter 6.

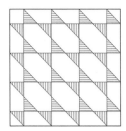

CHAPTER FIVE

Dirty Pixels

JULY 1989

I once saw a quotation hanging from someone's wall that went something like

> *Doing arithmetic with floating-point numbers is like moving piles of sand. Each time you do it, you lose a little sand and pick up a little dirt.*

If that's true for floating point, it's especially true for scaled integers. Since pixels must be given to display hardware as scaled integer values, this leads to several ways dirt can creep in. In this chapter I'll talk about two of them.

Integer Pixels

Let's start with something simple. We'll pretend that all pixel calculations are done in floating point, yielding a number between 0.0 and 1.0 as the desired intensity to display at that pixel. Now, a typical display stores a pixel as an 8-bit quantity, with a value from 0 to 255. How do we encode the desired intensity, which we'll call D, into an integer pixel value, which we'll call I? The most straightforward way is to scale the range (0.0–1.0) to the range (0–255) and pick the closest integer. This gives the formula

$$I = \text{int}(D \times 255. + .5)$$

The int function takes the integer part of a floating-point number. We must add .5 to round this to the nearest integer.

To show how errors can creep in, I'm going to plot some graphs in Figures 5.1 through 5.4. But I'm pulling a fast one for visualization (God, I love that word) purposes; even though I've written all the formulas with

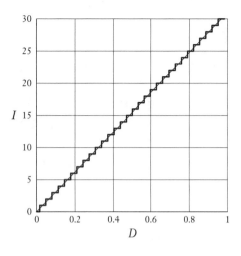

Figure 5.1 *Quantization error*

the number 255, I've generated the figures using a maximum pixel value of 31 (5 bits) to make the effects stand out better.

Anyway, the integerization process generates what is known as roundoff error. To show what it looks like, I have plotted D against I in Figure 5.1. Ideally we would want a straight line; what we get is stairsteps.

Gamma

The display hardware takes the 8-bit value and changes it into a proportional voltage to send to the monitor. The voltage is

$$V = I / 255.$$

Life gets more complicated when the monitor gets ahold of the voltage. The problem is that the intensity or brightness a monitor displays is not simply proportional to the voltage it sees. The actual result is something more like

$$B = aV^\gamma.$$

The brightness and contrast knobs effectively control the values of α and γ, but not in the way you might expect. Brightness controls γ and contrast controls α. Strange but true. The value of γ therefore varies, but in the monitors I have measured, it ranges between 1 and 3, with 2 a good average value. (You see some standard values mentioned in the literature like 2.4 or 2.7, but that doesn't change the net effect—it's not 1. I'll use $\gamma = 2$ from here on.)

The displayed intensity, normalized to a maximum value of 1.0, is

$$B = (I / 255.)^\gamma$$

Just feeding the pixels to the display results in the highly undesirable intensity response shown in Figure 5.2. It's a tribute to the human perceptual system that a picture displayed like this still looks recognizable, just dark and contrasty.

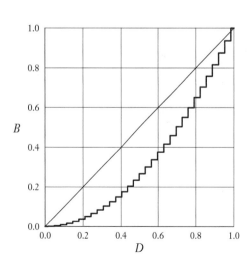

Figure 5.2 *Effect of gamma*

Gamma Correction

To fix this problem, we need to precorrect for the mangulation performed by the monitor. The most common approach is to use another hardware feature, the color map or color lookup table. This is an extra 256-word memory slapped on to the back end of the display. Each pixel value is used as an address into this memory; the memory contents are what are actually sent to the D/A converters. To correct for the gamma distortion, we just set up the table as an inverse gamma function. For example, a typical color map word has 8 bits, so its contents would be set up as

$$M_I = \text{int}\big((I\,/\,255.)^{1/\gamma} \times 255. + .5\big)$$

This integerization produces still more round-off error. The net result of starting with a *desired* intensity D, encoding it as an 8-bit number, passing it through the color map, and feeding the resultant voltage to the monitor is the *actual* intensity B plotted in Figure 5.3. It's sort of linear, but on closer inspection it really looks kind of ratty. Why?

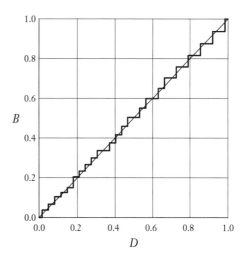

Figure 5.3 *Gamma correction with 8-bit color map*

Why I Don't Like This

Here is an important fact about the color map process. You typically have an 8-bit pixel in and only 8 bits out of the color map. So if you have *anything* other than an identity transformation in the color map, you are losing information.

For example, let's look at the first and last few entries in the color map for $\gamma = 2$. In Table 5.1, the middle column shows the floating-point value of $(i\,/\,255)^{1/\gamma} \times 255$ before it's rounded to the integer value M_I. Notice that, at the low end, the available hardware intensity levels from 1 through 15 can never be generated. Also, on the high end, every pair of frame buffer values maps to the same hardware intensity. In fact, this table constricts us to use only 194 out of the 256 possible hardware intensity levels. What a waste.

Table 5.1 *8-bit gamma correction lookup table*

I	$(I/255)^{1/\gamma} \times 255$	M_I
0	0.0000	0
1	15.9687	16
2	22.5832	23
3	27.6586	28
4	31.9374	32
…	…	…
251	252.9921	253
252	253.4956	253
253	253.9980	254
254	254.4995	254
255	255.0000	255

Cooperation

We can do better. We have the technology. We just cooperate with the hardware.

First, put an identity transform in the color map. Then encode D directly into that pixel value that generates the closest available hardware intensity. One (slow) way to do this is to use the formula

$$\tilde{I} = \text{int}(D^{1/\gamma} \times 255. + .5)$$

(The tilde indicates a pixel value that has gamma "burned into" it.) The net result of this non-linear encoding is the function in Figure 5.4— much less spastic.

The fact that the breakpoints between integer pixel values are not evenly spaced has another salutary effect. The bins get smaller and smaller as the value of D gets close to 0. This is good, since that's where we would like more resolution in intensity. It gives somewhat the same result as logarithmic quantization (which is used in high-quality film scanner output). I should have done this for my early space flyby movies since my pixels only had 32 intensity levels, but that little bit of optimization just fell between the cracks.

Anyway, the formula evaluation is a bit slow, so

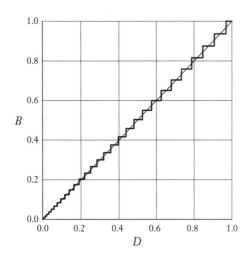

Figure 5.4 *Ideal non-linear quantization*

for a while I implemented it by a big table lookup. I scaled D by the length of the table and used the integer part as the table index. The table entries are only 1 byte long, so I figured I could afford a table that had 4096 entries. But even that's not really enough; the table lookup still lost resolution near the bottom. Pixel values 1, 2, 3, and 5 could never be generated. Table 5.2 shows a sample; again, the middle column is the floating-point value before being rounded into an integer byte I.

There is a better, but devious, way. To get there, let's first solve the inverse problem.

Getting Pixels Back

Suppose we want to combine a calculated image with an existing one in a frame buffer. Translating a pixel value into its effective intensity for some later arithmetic processing can best be done by table lookup too. There are, after all, only 256 possible pixel values, so the table isn't too big. The table contains the function

$$T_{\tilde{I}} = D = (I / 255.)^{\gamma}$$

The first and last few entries look like Table 5.3.

Encoding Pixels

Now we can reexamine the pixel encoding process as an inverse table lookup. Given a desired intensity value, we just find the table entry that is closest to it and use its slot number as the pixel value.

The transition points where a given value changes from being closer to pixel value $\tilde{I} - 1$ to being closer to pixel value I is the value midway between $T_{\tilde{I}-1}$ and $T_{\tilde{I}}$. So, first make an auxiliary table with entries

$$A_{\tilde{I}} = (T_{\tilde{I}-1} + T_{\tilde{I}}) / 2$$

and use the following very streamlined binary search cribbed from *Programming Pearls* by Jon Bentley (a really good book).[1] We start with floating-point value D and end with pixel value I.

Table 5.2 *High-resolution gamma correction table*

D*4096	$D^{1/\gamma} \times 255$	I
0	0.000000	0
1	3.984375	4
2	5.634757	6
3	6.901140	7
4	7.968750	8
5	8.909333	9
6	9.759686	10
7	10.541670	11
8	11.269510	11
...	...	...

Table 5.3 *DAC value to intensity*

$\tilde{I}$	$T_{\tilde{I}}$
0	.00000000
1	.00001538
2	.00006151
3	.00013841
4	.00024606
...	...
252	.97660900
253	.98437520
254	.99217220
255	1.00000000

---

1 Reading, Mass.: Addison-Wesley, 1986, page 87.

```
I = 0
if D > A(128)    then I = 128
if D > A(I + 64) then I = I + 64
if D > A(I + 32) then I = I + 32
if D > A(I + 16) then I = I + 16
if D > A(I + 8)  then I = I + 8
if D > A(I + 4)  then I = I + 4
if D > A(I + 2)  then I = I + 2
if D > A(I + 1)  then I = I + 1
```

Note that, as a trivial result of this algorithm, the pixel value is clamped between 0 and 255 (i.e., overflow is automatically handled). You can also do logarithmic quantization with this technique if you want, just by changing the entries in the table.

Now this *is* a bit slower than the table lookup, but it's a lot more accurate. I've found that its execution time is overshadowed by the time it takes a typical nontrivial rendering program to come up with a value for *D* for a given pixel anyway. But still, 8 floating-point comparisons per pixel encode is a bit much, which leads us to phase two of this discussion.

Scaled Integers

And now for something (almost) completely different. I've been talking so far as though the desired pixel intensity, *D*, is a floating-point number. And for me it has been, up until recently. When I graduated from a PDP-9 to a PDP-11 with floating-point hardware, I resolved to never again use scaled integer arithmetic. But now that I'm using PC clones, I'm getting back into it. And when you think about it, floating point is a bit of overkill anyway. I mean, how accurate do you need to be if you're just going to pack the value into 8 bits?

So, suppose we are going to represent our desired intensity as a 16-bit scaled integer. What should the scale factor be? It will be useful to have a representation of 1.0 that is an exact power of 2. It will also be useful to have the integer range small enough so that you don't have to worry about overflow into the sign bit. This all points to a scale factor of 16384. To convert from a floating point *D* to a scaled integer called *J*, use

$$J = \text{int}(D \times 16384. + .5)$$

A value of 1.0 is represented by the hexadecimal value 4000; the binary point is 2 bits in from the left end of the word. Most fractional numbers fit cozily into the low 14 bits. It seems, though, like you are throwing away two possible bits of precision. How bad is this? One way to find out is to look at the scaled integer representations of the available hardware intensities, shown in Table 5.4. These are just the scaled versions of what is in Table 5.3, the lookup table for $J_{\tilde{I}}$. Again, the middle column is the scaled intensity before being rounded into the integer value of $J_{\tilde{I}}$.

We have lost the use of pixel value $\tilde{I} = 1$ since its intensity maps into a J value of 0. But we would need two more bits to get enough resolution to distinguish these bottom two intensities. That means 17 bits (so that 1.0 is represented by hex 10000). Table 5.4 seems as good as we can do in 16 bits.

Anyway, now the encode operation takes eight integer comparisons per pixel encode, fairly reasonable.

How do conventional operations translate into this realm?

Table 5.4 *DAC value to 16-bit scaled intensity*

$\tilde{I}$	$T_{\tilde{I}} \times 16384.$	$J_{\tilde{I}}$
0	0.000	0
1	0.252	0
2	1.008	1
3	2.268	2
4	4.031	4
5	6.299	6
6	9.071	9
7	12.346	12
...	...	...
250	15747.79	15748
251	15874.02	15874
252	16000.76	16001
253	16128.00	16128
254	16255.75	16256
255	16384.00	16384

Addition

Just add:

$$J_{new} = J_1 + J_2$$

Multiplication

When multiplying two scaled integers, you have to remember that each one carries an implicit factor of 16384 along with it. So after you take the product, you have to divide out one of them to get back a result scaled only once by 16384. Since the division effectively gives you some fractional part, you also have to add one half (which corresponds to adding 8192) for rounding before dividing. The formula is

$$J_{new} = \frac{J_1 J_2 + 8192}{16384}$$

Now we see why the factor 16384 is so nice; the division can be done with just an arithmetic shift:

$$J_{new} = \text{ArithShiftRight}(J_1 J_2 + 8192, 14)$$

Lerping

Over the years we computer graphicists have identified the most commonly useful pixel operation as being linear interpolation between two values, known by the picturesque name of *lerp*. This is used in soft-edge matting, rendering transparency, and a lot of other things. In terms of floating-point numbers, the formula is

$$D_{new} = \alpha D_2 + (1-\alpha)D_1$$

A better implementation that avoids a multiplication is

$$D_{new} = D_1 + \alpha(D_2 - D_1)$$

If all these quantities (including α) are encoded as 16-bit integers, we just use our multiplication formula

$$J_{new} = J_1 + \mathrm{ArithShiftRight}(J_\alpha(J_2 - J_1) + 8192, 14)$$

Now, however, there is a subtlety. In this case, you *must* use the shift operation instead of a division. The reason for this is that $J_2 - J_1$ might be negative, and integer division doesn't give the answer we want for negative numbers; e.g., $-16000/16384 = 0$ while $ASR(-16000, 14) = -1$, and -1 happens to be what we need to get the right answer.

Error in Scaled Integers

But what other kinds of error can creep in with these operations? To see what happens, let's first make things more obvious by using a scale factor of 4 instead of 16384. Another way to think of the scaled integer process is that the five possible integer values are tokens for the floating-point ranges given in Table 5.5. (Also look at the number line plot in Figure 5.5.) The nice thing about this tokenization is that ordinary arithmetic on the tokens generates the correct token for the floating-point answer. Sort of.

To see how this can cause errors, I will make three pictures for each operation in Figures 5.6 through 5.8. Each figure has three parts. Part (a) shows what happens when you do the operation in infinite precision and then pack the result into an integer. Part (b) shows what happens when you pack the arguments into integers and do the operation using integer arithmetic. In each case, these are binary operations, so the entire universe of possible arguments is the square between 0.0 and 1.0 (scaled into tokens 0 through 4). The pictures

Table 5.5 *Quantization bins for each token value*

J	D range
0	.000–.125
1	.125–.375
2	375–.625
3	.625–.875
4	.875–1.00

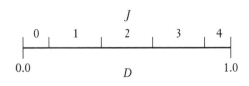

Figure 5.5 *Quantization bins for fixed point scale of 4*

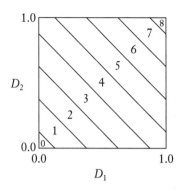
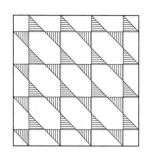

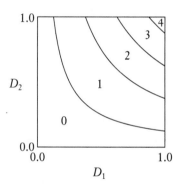
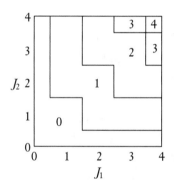
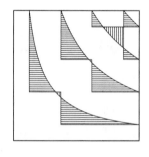

Figure 5.6 *Error regions for addition*

Figure 5.7 *Error regions for multiplication*

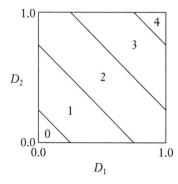
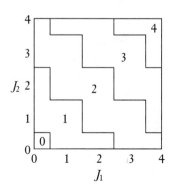
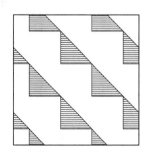

Figure 5.8 *Error regions for lerp with* $\alpha = \frac{1}{2}$

divide the square into regions where the answer is represented by the various integer tokens. We can see trouble spots by overlaying the two plots, as shown in part (c) of each figure.

Addition

In Figure 5.6 the desired answer makes diagonal stripes. The integer version is a checkerboard pattern, just an addition table. Overlaying the two, we see three types of regions: where the answer is correct, where it's too large by one (the dark, vertically shaded regions), and where it's too small by one (the lighter, horizontally shaded regions). We got the right answer 75% of the time; 12.5% we were too high and 12.5% too low. On the whole, statistically, we get some dirt but at least it's not biased as being too much one way or the other.

A note on Figure 5.6d (Color Plates). When my mother saw the original publication of this figure as a line drawing, she was struck by the pattern. Being an excellent quiltmaker as well as sweater knitter, she was inspired to create a quilt with the same pattern. What you see here is a photograph of the quilt.

Multiplication

Now look at Figure 5.7. Here we get the right answer 80.7% of the time, too big 17.8%, too small 1.5%. This looks bad. It seems as though there is a bias toward being too big. But it's really not that bad because, if we use more and more bits, it turns out that the too-small and too-big regions get more and more equal. It's a little hard to calculate exactly, but a Monte Carlo simulation shows that for a scale factor of 16384 the percentages are about 80, 10, and 10.

Lerping

Look at Figure 5.8, which shows lerping with $\alpha = \frac{1}{2}$. Here we have a real problem. It gives the right answer 75% of the time; 25% of the time it's too big, but it's never too small—in other words, it's biased. And it doesn't get better by just using more bits. The proportions stay exactly the same.

When I first wrote this article, I found this very disturbing. I thought it meant that the lerp operation was inherently unstable. But, upon further reflection, I realized that things were not so bad. It turns out that $\frac{1}{2}$ is the *only* value of α that has this problem. Almost all α values generate a perfectly symmetrical diagram as you can see in Figure 5.9, which illustrates the situation for $\alpha = \frac{1}{3}$. Here, we get the right answer $214/256 = 83.6\%$ of the time. The too-high and too-low regions are exactly equal and each represents $21/256 = 8.2\%$ of the time. The problem we had when $\alpha = \frac{1}{2}$ is that half the J_1, J_2 combinations result in a calculation that has an ambiguous rounding. For example, for $J_1 = 1$, $J_2 = 2$ the result is $\frac{1}{2} \times 1 + (1 - \frac{1}{2}) \times 2 = \frac{3}{2}$. We always round this to a value of 2 although half of the D_1, D_2 combinations that generate $J_1 = 1, J_2 = 2$ would give a result that should round to 1. This rounding bias will occur, in general, whenever any of the diagonal quantization threshold lines pass exactly through a point of the J_1, J_2 diagram at integral coordinates. It will, for example, happen to a lesser extent at $\alpha = \frac{1}{4}$. But, in general, the lerp operation is perfectly well behaved for almost all values of α.

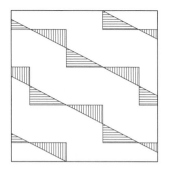

Figure 5.9 *Lerp with $\alpha = \frac{1}{3}$*

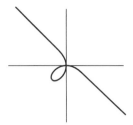

CHAPTER SIX

Cubic Curve Update

N O V E M B E R   1 9 8 9

After writing the column that became Chapter 4 of this book, I received a letter from William Waterhouse of Penn State answering some of the questions raised in that column and pointing out an error. This motivated me to another frenzy of cubic curve experiments, so here's an update.

A Look Back

Remember the problem: We want to catalog all the shapes that can be generated by the cubic equation

$$Ax^3 + 3Bx^2y + 3Cxy^2 + Dy^3$$
$$+ 3Ex^2w + 6Fxyw + 3Gy^2w$$
$$+ 3Hxw^2 + 3Jyw^2$$
$$+ kw^3 = 0$$

Also, remember that any two curves that can be made to match by any homogeneous transformation (possibly containing perspective) count as the same shape.

Degenerate Cubics

First, let's talk about the degenerate curves. Visually, these look like two or more low-order curves drawn on top of each other. Algebraically, it means that the cubic expression can be factored into the product of two or three lower-order expressions.

I listed all the combinations of factorizations that could make degenerate curves, but Waterhouse points out an error in the catalog. The errors are in type 5 (a circle and a disjoint line) and in type 7 (a circle and an intersecting line). I stated that each of these was really a family of different shapes parameterized by the distance of the line from the origin.

I was wrong; I should have known better. You should always be suspicious when distances show up in these equations, since distance by itself is not a meaningful concept in projective geometry. Actually, each of these types is just a single shape, not a parameterized family. To see why, let's try to transform a circle and line into the same circle with the line at a different position. First, do some sort of perspective transform on the circle, turning it into an ellipse. The line goes along for the ride and winds up somewhere new. Now, perform a non-uniform scaling and translation of the ellipse to turn it back into the original circle. The line moves again, but now it's in a different position. To be explicit, the transform might be

$$[x \quad y \quad w]\begin{bmatrix} 5 & 0 & 3 \\ 0 & 4 & 0 \\ 3 & 0 & 5 \end{bmatrix} = [x' \quad y' \quad w']$$

You can verify for yourself that, if $x^2 + y^2 = w^2$, then $x'^2 + y'^2 = w'^2$, so this transforms the circle to itself. But the vertical line $x / w = k$ transforms into

$$x / w = \frac{5k+3}{3k+5}$$

Notice that the lines $x / w = -1$ and $x / w = 1$ stay put; they are the tangents. Only the other vertical lines move—pretty magical.

So, anyway, all type 5s are really the same shape, and all type 7s are really the same shape. The list should be modified to read

5. a conic and a line that is disjoint; $(x^2 + y^2 - w^2)w = 0$
7. a conic and a line that intersects it; $(x^2 + y^2 - w^2)x = 0$

Non-Degenerate Cubics

Our second topic has to do with the possible shapes of non-degenerate curves. Again, to review, in addition to our 10 types of degenerate curves, there are several types of non-degenerate ones. After some fiddling, we came up with the fact that all non-degenerate curves could be forced into the form

$$y^2w = ax^3 + bx^2w + cxw^2 + dw^3$$

It's sometimes clearer to write this in non-homogeneous form by the substitutions $X = x / w$ and $Y = y / w$:

$$Y^2 = aX^3 + bX^2 + cX + d$$

Then, after further scaling Y and scaling and translating X, we were able to "freeze out" five distinct types of equations, the last two of which are continuous parameter families. The relationship between the values $a \ldots d$ determines which type; for example, if $3ac = b^2$, we get one of types 11, 12, or 13. (Remember this; we'll use it later.) The types are as follows:

11. a wiggle; $Y^2 = X^3 + 1$
12. a cusp; $Y^2 = X^3$
13. another wiggle; $Y^2 = X^3 - 1$
14. a continuum of wiggles; $Y^2 = X^3 + X + e$
15. other stuff; $Y^2 = X^3 - X + e$

Type 11 has a special property: the three tangent lines at its three inflection points all intersect at the same point. This is not true of the other wiggles. Type 15 breaks down into five subcategories based on the range of the parameter e. Naming the threshold value $e^0 = 2\sqrt{3} / 9$, the subcategories are

15a. a wiggle; $e > e_0$
15b. a loop; $e = e_0$
15c. an egg and a wiggle; $-e_0 < e < e_0$
15d. a dot and a wiggle; $e = -e_0$
15e. a wiggle; $e < -e_0$

These are illustrated in the left column of Figure 6.1 and in Figures 6.2 through 6.5. This is indeed a complete list and contains no duplications, but I complained about this categorization not being very "pretty." And pretty is *important* in mathematics. It turns out that this form disguises a basic pattern in the non-degenerate cubic catalog.

A New Form

Waterhouse points out that there is indeed a prettier formulation of the cubic equation devised by someone named Hesse, namely

$$x^3 + y^3 + w^3 - \lambda xyw = 0$$

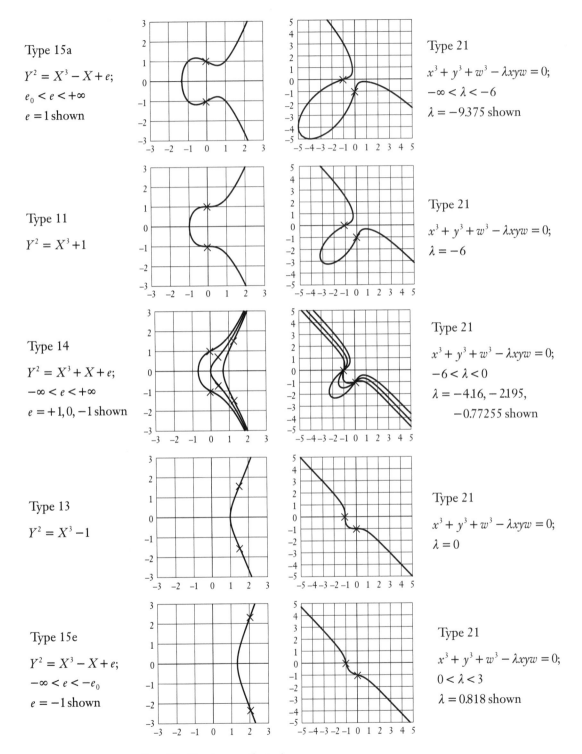

Type 15a

$Y^2 = X^3 - X + e;$

$e_0 < e < +\infty$

$e = 1$ shown

Type 11

$Y^2 = X^3 + 1$

Type 14

$Y^2 = X^3 + X + e;$

$-\infty < e < +\infty$

$e = +1, 0, -1$ shown

Type 13

$Y^2 = X^3 - 1$

Type 15e

$Y^2 = X^3 - X + e;$

$-\infty < e < -e_0$

$e = -1$ shown

Type 21

$x^3 + y^3 + w^3 - \lambda xyw = 0;$

$-\infty < \lambda < -6$

$\lambda = -9.375$ shown

Type 21

$x^3 + y^3 + w^3 - \lambda xyw = 0;$

$\lambda = -6$

Type 21

$x^3 + y^3 + w^3 - \lambda xyw = 0;$

$-6 < \lambda < 0$

$\lambda = -4.16, -2.195,$
$\qquad -0.77255$ shown

Type 21

$x^3 + y^3 + w^3 - \lambda xyw = 0;$

$\lambda = 0$

Type 21

$x^3 + y^3 + w^3 - \lambda xyw = 0;$

$0 < \lambda < 3$

$\lambda = 0.818$ shown

Figure 6.1 *Continuum of wiggles*

This form is nice and symmetric; each coordinate is treated the same as any other. It also has some nice geometric properties. Notice, for example, that all the curves in this formulation pass through the three points $[-1 \ 0 \ 1]$, $[1 \ -1 \ 1]$, and $[1 \ -1 \ 0]$. Furthermore, these three points happen to be the three inflection points of the curve, and they are of course colinear.

This equation has two degenerate special cases. When $\lambda = 3$, it degenerates to a line and a dot (type 9 from Chapter 4); the line is $X + Y = -1$ and the dot is at $[1 \ 1]$. I originally saw this by plugging in numbers and plotting them; with some work, you can also see it algebraically by factoring

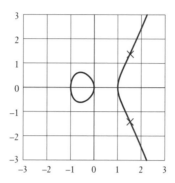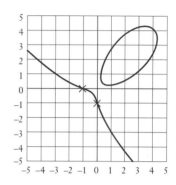

Figure 6.2 *Continuum of egg and wiggles: left, type 15c,*
$Y^2 = X^3 - X + e, -e_0 < e < +e_0, e = 0$ *shown; right, type 22,*
$x^3 + y^3 + w^3 - \lambda xyw = 0, 3 < \lambda < +\infty, \lambda = 8.195$ *shown*

$$x^3 + y^3 + w^3 - 3xyw = (x + y + w)(x^2 + y^2 + w^2 - xy - yw - wx)$$

When $\lambda = \infty$, the curve degenerates into three distinct lines (type 4). How do we deal algebraically with an infinite value for λ? Just divide the equation by λ and *then* let it go to infinity. The equation you get is

$$xyw = 0$$

This gives the three lines: the X axis, the Y axis, and the line at infinity.

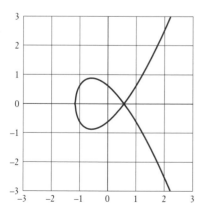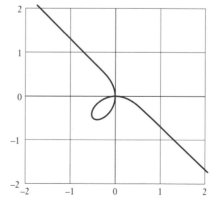

Figure 6.3 *Loop: left, type 15b, $Y^2 = X^3 - X + e_0$; right, type 23, $x^3 + y^3 + xyw = 0$*

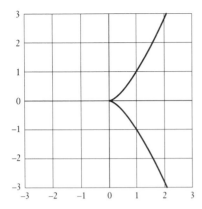

Figure 6.4 *Cusp: type 12; type 24,* $Y^2 = X^2$

I actually played with this symmetric form a lot when writing the first column, trying to see if I could get *all* of the non-degenerate cubics to be expressible in this form. Unfortunately, I started with the cusp (it's the simplest algebraically) and found that it *cannot* be transformed into this symmetric form. I got discouraged and gave up. Well, guess what . . . all of them *can* be transformed into this form *except* for the cusp (type 12), the loop (type 15b), and the wiggle-and-dot (type 15d). So I gave up too soon. I guess there's a lesson here.

Correspondence

Anyway, what I want to do now is to show the correspondence between the $Y^2 = \ldots$ form and Hesse's symmetric form. To make the correlation, let's start with the symmetric form and try to transform it to the Y^2 form. First for some visual inspiration: Look at a sampling of the sorts of shapes the symmetric form can generate in the right column of Figure 6.1. All the shapes are tilted by 45 degrees, so our first guess is to tilt the symmetric equation back by 45 degrees. Actually, it's simpler to use the following transform:

$$x \mapsto x + y$$
$$y \mapsto x - y$$

The symmetric equation turns into

$$y^2(\lambda w + 6x) + 2x^3 - \lambda x^2 w + w^3 = 0$$

Now, remember, we're trying to put this into the form $Y^2 = $ (a cubic polynomial in X). So let's try to turn the factor $(\lambda w + 6x)$ into a simple w. With blinding inspiration, we try replacing

$$w \mapsto (w - 6x)/\lambda$$

Warning! Danger! What happens if $\lambda = 0$? If this happens, our intermediate form is

$$y^2(6x) + 2x^3 + w^3 = 0$$

and we can bash it into the desired form by simply exchanging x and w. After fiddling we get the equation for a type 13 curve:

$$Y^2 = X^3 - 1$$

This is our first match between the old world and the new.

Whew! Back to $\lambda \neq 0$. Make the $(w - 6x)/\lambda$ substitution, algebrize a bit, go to non-homogeneous coordinates, and you wind up with

$$Y^2 = X^3\left(\frac{8(3^3 - \lambda^3)}{\lambda^3}\right) + X^2\left(\frac{\lambda^3 - 4\cdot 3^3}{\lambda^3}\right) + X\frac{18}{\lambda^3} + \frac{-1}{\lambda^3}$$

so

$$a = 8(3^3 - \lambda^3)/\lambda^3$$
$$b = (\lambda^3 - 4\cdot 3^3)/\lambda^3$$
$$c = 18/\lambda^3$$
$$d = -1/\lambda^3$$

Now for a reality check. If $\lambda = 3$, the cubic term evaporates and we have a degenerate curve. Check. If $3ac = b^2$, we should get one of types 11, 12, or 13. So substitute in and solve for λ. You get two solutions: $\lambda = 0$ and $\lambda = -6$. We already saw that $\lambda = 0$ leads to type 13. Double check. $\lambda = -6$ turns out to give type 11. Triple check.

Other values of λ give various cases of types 14 and 15. Solving for the parameter e in terms of λ gives some algebra too horrible to contemplate, so I did some numerical experiments and summarized the results in Table 6.1. Notice that it shows our old types 15a, 11, 14, 13, and 15e are part of one continuous gradation of wiggles. Also pay attention to the relative or-

Table 6.1 *Correspondence between old and new forms*

Old style		New style		
Type	e	**Type**	λ	**Description**
15a	$e_o \ldots +\infty$	21	$-\infty \ldots -6_0$	Wiggle
11		21	-6	Special wiggle
14	$+\infty \ldots -\infty$	21	$-6 \ldots 0$	Wiggle
13		21	0	Wiggle
15e	$-\infty \ldots -e_0$	21	$0 \ldots 3$	Wiggle
9		9	3	Degenerate: line and dot
15c	$-e_0 \ldots e_0$	22	$3 \ldots \infty$	Egg-and-wiggle
4		4	$+\infty$	Degenerate: three lines
15b		23		Loop
12		24		Cusp
15d		25		Wiggle-dot

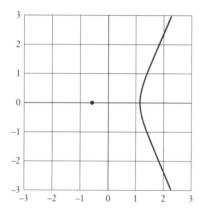

Figure 6.5 *Dot and wiggle: type 15d, type 25,* $Y^2 = X^3 - X - e_0$

dering of λ with respect to e. For example, as λ increases from −6 to 0, you get a type 14 curve with e decreasing from $+\infty$ to $-\infty$.

Orphans

There are some curves left out in the cold, though: the cusp (type 12), the loop (type 15b), and the wiggle-dot (type 15d). These cannot be generated by just finding a magic value for λ. Their algebraic form just won't be symmetric. So how close can we come?

After some tinkering, I was able to transform the loop into the approximately symmetrical form

$$x^3 + y^3 + xyw = 0$$

Notice that there's no parameter here. The λ can be absorbed by scaling x and y. So all loops are the same shape (projectively).

Is there a sort of symmetric formulation for the cusp and wiggle-dot? I've flailed around for a while but haven't come up with one. (You can make the wiggle-dot a bit prettier by translating it so that it's $Y^2 = X^3 - X^2$.)

Punchline

Here's the prettier catalog of non-degenerate cubics. I'll start numbering from 21 to avoid confusion with the old catalog.

21. a continuum of wiggles; $x^3 + y^3 + w^3 - \lambda xyw = 0$; $\lambda < 3$ (Figure 6.1)
22. a continuum of egg-and-wiggles; $x^3 + y^3 + w^3 - \lambda xyw = 0$; $\lambda > 3$ (Figure 6.2)
23. a loop; $x^3 + y^3 + xyw = 0$ (Figure 6.3)
24. a cusp; $x^3 - y^2w = 0$ (Figure 6.4)
25. a dot and a wiggle; $x^3 - x^2w - y^2w = 0$ (Figure 6.5)

CHAPTER SEVEN

Triage Tables

Triage is the somewhat grim process applied to victims of a medical disaster. They're divided into three categories:

- those who will get better by themselves
- those who will die, no matter what you do
- those who will survive only if they are treated

You can apply the same principle in computer graphics to speed up certain types of algorithms. For example, most clipping algorithms have a "trivial accept" and "trivial reject" test. This is a quick-and-dirty calculation to tell if a line is grossly outside the screen or completely inside the screen region. (This process also goes by the name *culling*.) More detailed intersection tests are only done for the far fewer remaining cases that need such attention.

Things get more interesting in hidden line and hidden surface calculations. (Why are they called "hidden" line and surface algorithms instead of "visible" line and surface algorithms? Does this mean that all computer graphicists are pessimists?) Ultimately, any hidden line or hidden surface algorithm involves comparing some candidate line or polygon against the other lines or polygons in a scene to see if any of them hide it. This tends to make n^2 types of time dependence—each line versus each other line.

Triage, or culling, can help speed this up by making most of the tests very fast. But what can help even more is to retain some information about the results of triage for one line or polygon in a form that helps speed up the triage for other lines or polygons. This is the goal of most of the classical rendering algorithms that involve spatial sorting, and it leads to $n \log n$

types of time dependence. In this chapter I'll describe a very simple data structure that I've used to keep track of triage information in several situations. It's an example of an idea whose implementation is very simple and fast, but it takes a while to explain why it works. In the explanation, I'm not going to dwell on the exact algebra of spatial testing; I'll just talk about list management.

Warnock's Algorithm

One of the classic algorithms in computer graphics is Warnock's algorithm. The general technique has been given the much more descriptive name *recursive windowing* by Bruce Baumgart. It is one of the first techniques to introduce the concept of $n \log n$ time growth. The main idea is to consider a window on the screen and to divide all the polygons into three categories:

- those that completely surround the window
- those that are completely disjoint from the window
- those that intersect the window in some way

This categorization portion of the algorithm is sometimes called the *looker*. Only the intersectors and surrounders can be visible. You can render them by comparing each with the other, an n^2 type of operation, but with a smaller n. On the other hand, you could recurse. (Recursion is the ultimate tool of the procrastinator. If you don't want to do any work, just subtract 1 and recurse.)

To recurse, you subdivide the main window into some number of smaller subwindows. In each smaller subwindow, fewer polygons will intersect; more of them will be disjoint or surrounders. The algorithm keeps subdividing and recursing until some very small and easy-to-handle number of polygons intersect the window. For more details, you can look in Newman and Sproull[1] or Rogers.[2]

What makes this algorithm even more interesting is the following observation: When you start with a window and its categorized polygons and then proceed to look at a subwindow, the following things may happen.

1. Any disjoint polygon remains disjoint from the subwindow.
2. Any surrounder remains a surrounder of the subwindow.

---

1 W. Newman and R. Sproull, *Principles of Interactive Computer Graphics* (New York: McGraw-Hill, 1979), page 377.

2 D. Rogers, *Procedural Elements for Computer Graphics* (New York: McGraw-Hill, 1985), page 240.

3. Some intersectors may be surrounders of the subwindow; some intersectors may be disjoint; others will remain intersectors.

This is shown in Figure 7.1, where all the polygons are intersectors of window 1, but in the process of going to window 2, polygon A becomes disjoint, polygon B becomes a surrounder, and polygons C and D remain as
intersectors. So, to recategorize you only have to look at the intersector
list; you don't have to look at the disjoints or surrounders at all. And when
you are deeply nested in the recursion, processing a fairly small sub-
subwindow, most of the polygons will be in the disjoint or surrounder lists.
This economy is called making use of *ancestral information.*

Now comes the tricky part. When you pop back to the main window
and prepare to examine any of the other subwindows, you want the categorization to revert back to the state it was in before you did the recategorization to the first subwindow. How do you push and pop this entire state?
With the following nifty data structure.

List the names of all polygons in a big, contiguous table of length N.
(A name can be a pointer to a polygon descriptor block, an index into another polygon table, or whatever.) Represent the three types of polygons
by sorting the table into three regions: the surrounders are at the beginning, the intersectors are in the middle, and the disjoints are at the
end. Mark the boundaries between these sets with just two pointers—one,
`FI`, to the first intersector and the other, `FD`, to the first disjoint. This is
shown in Figure 7.2; the disjoint and surrounder portions of the table
are shaded to make them stand out. The names of the surrounders are
in `table[0]` ... `table[FI-1]`, the names of the intersectors are
in `table[FI]` ... `table[FD-1]`, and the names of the disjoints are in
`table[FD]` ... `table[N-1]`.

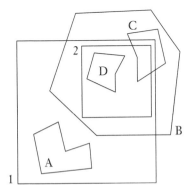

Figure 7.1 *Polygon categorization*

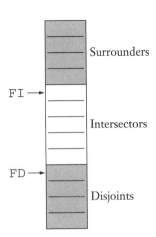

Figure 7.2 *Triage table*

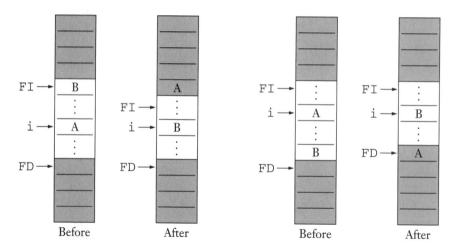

Figure 7.3 *Moving polygon A to surrounder list*

Figure 7.4 *Moving polygon A to disjoint list*

Now, when we do a recategorization ("look"), here's how to implement the movement of polygons from one sublist to another. The two possibilities come from case 3 above.

3a. To move polygon `table[i]` from the intersector subset to the surrounder subset: exchange `table[i]` and `table[FI]` and add 1 to `FI`. See Figure 7.3.

3b. To move polygon `table[i]` from the intersector subset to the disjoint subset: exchange `table[i]` and `table[FD-1]` and subtract 1 from `FD`. See Figure 7.4.

Now here's the neat part. How do we save the ancestral information? Since the only thing that can happen when we go from a window to a subwindow is for some of the intersectors to percolate outward into the surrounder or disjoint lists, we can save the entire state by simply pushing and popping the `FI` and `FD` pointers.

Let's see how this works. We start with the polygons shown in Figure 7.1, represented by the data structure in Figure 7.5a. First, push the pointers. Then go through the intersector list, comparing it with subwindow 2 and percolating the necessary polygons into the disjoint and surrounder lists. You get the situation in Figure 7.5b. After processing the new, improved, smaller intersector list (possibly involving some more recursion), you may wish to return to the status of window 1. Just pop the pointers, giving Figure 7.5c. Notice that all the intersectors we had shoved outward to the surrounder or disjoint lists are now back in the intersector list. True, they might be in a different order, but that's OK; the order within the in-

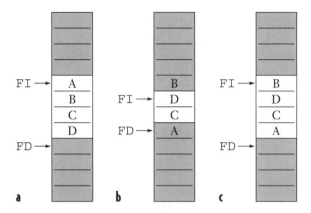

Figure 7.5 *Ancestral information: a, before; b, during; c, after*

tersector list is arbitrary. So, what we will have at any stage is a set of concentric layers of surrounder/disjoint lists, sort of like rings on a tree. Each layer is represented simply by a pair of numbers on the stack.

Note that, all during the processing, the total number of polygons, N, doesn't change. The list stays the same size; just the order of polygons in the list gets continuously reshuffled.

Well, this is pretty neat. When I came up with it I said to myself, "This smacks of originality." But when I recently described it to John Warnock, he said, "Oh yes. That's exactly how I did it." Rats! And he said that the idea probably came originally from Ivan Sutherland. It figures.

Sliding Windows

Anyway, on to another use of the triage table concept, one motivated by a fairly standard hidden line elimination algorithm. The basic algorithm involves comparing a list of potentially visible (PV) edges against a set of boundary (or silhouette) edges. Intersections are places where a PV edge might become visible or invisible. See Chapter 10, "Fractional Invisibility," from *A Trip Down the Graphics Pipeline* for more description.

The important part here is that we are going to intersect a bunch of PV edges with a bunch of boundary edges. Now, we would like to spend our time testing PV edges only against those boundary edges that do indeed intersect it. A simple culling test is the x overlap test: only consider boundary edges whose x extent overlaps the x extent of the PV edge.

As the algorithm progresses, we will process each PV edge, deciding which (visible) parts of it to draw, and proceed to the next PV edge. The next PV edge is chosen to connect with the previous PV edge, if possible.

So its x extent is close to the x extent of the previous edge. Can we take advantage of the triage from one PV edge when we progress to the next one? Of course we can. Otherwise I wouldn't have brought it up, would I?

OK, now for the data structure. While a given PV edge is being considered, there are three disjoint sets:

- left—boundary edges completely to the left of the PV edge
- overlap—boundary edges whose x extent overlaps the PV edge's x range
- right—boundary edges completely to the right of the PV edge

These are placed in a linear table just like before, and the boundaries between the three regions are marked by pointers to the first overlap edge, FO, and to the first right edge, FR. Take a look at Figure 7.6. Here, instead of drawing boxes and arrows, I've represented the structure by drawing the x extent of each edge. The vertical lines show the x range of the current PV edge. The dotted lines represent the positions of the FO and FR pointers.

Now, when processing, only the overlap edges need to be tested against the PV edge. And, if we are lucky (e.g., for a large, complicated scene with lots of small edges), most of the edges will be in the left or right part of the table so we will save a lot of time.

Then, as we move on to the next PV edge, the x region we wish represented by the overlap subset changes. I'll denote the original x range of the overlap list as XLold and XRold and the desired x range as XLnew and XRnew. The update operations are then as follows. There are four steps.

1. Suppose XLnew < XLold (i.e., XL moves left). Some of the left edges will need to move to the overlap list. The big trick to make this type of reshuffling fast is to keep the left edges sorted on their maximum x (as you see has been done in Figure 7.6). This means that all the edges we need to move will be at the end of the left list. You don't even need to touch the table entries. Just keep moving the FO pointer back until the

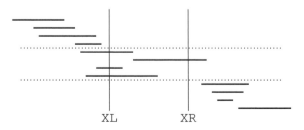

XL   XR

Figure 7.6 *The x overlap list*

Xright of the next list element is to the left of XLnew. Compare Figure 7.7 with Figure 7.6.

2. Similarly, if XRnew > XRold, we need to move some edges from the right list to the overlap list. If we keep the right edges sorted on their minimum x, all the edges we need to move will be at the beginning of the right list. Just keep moving the FR pointer forward until the Xleft of the next list element is to the right of XRnew. No diagram for this; it's similar to the one above.

3. Now if XLnew > XLold, some of the overlappers can move to the left list. You must scan the entire overlap list for such edges, but that's OK; it will be pretty small. Percolate all new left edges to the beginning of the overlap list by our exchange technique and then move the FO pointer down beyond them, thus placing them in the left list (see Figure 7.8). Now we must make sure the left list is still sorted on the XR of each edge. But notice that we only need to sort those edges that we have just moved. An edge newly added to the left list must have had its XR greater than all those that used to be in the list or it wouldn't have been in the overlap list to begin with. So . . . we only need to sort the edges in the range from the old FO to the new FO (see Figure 7.9).

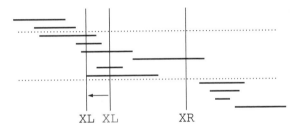

Figure 7.7 XL *moves left*

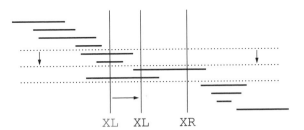

Figure 7.8 XL *moves right, part 1*

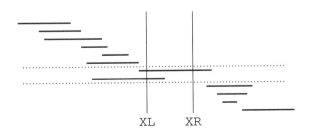

Figure 7.9 XL *moves right, part 2*

4. Finally, for XRnew > XRold, some overlappers can move to the right list. You can take care of these in a manner similar to the way we did it above.

Doing things in the above order ensures that things enter the overlap list before they are tested for exiting it. This means that we are safe, even if the

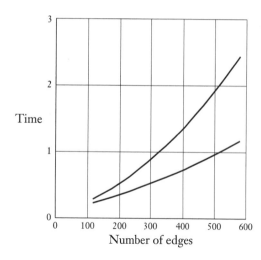

Figure 7.10 *Timings*

new *x* range is completely disjoint from the old *x* range. Notice that there's not going to be any pushing or popping of boundary pointers here, just a continual flow of boundary edges into and out of the overlap list as the *x* range of the candidate PV edge changes when we go from edge to edge.

The plot in Figure 7.10 shows how much time we save by this technique. The upper curve is without the triage process, the lower curve is with it. The important feature is not just that it's faster with triage but that the speedup gets better the more edges you have.

Data Structure Design Wisdom

Here's some wisdom about designing data structures: Data structures should be designed by first looking at the operations you plan to perform on the data and then devising the structure so it is easy and quick to perform those operations. We gained a lot by making the lists out of a contiguous table. No storage was needed for link pointers. The operations of moving items from one list to another just consist of the exchange of two table entries and incrementing or decrementing a pointer. No wholesale list copying is ever required.

Now, is it feasible to extend the sliding window technique in *x* to a further sliding window in *y?* The overlap sublist itself could perhaps be divided into three sub-sublists: above, overlap, and below. I've thought about this, but it seems to get overly complicated.

CHAPTER EIGHT

The Wonderful World of Video

M A Y   1 9 9 0

I hate film.

I don't mean I hate looking at it; I mean I hate *using* it. But in the bad old days, it was the only thing available to record animation. It was agony. You had to manufacture your own camera controller—there weren't any commercially available ones. You had to set up a camera in a darkened room, aim it at the screen, and hope nobody bumped into it. You never knew if the exposure was right. You had to wait for a day or two to get the film developed and see if it worked. And if there was so much as one bad frame, you had to do the whole thing over again.

But nowadays it's so easy to record animation on video that I never have to deal with film again. Well, maybe not all that easy. Video is a complex and fascinating process, and there's a lot that can go wrong. So in this chapter I'll give you an overview of video animation for computer graphics. A lot of it is terminology, so you'll see a bunch of definitions here.

Signal Timing

The first step in recording video is to generate a recordable television signal. There are three main video standards in the world: NTSC (the one used in the U.S. and Japan), SECAM (used primarily in France), and PAL (used about everywhere else). I'll stick pretty much to NTSC here, but I won't go into incredible detail. That's the subject of Chapter 13 ("NTSC: Nice Technology, Super Color").

The basic scan rate for NTSC is 525 scan lines per screen, 485 of which are visible; the remainder are blanked during the vertical retrace. The screen is refreshed 29.97 times per second (not 30—the reason has to do with avoiding interference with the carrier frequency of the sound portion of the program). A screen flashing at this slow a rate would be very obnoxious, so the lines are scanned out "interlaced": the even-numbered lines first, then the odd ones. This breaks the picture into two half-frames (called fields) of 262.5 lines each (242.5 visible lines).

Until recently, computer manufacture had an appalling disregard for these video standards. They made frame buffer displays with whatever scan rates and resolution suited them. Well, there actually was a reason for this. NTSC video was designed back in the fifties with technology and bandwidth restrictions that don't apply to computers today. Interlace is, after all, a compromise to lower the bandwidth of the signal. A 60-Hz non-interlaced scan rate with 768 scan lines is obviously much better, but if you need to record video you have to stick to the standards. Nowadays it's possible to get NTSC-compatible frame buffers from various manufacturers. You just have to be careful to make sure the scan rates match those mentioned above. It's even possible to get external rate converters that take any old random signal and resample it (in both space and time) to the NTSC standard.

Color Encoding

Different types of video equipment can expect the color TV signal to be in any of a number of different formats. Here is a catalog of the types of video signals you might encounter.

RGB

Computer displays start by generating a color image with separate wires for each of the red, green, and blue signals, although video people usually name them in the order GBR. These signals are presumed to be already gamma corrected (see Chapter 5, "Dirty Pixels"). This is often denoted in the video literature by naming the signals E'_R, E'_G, and E'_B (the primes indicate gamma correction). Horizontal and vertical synch signals can be on two more separate wires, or merged into one combined synch signal, or, possibly, merged with the green signal.

Component

This color space is used by modern Betacam, MII, and digital D1 standard recorders. It too consists of three separate signals, but they are related to RGB by the transformation

$$Y = .299R + .587G + .114B$$
$$C_R = R - Y$$
$$C_B = B - Y$$

The Y signal is called *luminance* (not yellow) and represents the perceived brightness of the color. (The letter designation comes from a color space devised by the CIE, which names its color primaries X, Y, and Z. Luminance is the same as the CIE Y component.) The other two signals contain the color information. If $R = G = B$, the chrominance values are both zero, and you get a shade of gray.

Devices that convert RGB into YC_RC_B are called *transcoders*. They are basically analog matrix multipliers, but they also have to combine synch with the Y signal so that it, by itself, is a perfectly respectable black-and-white video signal.

YIQ

Another similar color space is older and is the first step in going to the full composite video that is the NTSC standard. The luminance signal is the same as above, and the color signals are

$$I = .596R - .275G - .321B$$
$$Q = .212R - .523G + .311B$$

I is short for *intermodulation* and Q stands for *quadrature*. (Who makes up these names?) Another way to generate I and Q is

$$[I \quad Q] = [C_R \quad C_B] \begin{bmatrix} .877 & 0 \\ 0 & .493 \end{bmatrix} \begin{bmatrix} \cos 33 & -\sin 33 \\ \sin 33 & \cos 33 \end{bmatrix}$$

In other words, a scaling and rotation of the component chroma signals. This coordinate space was chosen based on psychophysical measurements of the human visual system; the eye is less sensitive to spatial variations in the Q direction, so the signal can get away with less bandwidth along that axis.

S-Video

Next, the video people tell us to combine I and Q into one signal by modulating a color carrier having a frequency of $f_{sc} = 3.579545$ MHz (and they mean every last decimal point).[1] The combined chroma signal is then

$$C = I\cos(2\pi f_{sc}t) + Q\sin(2\pi f_{sc}t)$$

The two-wire signal (Y,C) is called S-Video and is an option on high-end home video equipment.

The frequency of the color carrier is a very magic number in video. Most video timing is an integer multiple of four times this frequency, so 14.31818 MHz forms a natural clock frequency for digital video applications. For example, one scan line is 910 clocks long with 756 clocks visible and the rest devoted to horizontal blanking and synch pulses.

Composite

Composite NTSC just adds the luminance and chrominance to get the one-wire signal that you get on your home TV. (It's unfortunate that the words "component" and "composite" are so similar. It's too easy to get them confused.) Now, your TV must be able to pull the composite signal apart to convert it to RGB for the tube. It can do this because the frequency ranges don't overlap (a subject I will delve into in Chapter 13). This is often done imperfectly, however, and imperfect separation of luminance and chroma is responsible for such artifacts as chroma crawl and rainbows on finely patterned objects. This is why S-Video was invented—to eliminate the problems caused by cross-talk between the luminance and chroma.

Tape Formats

ow for a brief primer on video recording techniques. There are lots of formats of VTRs (video tape recorders). They differ primarily in recorded image quality and the types of input signals they can handle. I'll just list those that are most popular, roughly in order of quality. Almost all of them come in two flavors: original recipe and extra crispy, which gives an enhanced picture. These are cross-compatible in the obvious way: The only thing you can't do is play back an extra crispy tape on an original recipe machine. (Well, you can do it, but it doesn't give a particularly good picture.)

---

1   The exact definition of this frequency is $227.5 \times 525 \times 30 \times 1000/1001$.

VHS

This is the standard home system in the U.S. It's the lowest quality of the bunch, partly because it works all kinds of perversions on the video signal in order to cram 6 hours on a tape. Extra crispy VHS is called SVHS.

8 mm

This is a new format for home systems. It uses teeny cassettes but gets somewhat better quality than VHS. The higher-quality version is called Hi8. Rumor has it that the functionality of these recorders is artificially crippled to keep them below Umatic in quality.

Umatic

This is the oldest format but is still popular. It uses ¾-inch-wide tape on cassettes. The enhanced version is called Umatic-SP (for superior performance).

Betacam and MII

Betacam and MII are very similar, but incompatible, formats that are replacing top-of-the-line professional formats. Betacam seems to have caught on a lot more than MII. (Note that Betacam is not the same as Betamax, a home format that is falling into disuse.) Betacam also has an SP mode.

The main attraction of these formats is that they record on the tape in component format. That is, the Y, C_R, and C_B signals are actually placed on different tracks of the tape rather than being crammed together into one signal with its attendant noise and cross-talk problems. You can also feed these decks NTSC composite and they will split it into components before recording.

1-Inch Type C

This is a professional format that has largely been replaced by Betacam. It uses open reels of 1-inch-wide tape. It only accepts NTSC composite signals but is still about the best quality available.

D1

This is the first fully digital recording technique. It basically records a digitized version of the component signals that Betacam uses. For reasons of compatibility with PAL and SECAM systems, it uses a basic pixel clock that is $\frac{33}{35}$ times that of NTSC. This works out to 13.5 MHz. The exact format of the digital byte stream is standardized for use in other types of digital processing systems and is variously referred to by the names CCIR 601, RP 125, or 4:2:2. A standard scan line has 720 pixels (bytes) of luminance, but only every other pixel has an additional 2 bytes of digitized chroma. Thus, the ratio of numbers of pixels of $Y:C_R:C_B$ is 4:2:2. Further details of this are in Chapter 11 ("The World of Digital Video").

Digital video sounds like the world of the future, but I understand that there is still a bit of a problem: 8 bits don't really give enough resolution in the darker areas to prevent contouring or banding. Some digital video equipment resorts to proprietary dithering techniques to minimize this problem.

D2 and D3

These two digital formats simply record composite NTSC, digitized at four times the color carrier frequency. The D3 format has the same digital signal standards as D2; it's just recorded on a different sized cassette. These formats were developed more recently than D1 and might seem to be a step backward, but they're more popular in video editing situations since they're easier to integrate with older-style analog NTSC.

Another notable feature of D2 machines is that the read and write heads are separate and can operate concurrently. This makes it possible to read a frame, digitally process it in some way, and then write it back onto the same frame of the tape, all in one pass. This in-place editing ability is very useful in postproduction.

Making Tracks

Picture information isn't the only thing being recorded on the tape. There are also two or more tracks of audio and possibly other low-frequency information such as time codes and control tracks (described below). These are all recorded longitudinally, in a continuous stripe down the tape.

Video signals, however, have bandwidths in the 4- to 5-MHz range; recording them longitudinally would require very fast tape speeds. I remember ads for experimental longitudinal video tape machines in the back of electronics magazines when I was a kid. They would zip through a large reel of $\frac{1}{4}$-inch tape in a few minutes. If the tape got caught, you got a roomful of tape almost instantly.

To avoid these problems, all video tape formats use helical scanning. The video heads are mounted on a drum that spins 30 or 60 times per second, and the tape is wrapped around the drum in a roughly helical pattern. As the tape moves forward, the heads stroke across the tape in a diagonal path with everything timed so that one field (or one frame, depending on the format) makes one diagonal stripe. When the tape is played back, the spinning drum must be adjusted to track across the same place where the signal is recorded. This is done by reference to a *control track*, a 59.94-Hz signal recorded longitudinally and timed to the start of each field. (I understand that 8-mm recorders don't use a control track; they find the video tracks by some other mechanism.)

Genlock

For this to work with a frame buffer, there is still another thing you must do. Your frame buffer must, of course, generate scan lines at the proper rate for NTSC video, but it must also must generate them at the proper time. That is, the frame buffer must be scanning out the upper left of the screen at the same time the VTR is beginning a video track on the tape. Any decent piece of video equipment is prepared for this; the process is called *genlocking*. A genlockable device looks at the synch pulses of a separate input signal (often labeled *reference video*) and adjusts itself so that its frames and scan lines are in synch. Genlock also keeps two video boxes in synch in case they drift ever so slightly apart due to microscopic differences in scan rate. In fact, the ability to genlock is a good test of whether your frame buffer is really generating NTSC-compatible video.

Often, in big video setups, there is one main synch generator, and all the other equipment genlocks to it. But if you only have one video source (frame buffer) and one recorder, you can get away with using one as the reference video and genlocking the other to it. For example, a Betacam machine has a built-in synch generator that goes into operation if it sees no reference video, so I genlock my frame buffer to the Betacam. Theoretically, I could go the other way too, genlocking the tape machine to the frame buffer, but for some reason this doesn't seem to work as well.

Time Code

Time code is a mechanism for labeling each frame on the tape with an hour, minute, second, and frame number. Since it was originally an add-on to existing machines, time code can show up in any of three locations on the tape. It can be encoded into an audio signal and recorded on one of the audio tracks (if you play it accidentally through the speaker, you get a horrible screeching sound). In newer machines, it can be recorded on a special longitudinal track reserved for just that purpose. Finally, it can be recorded onto one of the scan lines that is normally blanked during vertical retrace.

This latter method, called vertical interval time code, was originally meant to solve one of the problems of longitudinal time code: you can't read it if the tape isn't moving at some minimal speed. Nowadays, longitudinal time code readers are smart enough to count control track pulses if necessary and update themselves to keep properly in synch. The effect is that longitudinal time code works fine for the type of editing done during animation recording.

Editing

The process of recording a single isolated frame on a video tape takes advantage of a capability of tape machines that was originally intended for another purpose: *insert editing*. The idea is that, when a machine plays back an already recorded tape, it is possible to switch the video heads briefly into and out of record mode. Only the video information is overwritten; the control track timing pulses are left intact.

Switching at exactly the right time can be tricky, but nowadays VTRs are internally microprocessor controlled and can come equipped with a further capability called *auto edit*. You simply have your computer send instructions to the VTR to tell it the time code where you want to start recording (called the *in point*), the time code where you want to stop recording (called the *out point*), and then send the auto edit command. The VTR takes over. It rewinds the tape to a few seconds before the in point (called prerolling), starts playback, and watches the time code. When it gets to the in point, it kicks over into record mode until it sees the out point. Sawing the tape back and forth for each recorded frame (or burst of frames) seems a bit gross, but it works. Tape machines are now rugged enough (barely) to handle it. (I understand that digital recorders are a lot less rugged, though, and won't stand up to a lot of insert editing.)

This means, incidentally, that you have to prerecord a control track and time code track on the tape you plan to animate onto. The video signal you record doesn't really matter much, but it is usual to just record a blank screen. This action is variously called *striping* or *blacking* a tape and is analogous to formatting a floppy disk.

A Hum Danger

When you're recording frames at 5- to 10-second intervals, there's another creepy thing that can cause problems: 60-cycle hum. Remember that our frame rate is 29.97 frames per second, not 30. So any portion of the power supply frequency that creeps into the video signal will crawl slowly up the screen, taking about 17 seconds to cycle once. If it's low amplitude, you may not even notice it. But if you record one frame every 5 seconds and then play it back at normal speed, it will now be moving quite rapidly and become much more noticeable. So the moral of the story is, filter out all possible 60-Hz noise.

Special Effects

The helical scan process gives us another interesting capability. If the tape isn't moving, the playback head can repeatedly stroke over and over on the same frame (or field). This is how freeze frame and slow motion works. Unfortunately, it's not quite so simple. Think about it for a second; if the tape is standing still, the effective path of the head over the tape is slightly different from when the tape is moving forward. The angle of attack is different, and the total time it takes to pass over the track is different. This isn't so bad for home units; the place where the head wanders off the track can be adjusted to fall near the top or bottom of the screen. (If it's not, you get the familiar few lines of snow in the middle of the screen somewhere.) And if the signal is sped up a bit, it's no big deal since TV sets can adjust to quite a wide range of scan rates. On professional machines, though, you can't get away with such sloppiness. (Life is so difficult if you try to be professional. In fact, professional video equipment is often a nuisance since it is a lot more picky about signal quality and refuses to work at all for signals that home video equipment can still muddle through.) We can fix the problems using two mechanisms: a time base corrector and dynamic tracking.

A time base corrector (TBC) is basically a signal laundry. It's useful even when the tape is moving forward. It's designed to correct for those tiny irregularities in speed that come from any mechanical device as well as from the unavoidable stretching and shrinking of the physical tape itself. A TBC is basically a digital memory several scan lines long, arranged like a circular buffer with an input pointer and an output pointer. The video off the tape is continuously digitized into the buffer through the input pointer, and an output signal is continuously analogized through the output pointer. The clock rate of the output pointer is electronically adjusted by some magical process to correct for speed fluctuations in the spinning heads. This same device can also correct for the somewhat faster scan-out of the video frame when the tape is stationary. Most time base correctors also have a built-in *dropout compensator* (DOC) that helps if there is a dropout on the tape. These usually fill in the gap with video from the preceding scan line (conveniently available from the TBC buffer).

Dynamic tracking (DT) is a mechanism to allow variable-speed playback. The video head is mounted on a piezoelectric crystal that can vibrate it sideways within its mounting. Now, imagine that the tape is moving forward at one-half speed. If we vibrate the head with a sawtooth wave at half the frame rate, it will effectively follow the tape forward, scanning out the same frame twice, and then suddenly snap over to the next frame. Voila—clean half-speed playback. By adjusting the vibration signal, you can play the tape backward or forward at up to three times normal speed and still get a perfect picture.

An extension of these mechanisms can enable a VTR to record a frame without moving the tape. So far, the only machine that does this is the Sony BVH2500, a 1-inch machine designed for animation. First, it uses dynamic tracking to make the heads track the tape at the correct angle, with the tape stationary. Then it uses a sort of inverse time base corrector to predistort the signal in time so that it is laid down on the tape at the correct rate for standard-speed playback. The recorded signal is still pretty ratty, but barely within the range that a normal playback time base corrector can clean up. Every now and then, though, a recorded frame is just outside this range; the image seems to jump when this frame is played. It can be repaired, though, by simply re-recording the bad frame. It's helpful to have recording software that makes this easy.

Other ways to record in place are beginning to become available. Machines designed for surveillance applications claim to record one frame at a time. Also, some camcorders can record bursts of two or three frames, but they're not really high quality. I believe they do this simply by being able to bring the tape up to speed in a very short time.

VTR Communication

The next big question is, how does your computer give commands to the VTR? For older machines, this required a special interface board, and there are several companies that make such boards. Nowadays, however, these often are not necessary. After all, the VTR *is* microprocessor controlled. Recent tape recorders provide some more or less standard computer port built into the machine. The two communications protocols I have encountered use either the EIA RS422 standard or something called a *Control L* interface. (I've seen VHS machines advertised with an RS232 interface, but I don't know anything about them.)

RS422 is very similar to the more familiar RS232, except that it uses different voltage levels and differential line drivers so that there are two wires each for transmit and receive. Otherwise, it is just like RS232; the basic unit is an 8-bit byte with additional start and stop bits.

Most Sony machines build a communications protocol on top of this that's uniform over their entire product line. Communication is via a stream of bytes transmitted at 38,400 baud. A command consists of a 2-byte opcode followed by 0 to 15 data bytes and a checksum byte. The VTR immediately sends back a response, which may be just an acknowledgment or which may contain some requested data. There are no asynchronous messages. Bytes are binary values rather than ASCII characters, so your serial interface routines must be prepared to handle this.

The other communication protocol, Control L, is commonly found on 8-mm camcorders and is meant to be part of a general-purpose bus system for home electronic devices. It's a bit more bizarre from the computer point of view. It consists of a burst of 8 bytes transmitted at 9600 baud starting at the beginning of each video field. The tricky part is that all devices on the bus transmit and receive on the same wire, using open collector TTL levels. The VTR generates the start bit of a byte, and then the computer or other device can, if it desires, pull down the line at the appropriate time to generate the data bits. Two devices might, in fact, try to pull down the data line at the same time. That would create a conflict, so each device is supposed to monitor the data line too. If someone else is pulling down the line when it itself isn't, it's supposed to realize there's a conflict, shut up, and try again later. The UART in most computers cannot deal with this properly. I understand that the one in a Macintosh can do this with some fancy programming.

Anyway, if you get a machine that uses either of these protocols, a separate manual available from the manufacturer gives all the details necessary to wire up connectors and program your computer to send commands. The key thing to know is to request the "protocol" manual.

Software

I've found that recording is the most boring part of animation, and it's good to make it as idiotproof as possible or there will be trouble. The recording process is basically a loop: read a frame into the frame buffer, command the VTR to record it, read, record, etc. This sounds simple enough. But one of the main advantages of video over film is the ability to repair bad frames, or overwrite short sections with new versions of an animation. For all but the simplest type of recording, the bookkeeping can be a killer. Each frame can be located three different ways: by the file name, by the frame number within a sequence, and by time code number. You need to be able to translate back and forth between any of these.

The recording software I've developed elaborates this into a whole video database system. It maintains a directory of scenes on each video tape that gives the frame number–to–time code correspondence (via directory files kept on the computer disk). For each scene, an *exposure sheet* file gives the file name–to–frame number correspondence and describes such things as double framing and frame cycles. The recording program then interprets the exposure sheet and checks everything for consistency to ensure that you don't accidentally record over something.

Things to Remember

Video is not without its problems. Certainly, it has less resolution than film. Equipment to record video properly is still a bit expensive (but getting cheaper by the minute). And it's still not quite at the black box stage where you just get some equipment, plug it in, and it works. Video is an example of a system that is complicated enough so that nobody really knows exactly what's going on. This is the sort of situation that creates superstitions. Here are a couple of mine:

- Don't leave a tape in the machine for extended periods of time, especially the open reel tape of a 1-inch machine. This allows dust to get into it and also bends the tape, causing dropouts.

- Don't leave the heads spinning against the tape for more than a couple of minutes. Don't spin down the heads in the middle of a scene; park the tape in a blank area between scenes first.

- Sometimes video equipment hides problems since each module tries hard to compensate for a less-than-perfect input. A good waveform monitor can tell you amazing things about your signal.

- Some features of a particular machine might seem redundant, but often they are included just to maintain compatibility with older formats and recording techniques.

Remember, life could be worse. You could be using film.

$$A_\alpha \varepsilon^{\alpha\gamma\kappa} \varepsilon_{\beta\gamma j} B^\beta = T^k_j$$

CHAPTER NINE

Uppers and Downers, Part I

MARCH 1992

Tenser said the tensor.
Tenser said the tensor.
Tension, apprehension,
and dissension have begun.
—Alfred Bester, *The Demolished Man*

M athematical research is largely a process of successive generalization. Generalizing the square root operation to negative values leads to complex number theory. Generalizing Euclidean transformations to perspective transformations leads to projective geometry and homogeneous coordinates. Often, stuff we use in day-to-day calculations is just a special case of some more general theory that we aren't even aware of. In fact, sometimes this can lead to confusion—an example of "too little knowledge is a dangerous thing." But once you see the generalization, what was a problem before now becomes a thing of beauty. This is the case for the standard vector/matrix formulation used to solve geometric problems in homogeneous coordinates. So, this time I'm going to discuss what's *really* going on with homogeneous coordinates.

We are going to adopt a new notational scheme for vectors and matrices. The whole story is a bit lengthy, so I am going to split it over two chapters. This chapter is a review of the old notation, an exposé of its deficiencies, and the introduction of the new notation. In Chapter 10 I'll show how the new notation solves some complex problems easily, and I'll discuss an interesting representation based on graph theory.

First, some ground rules. We're dealing with pure projective geometry and homogeneous coordinates here. That means that such concepts as distance, angle measurement, and parallelism are meaningless. We are only interested in the things that remain constant after a perspective transformation: intersections, tangency, etc. Also, any non-zero scalar multiple of any of our entities still represents the same entity. Sometimes I will discard troublesome scales without much comment.

Naming Conventions

Since this is all about notation, let's review some typical conventions for naming things to give you a taste of the things we are trying to unify.

We'll start with the distinction between scalars, vectors, and matrices. For the time being, I will write scalars, vector components, and matrix elements using italic letters: a, p_i, T_{ij}. I'll use roman letters for vectors: P. Different vectors of the same type will sometimes be distinguished with subscripts: P_1, P_2. I'll use boldface letters for matrices: **T**. We see right away that there is some potential for confusion with the meaning of subscripts; they can either identify vector elements or they can name different vectors. This is one of the things we want to avoid when we get to our improved technique.

Often, we will need to represent vectors or matrices that are simple modifications of other vectors or matrices. I'll represent these by using the letter of the original with some diacritical mark appended. (The definitions of some of these operations are given below.) A transformed version of a vector P is P′. The adjoint of matrix **M** is written **M***. The transpose of matrix **M** is $\mathbf{M}^\top$. The dual of matrix **M** is $\tilde{\mathbf{M}}$.

2DH Review

First, let's go through the standard litany of homogeneous representation in two dimensions. We represent two-dimensional homogeneous (2DH) entities in three-dimensional space.

Points and Lines

Points are three-element row vectors:

$$P = \begin{bmatrix} x & y & w \end{bmatrix}$$

Lines are three-element column vectors:

$$L = \begin{bmatrix} a \\ b \\ c \end{bmatrix}$$

The matrix (or dot) product of the row and column vector is a scalar:

$$P \cdot L = ax + by + cw$$

If the value is zero, the point lies on the line.

Transformations

We transform points by multiplying on the right by a 3×3 matrix

$$P' = PT$$

and transform lines by multiplying on the left by the adjoint of the matrix we used to transform points

$$L' = T^*L$$

The adjoint is the transpose of the matrix of co-factors of the original matrix. An example element of the adjoint of T is

$$(T^*)_{23} = T_{21}T_{13} - T_{11}T_{23}$$

The adjoint is the same as the inverse except for a scale factor. But we don't care about scale factors, so the adjoint and inverse are all the same to us.

Intersections

To find the line containing two given points, take their 3D cross product and write the result as a column vector:

$$P_1 \times P_2 = \begin{bmatrix} x_1 & y_1 & z_1 \end{bmatrix} \times \begin{bmatrix} x_2 & y_2 & z_2 \end{bmatrix} = \begin{bmatrix} y_1 w_2 - y_2 w_1 \\ w_1 x_2 - w_2 x_1 \\ x_1 y_2 - x_2 y_1 \end{bmatrix}$$

To find the intersection of two lines, take their 3D cross product and write the result as a row vector:

$$L_1 \times L_2 = \begin{bmatrix} a_1 \\ b_1 \\ c_1 \end{bmatrix} \times \begin{bmatrix} a_2 \\ b_2 \\ c_2 \end{bmatrix} = \begin{bmatrix} b_1 c_2 - b_2 c_1 & c_1 a_2 - c_2 a_1 & a_1 b_2 - a_2 b_1 \end{bmatrix}$$

Quadrics

Now for something a little less well known. A second-order algebraic equation such as

$$Ax^2 + 2Bxy + 2Cxw + DY^2 + 2Eyw + Fw^2 = 0$$

represents an arbitrary conic section (also called a quadric curve). This equation can be written in matrix form as

$$[x \quad y \quad w]\begin{bmatrix} A & B & C \\ B & D & E \\ C & D & F \end{bmatrix}\begin{bmatrix} x \\ y \\ w \end{bmatrix} = [x \quad y \quad w]\mathbf{Q}\begin{bmatrix} x \\ y \\ w \end{bmatrix} = 0$$

That is, a point P is on the conic if

$$\mathbf{PQP}^\mathrm{T} = 0$$

Note that the matrix $\mathbf{Q}$ is symmetric.

There is a variant of $\mathbf{Q}$ that is good for testing line tangency. We'll call this the *dual* of $\mathbf{Q}$ and write it as $\tilde{\mathbf{Q}}$. It so happens that the dual of $\mathbf{Q}$ is equal to the adjoint of $\mathbf{Q}$. A line L is tangent to the conic if

$$\mathbf{L}^\mathrm{T}\tilde{\mathbf{Q}}\mathbf{L} = 0$$

Note that we had to put in a few transposes in the above two equations to make the row and column conformability rules of matrix multiplication work out.

Starting from an arbitrary point, we can draw two lines tangent to a given quadric. Connecting these two points of tangency gives a line called the *polar line*. The vector for this line is just the product of the quadric matrix and the point vector:

$$\mathbf{PQ} = \mathbf{L}^\mathrm{T}$$

What you get, according to the rules of matrix multiplication, is a row vector. You have to transpose it to get the line into the column vector notation.

To transform a conic section, we transform the $\mathbf{Q}$ matrix by

$$\mathbf{Q}' = \mathbf{T}^\star \mathbf{Q}(\mathbf{T}^\star)^\mathrm{T}$$

that is, by pre- and postmultiplying by the adjoint of the point transformation matrix $\mathbf{T}$. To transform the dual of $\mathbf{Q}$, we must multiply by the point transformation matrix

$$(\mathbf{Q}^\star)' = \mathbf{T}^\mathrm{T}(\mathbf{Q}^\star)\mathbf{T}$$

Oops

Now wait a minute—there's something fishy here. I've been preaching all along that points are row vectors and lines are column vectors. But the above equations have points showing up sometimes as columns and lines showing up sometimes as rows. It gets even worse when we go to three dimensions.

3DH Review

n ow, let's generalize this to 3D homogeneous.

The Obvious Part

All the 2DH stuff generalizes pretty easily to three dimensions: just make the vectors four elements long and the matrices 4×4. You then have to re-interpret the geometric meaning of things a bit. What was a line in 2DH (column vector) is now a plane in 3DH. I will typically use the letter E for 3DH planes.

$$E = \begin{bmatrix} a \\ b \\ c \\ d \end{bmatrix}$$

What was a conic section in 2DH (symmetric matrix) is a family of 3DH surfaces consisting of ellipsoids, cones, cylinders, saddle points, and the like. Tangency of lines with a conic section becomes tangency of planes against the above surfaces.

The only slightly tricky part in going to 3DH involves the four-dimensional generalization of the cross product. Geometrically, this is the problem of finding a plane passing through three points. We can write the three-dimensional cross product of P_1 and P_2 as

$$P_1 \times P_2 = \begin{bmatrix} a \\ b \\ c \end{bmatrix}$$

where

$$a = \det\begin{bmatrix} y_1 & w_1 \\ y_2 & w_2 \end{bmatrix}, \quad b = \det\begin{bmatrix} w_1 & x_1 \\ w_2 & x_2 \end{bmatrix}, \quad c = \det\begin{bmatrix} x_1 & y_1 \\ x_2 & y_2 \end{bmatrix}$$

By analogy, the four-dimensional cross product of P_1, P_2, and P_3 is a four-element column vector with components

$$a = \det \begin{bmatrix} y_1 & z_1 & w_1 \\ y_2 & z_2 & w_2 \\ y_3 & z_3 & w_3 \end{bmatrix}, \quad b = -\det \begin{bmatrix} x_1 & z_1 & w_1 \\ x_2 & z_2 & w_2 \\ x_3 & z_3 & w_3 \end{bmatrix}$$

$$c = \det \begin{bmatrix} x_1 & y_1 & w_1 \\ x_2 & y_2 & w_2 \\ x_3 & y_3 & w_3 \end{bmatrix}, \quad d = -\det \begin{bmatrix} x_1 & y_1 & z_1 \\ x_2 & y_2 & z_2 \\ x_3 & y_3 & z_3 \end{bmatrix}$$

A symmetric formulation finds the four coordinates of a point common to three planes.

Lines

Again, less well known is a homogeneous formulation for lines in three dimensions. I babbled about this in a SIGGRAPH paper in 1977.[1] Here are the highlights.

We represent a 3DH line as an antisymmetric 4×4 matrix. Giving the six unique elements of the matrix the names p, q, r, s, t, u, we can write the matrix as

$$\mathbf{L} = \begin{bmatrix} 0 & p & -q & r \\ -p & 0 & s & -t \\ q & -s & 0 & u \\ -r & t & -u & 0 \end{bmatrix}$$

Given two points P_1 and P_2, you can calculate the values of p, q, r, s, t, u for the line connecting them by

$$p = \det \begin{bmatrix} z_1 & w_1 \\ z_2 & w_2 \end{bmatrix}, \quad q = \det \begin{bmatrix} y_1 & w_1 \\ y_2 & w_2 \end{bmatrix}, \quad r = \det \begin{bmatrix} y_1 & z_1 \\ y_2 & z_2 \end{bmatrix}$$

$$s = \det \begin{bmatrix} x_1 & w_1 \\ x_2 & w_2 \end{bmatrix}, \quad t = \det \begin{bmatrix} x_1 & z_1 \\ x_2 & z_2 \end{bmatrix}, \quad u = \det \begin{bmatrix} x_1 & y_1 \\ x_2 & y_2 \end{bmatrix}$$

Given two planes E_1 and E_2, you can calculate p, q, r, s, t, u for the intersection line by using a similar set of expressions.

It turns out that these calculations will always generate a singular matrix for $\mathbf{L}$. Calculating the determinant of the matrix gives the value

1 J. F. Blinn, A homogeneous formulation for lines in 3 space, *SIGGRAPH '77 Conference Proceedings* (New York: ACM), pages 237–241.

$(pu - qt + sr)^2$. This means that the components of the line matrix will always satisfy the constraint

$$pu - qt + sr = 0$$

A given point $\begin{bmatrix} x & y & z & w \end{bmatrix}$ lies on the line $\mathbf{L}$ if their vector/matrix product gives four zeros:

$$\begin{bmatrix} x & y & z & w \end{bmatrix} \mathbf{L} = \begin{bmatrix} 0 & 0 & 0 & 0 \end{bmatrix}$$

If the point is not on the line, the two of them together determine a plane in space. The four numbers you get out of the product will be the components of the plane.

$$\begin{bmatrix} x & y & z & w \end{bmatrix} \mathbf{L} = \begin{bmatrix} a & b & c & d \end{bmatrix}$$

You just have to transpose the result to get it to be a column vector.

There is a different form of the line matrix that is good for intersections with planes. We'll call this $\tilde{\mathbf{L}}$. This consists of the same six values as $\mathbf{L}$ but arranged differently:

$$\tilde{\mathbf{L}} = \begin{bmatrix} 0 & -u & -t & -s \\ u & 0 & -r & -q \\ t & r & 0 & -p \\ s & q & p & 0 \end{bmatrix}$$

A given plane includes the line $\mathbf{L}$ if the vector/matrix product with the $\tilde{\mathbf{L}}$ form gives four zeros. If it doesn't, the four values give the point of intersection of the line and plane.

$$\tilde{\mathbf{L}} \begin{bmatrix} a \\ b \\ c \\ d \end{bmatrix} = \begin{bmatrix} x \\ y \\ z \\ w \end{bmatrix}$$

Again, you must rewrite the result as a row vector.

It so happens that $\tilde{\mathbf{L}}$ is *almost* the adjoint of $\mathbf{L}$. In fact, if you go through the adjoint calculation machinery, you find that

$$\mathbf{L}^* = (pu - qt + sr)\tilde{\mathbf{L}}$$

If it weren't for the embarrassing fact that $pu - qt + sr = 0$, we'd be in business. As it is, we find the dual by just rearranging the elements.

You transform a line matrix by

$$\mathbf{L}' = \mathbf{T}^* \mathbf{L} (\mathbf{T}^*)^{\mathsf{T}}$$

You transform its dual form by

$$\tilde{\mathbf{L}}' = \mathbf{T}^{\mathrm{T}}\tilde{\mathbf{L}}\mathbf{T}$$

Yikes!

So what's going on here? Our whole concept of row and column vectors distinguishing between points and planes is crumbling! And well it should. It turns out that the somewhat pictorial matrix representation of all these geometric entities is simply not powerful enough to express all the things that can happen.

The Solution

In order to do this right, we have to borrow some notation from the world of tensor analysis. It turns out that physicists have been faced with this sort of thing for some time. They are concerned with somewhat different problems than we are here, but their notation is readily adaptable. Let's build up to this gradually.

We recognize that there are two kinds of things: point-like and plane-like. Rather than cloud our minds with such concepts as rows and columns, we'd like to identify which kind of vector something is by some other sort of notational mechanism. Hmm . . . how about writing points in green and planes in red? Well, that's a bit impractical. What to do . . .

The physicists' solution, translated into our terms, is to write the point-like things with superscript indices (the uppers of the title) and the plane-like things with subscript indices (the downers). The point-like indices are called *contravariant* and plane-like ones are called *covariant*.

Putting the two different types of indices in two different locations keeps them distinguishable but also creates an ambiguity: Superscripts used to mean exponentiation; now they are contravariant coordinate indices. Subscripts used to be available to construct different names; now they are covariant coordinate indices, and we have to use entirely different letters for different names. This ambiguity is another example of a growing problem with mathematical notation:

There aren't enough squiggles to go around.

Anyway, we can now write our point as

$$P = \begin{bmatrix} P^1 & P^2 & P^3 & P^4 \end{bmatrix}$$

and a 3DH plane as

$$E = \begin{bmatrix} E_1 & E_2 & E_3 & E_4 \end{bmatrix}$$

Matrices have two indices. Each one can be either covariant or contravariant. This makes for three possibilities: pure covariant (M_{ij}), pure contravariant (M^{ij}), and what are called *mixed* (M^i_j). It is the inability to distinguish between these that has been causing all our troubles.

One further note. The different type styles we previously needed to distinguish between scalars, vectors, and matrices are no longer necessary. Since we can now easily determine the species of creature by how many indices it has, I'll just use italic letters when indices are used. Anything with one index is a vector; anything with two indices is a matrix. In fact, we can now have triply indexed critters (cubical matrices?) or quadruply indexed critters. These actually have practical uses, as we will see below.

The Multiplication Machine

We will now represent vector and matrix multiplication in a different way. Remember, in the old style, the laws of matrix multiplication are just a shorthand notation for

$$\begin{bmatrix} x & y & z & w \end{bmatrix} \begin{bmatrix} a \\ b \\ c \\ d \end{bmatrix} = ax + by + cz + dw$$

Now, instead of using single-letter names, we are using index numbers for the components:

$$P \cdot E = \begin{bmatrix} P^1 & P^2 & P^3 & P^4 \end{bmatrix} \begin{bmatrix} E_1 \\ E_2 \\ E_3 \\ E_4 \end{bmatrix} = P^1 E_1 + P^2 E_2 + P^3 E_3 + P^4 E_4 = \sum_i P^i E_i$$

In fact, we can save valuable ink by noticing that the summation occurs so often that we can declare that it is implied by the fact that the point index and plane index are the same letter. This is often emphasized by the convention of using Greek letters for indices that are summed over. Thus, the product of a point and a plane is

$$P^\alpha E_\alpha$$

This expression is a sort of prototype of the terms that are summed over. This might take a bit of getting used to, but it's worth it. This notation is credited to Albert Einstein, who invented it to shorten his calculations for general relativity; it is therefore called *Einstein index notation*.

We can make all of our row/column confusion go away by the following rule:

> *Each index that is summed over must occur someplace in the prototype term exactly once as a covariant index and once as contravariant index. These indices "annihilate" each other, and the resultant product has one less of each kind of index.*

Indices that are *not* summed over are called *free indices*. They must occur just once in the prototype term, and the same index must occur in the resultant term. For example, the product of two matrices in the old notation is

$$\mathbf{T} = \mathbf{MN}$$

In the new notation this would be

$$T_i^{\;j} = M_j^{\alpha} N_{\alpha}^i$$

Now for a shocker:

$$M_j^{\alpha} N_{\alpha}^i = N_{\alpha}^i M_j^{\alpha}$$

But, you say, matrix multiplication is not commutative! And you are right. The above expression is not the whole matrix product; it is a prototype for each term in the product. Within the term, you just have numbers being multiplied—that *is* commutative. So, to mix metaphors somewhat, the two possible matrix products are

$$\mathbf{MN} = M_j^{\alpha} N_{\alpha}^i = N_{\alpha}^i M_j^{\alpha}$$

and

$$\mathbf{NM} = N_j^{\alpha} M_{\alpha}^i = M_{\alpha}^i N_j^{\alpha}$$

The New Order

Let's now reinterpret all of the above confusion in terms of this notation. First, let's do the obvious stuff.

Points and Planes

A point has a single contravariant index,

$$P^i$$

A 2DH line or 3DH plane has a single covariant index,

$$E_i$$

A point times a line/plane is a scalar

$$P^\alpha E_\alpha = s$$

If it's zero, the point lies on the line.

Quadrics

A quadric curve or surface has a pure covariant form for dealing with points. Note that both the points have their accustomed contravariant indices:

$$P^\alpha Q_{\alpha\beta} P^\beta = 0$$

The polar line to a quadric curve and the polar plane to a quadric surface is

$$E_i = P^\alpha Q_{\alpha i}$$

Note again the delightful consistency of indices.

The dual form of the quadric for testing line/plane tangency is pure contravariant:

$$E_\alpha \tilde{Q}^{\alpha\beta} E_\beta = 0$$

Both line/planes have their accustomed covariant indices. The tilde over the Q is kind of redundant since the placement of the indices tells us everything: covariant for the normal form and contravariant for the dual form. We won't bother with the tildes anymore—yet more cleanups.

The contravariant form of **Q** is the adjoint of the covariant form. This leads to another convenient rule that we will expand upon later. For now I'll just state:

Taking an adjoint flips the type of its indices.

This means that the adjoint of a mixed tensor (which is a transformation matrix) is also a mixed tensor. If the only type of matrix you encountered was a transformation matrix, you wouldn't know there was such a thing as covariant or contravariant tensors.

3DH Lines

A 3DH line has a pure covariant tensor or a pure contravariant tensor. The plane containing the line and a point P uses the covariant form

$$P^\alpha L_{\alpha j} = E_j$$

The point of intersection of the line and a plane E uses the contravariant form

$$L^{\alpha i} E_\alpha = P_i$$

Transformations

A transformation matrix is a mixed tensor. It can transform a point

$$(P')^i = P^\alpha T_\alpha^i$$

or it can transform a line (2DH) or a plane (3DH):

$$(E')_i = T_\alpha^i E_\alpha$$

The covariant form of **Q** transforms like

$$(Q')_{ij} = \left(T^*\right)_i^\alpha Q_{\alpha\beta} \left(T^*\right)_j^\beta$$

Notice that we no longer need to use the superscript T to express transpose; the relevant indices are just swapped. Yet more economization. Explicit notation for adjoints, however, is still necessary for now.

The contravariant form of **Q** transforms using **T**

$$(Q')^{ij} = T_\alpha^i Q^{\alpha\beta} T_\beta^j$$

Likewise, the covariant form of the 3DH line L transforms like

$$(L')_{ij} = (T^*)_i^\alpha L_{\alpha\beta} (T^*)_j^\beta$$

The contravariant form transforms like

$$(L')^{ij} - T_\alpha^i L^{\alpha\beta} T_\beta^j$$

This is an example of the general transformation rule:

*To transform something, multiply in a **T** for each contravariant (point-like) index and a **T*** for each covariant (plane-like) index.*

In fact, all these things are called tensors precisely because they transform according to this rule.

There is an interesting consequence of this. In order to transform a *transformation matrix* we must multiply both **T** and **T***. Calling the transformation matrix **M**,

$$(M')^i_j = (T^*)^\beta_j M^\alpha_\beta T^i_\alpha$$

This is a nice way of representing the standard trick of scaling about an arbitrary point by transforming the point to the origin (**T***), scaling about the origin (**M**), and transforming back (**T**).

The Magic Epsilon

You may have noticed that we've encountered a lot of expressions of the form

$$\det \begin{bmatrix} p_1 & p_2 \\ r_1 & r_2 \end{bmatrix}$$

There's another gimmick that the physicists have come up with that's useful to abbreviate this type of thing: it's the Levi-Civa epsilon. In this chapter I can give just a hint of the wonders in store for us when using epsilon. To start out, let's discuss this just in 2DH (3D) terms.

The 3D (2DH) Epsilon

The three-dimensional epsilon tensor has three indices, so it looks like

$$\varepsilon_{ijk}$$

Its elements are defined to be

$$\varepsilon_{123} = \varepsilon_{231} = \varepsilon_{312} = 1$$
$$\varepsilon_{321} = \varepsilon_{213} = \varepsilon_{132} = -1$$
$$\varepsilon_{ijk} = 0 \text{ otherwise}$$

You can visualize ε by thinking of it as a cube of numbers made by stacking up the matrices:

$$\begin{bmatrix} 0 & 0 & 0 \\ 0 & 0 & 1 \\ 0 & -1 & 0 \end{bmatrix}, \begin{bmatrix} 0 & 0 & -1 \\ 0 & 0 & 0 \\ 1 & 0 & 0 \end{bmatrix}, \begin{bmatrix} 0 & 1 & 0 \\ -1 & 0 & 0 \\ 0 & 0 & 0 \end{bmatrix}$$

Multiplying two points P and S by epsilon gives

$$P^\alpha S^\beta \varepsilon_{\alpha\beta i} = L_i$$

a covariant vector. What is it? To find, say, the first element, let's write down all the terms containing an epsilon that is non-zero.

$$L_1 = P^\alpha S^\beta \varepsilon_{\alpha\beta 1}$$
$$= P^2 S^3 \varepsilon_{231} + P^3 S^2 \varepsilon_{321} = P^2 S^3 - P^3 S^2$$

The other elements look similar. L is, in fact, the cross product of P and S, that is, the line connecting them.

There is also a contravariant epsilon that has the same numerical values. You can use it to take cross products of lines to find their point of intersection.

$$L_\alpha K_\beta \varepsilon^{\alpha\beta\iota} = P^i$$

Notice that I didn't even need to tell you that K was a line. You could tell by seeing that it has a single covariant index.

The epsilon can also be used to calculate adjoints. It turns out that

$$(M^*)^{ij} = \frac{1}{2} \varepsilon^{i\alpha\beta} \varepsilon^{j\gamma\delta} M_{\alpha\gamma} M_{\beta\delta}$$

Where does the ½ come from? Well, as an exercise, write down all the non-zero epsilon terms implied by the summation over α, β, γ, and δ. You will find that each product of the M terms will appear twice, requiring ½ to compensate. We can, however, ignore the ½ since we are being homogeneous.

The above is for pure covariant matrices; note how the result is contravariant. If you start with a contravariant matrix, you multiply by two covariant epsilons and get a covariant result. For a mixed matrix, you must multiply by one covariant and one contravariant epsilon, and you will get a mixed result.

The 4D (3DH) Epsilon

There is also a four-dimensional epsilon that has four indices. It's defined by

$$\varepsilon_{ijkl} = \begin{cases} 1 & \text{if } ijkl \text{ is an even permutation of 1234} \\ -1 & \text{if } ijkl \text{ is an odd permutation of 1234} \\ 0 & \text{otherwise} \end{cases}$$

Given this, we can compactify a lot of the formulas for 3DH stuff.

The plane through three points is

$$E_i = P^\alpha S^\beta R^\gamma \varepsilon_{\alpha\beta\gamma i}$$

The point common to three planes uses the contravariant form

$$P^i = E_\alpha F_\beta G_\gamma \varepsilon^{\alpha\beta\gamma i}$$

The adjoint of a 4×4 matrix is

$$(M*)^{ij} = \frac{1}{6} \varepsilon^{ja\beta\gamma} \varepsilon^{iabc} M_{\alpha a} M_{\beta b} M_{\gamma c}$$

Again, this is for a covariant matrix. Contravariant and mixed matrices require the same treatment as for 2DH.

The 3DH line through two points P and R is the covariant matrix

$$L_{ij} P^\alpha R^\beta \varepsilon_{\alpha\beta ij}$$

The plane containing this line and another point S is

$$E_i = S^\alpha L_{\alpha i}$$

You find the contravariant version of a line by intersecting the two planes E and F:

$$L^{ij} = E_\alpha F_\beta \varepsilon^{\alpha\beta ij}$$

The point of intersection of this line with another plane G is

$$P^i = L^{i\alpha} G_\alpha$$

The covariant and contravariant line forms are related by

$$L_{ij} = \varepsilon_{ij\alpha\beta} L^{\alpha\beta}$$

Admittedly implementing some of the above calculations by explicitly multiplying by epsilon is a bit idiotic. You wind up multiplying by a whole lot of zeros and ones. The epsilon notation is good as a bookkeeping convenience. I'll describe even more uses for it in the next chapter.

So What

We just reduced all of geometry to tensor multiplication (well, almost all). And there are no embarrassing transposes. Row-ness or columnness is superseded by the more general concept of covariant and contravariant indices. Plus, we can feel really cool by sharing notation with general relativity.

CHAPTER TEN

Uppers and Downers, Part II

MAY 1992

In Chapter 9 I began talking about Einstein index notation, a way of abbreviating vector/matrix multiplication that simplifies a lot of algebra and cleans up some inconsistencies in notation. In this chapter I want to continue this discussion and to adopt another trick of theoretical physics, the Feynman diagram. This is an incredibly nifty way to turn nasty, complex tensor equations that confuse us into simple, elegant stick figures that amuse us.

First, a Review

Everything is a tensor. A tensor is a multiply indexed array of numbers that transforms in a certain special way. Each index of a tensor can be one of two types: covariant or contravariant. We write covariant indices as subscripts and contravariant indices as superscripts.

A column vector in the old matrix notation becomes a tensor with a single covariant index and is called a co-vector. These typically represent lines (2DH) or planes (3DH). A row vector in matrix notation becomes a tensor with a single contravariant index. I'll simply call them vectors. These typically represent points in 2DH or 3DH.

Now, in standard 3D geometry you can form dot products of vectors and you can form cross products of vectors. There are a lot of calculations (notably, lighting calculations) that take place in this Euclidean 3D space.

In our homogeneous scheme, however, you can only form the dot product of a vector with a co-vector; you can't take the dot product of a vector with another vector. You use the cross product to combine two vectors, and the result is a co-vector. I'll stick with these rules throughout this chapter.

Tensor multiplication (a generalization of the dot product) involves summing over a pair of covariant and contravariant indices. A typical expression looks like

$$A^i_{\alpha j} B^\alpha = C^i_j$$

Summed indices (here, α) are called bound indices and disappear from the result. Unsummed (free) indices (the i and j) survive in the result. Since bound indices are purely local to the summation, we can arbitrarily change their name; we could just as well have written the above equation as

$$A^i_{\beta j} B^\beta = C^i_j$$

Free indices, however, can only be renamed globally; you have to do it consistently for each term on each side of an equation. Index name bookkeeping is one of the biggest pains of this method.

In the last chapter I also introduced the special tensor called ε. We can use ε to abbreviate the following tensor operations.

The cross product

$$A \times B = C$$

becomes

$$A^\alpha B^\beta \varepsilon_{\alpha\beta i} = C_i$$

The adjoint of a 3×3 matrix becomes

$$(M^*)^{ij} = \frac{1}{2} \varepsilon^{j\alpha\beta} \varepsilon^{i\gamma\delta} M_{\alpha\gamma} M_{\beta\delta} \qquad \textbf{(1)}$$

In homogeneous land, we can drop the factor of $\frac{1}{2}$.

A Programming Application

This vector/co-vector distinction can take on practical significance in the programming arena. One game that's currently played with modern programming languages is to define compound data types and to overload all the language's arithmetic operators to do arithmetic on the new data type. For example, you might define a data type for vectors (as a triple or a quadruple of numbers) and then define vector addition for the "+" operator, vector subtraction for the "−" operator, and so forth, in the obvious way. The problem comes when you get to multiplication. Of the two types of vector multiplication, the dot product and the cross product, which one should be meant by the "*" symbol? Now that we realize that there are two types of vectors, we can remove the ambiguity. We need to define two different data types: vectors and co-vectors. The storage structure, addition, and subtraction operators are the same for both of these, but multiplication depends on the operand type. Suppose the variable S is declared to be a scalar, V1 and V2 are vectors, and C1 and C2 are co-vectors. Expressions containing the multiplication operator should be interpreted as shown in Table 10.1.

The Epsilon-Delta Rule

If you multiply two epsilons together along one index, the rules of tensor multiplication give a four-index mixed tensor,

$$\varepsilon_{\alpha jk}\varepsilon^{\alpha lm} = D^{lm}_{jk}$$

Since ε is filled with a fixed pattern of 0s, +1s, and −1s, you can work out the values of **D**. They turn out to be

$$D^{lm}_{jk} = \begin{cases} +1 & \text{if } l = j;\ m = k;\ l \neq m \\ -1 & \text{if } m = j;\ l = k;\ l \neq m \\ 0 & \text{otherwise} \end{cases}$$

You can write this in a more compact form by inventing yet another special tensor called δ.

$$\delta^i_{\ j} = \begin{cases} 1 & \text{if } i = j \\ 0 & \text{otherwise} \end{cases}$$

Table 10.1 *Product and result type for various vector/co-vector products*

Expression	Product	Result
S*V1	Scalar	Vector
S*C1	Scalar	Co-vector
V1*C1	Dot	Scalar
V1*V2	Cross	Co-vector
C1*C2	Cross	Vector

In other words, δ is just an identity matrix. This might seem a bit pointless at first, but it lets us write the above as

$$\varepsilon_{\alpha jk}\varepsilon^{\alpha lm} = \delta^l_j \delta^m_k - \delta^m_j \delta^l_k \qquad (2)$$

This fundamental identity is called the epsilon-delta rule and is useful as a way to simplify any expression you come across that contains the product of two epsilons.

A Simple Application

Take, for example, the following common 3D vector identity:

$$A \times (B \times C) = (A \cdot C)B - (A \cdot B)C \qquad (3)$$

First, let's see if this makes sense in our homogeneous world of vectors and co-vectors. **B** and **C** can be vectors (that is, 2DH points). Their cross product is a co-vector (a 2DH line). We cross this with **A,** which means that **A** must be a co-vector too. The result is a vector. Now look at the right side of the equation. It's also a vector, a weighted sum of the two vectors **B** and **C.** The weighting factors are dot products between vector–co-vector pairs. Everything fits in consistently with our scheme.

Writing the left side in Einstein index notation, we get

$$A_i\left(B^j C^k \varepsilon_{jkl}\right)\varepsilon^{ilm}$$

In this expression the letters i, j, k, and l are all bound indices (since they each appear exactly twice), indicating that they are implicitly summed over. The letter m is a free index, indicating that the net result is a vector with the single superscript index m.

We are going to want to apply the epsilon-delta rule, but its definition (equation 2) has different letters for the indices on the epsilons. We can make our expression more similar to it by shuffling the indices of the epsilons to get the common summed index, l, as the first one. This is legal as long as we do an even permutation of the indices.

$$A_i B^j C^k \varepsilon_{ljk}\varepsilon^{lmi}$$

Then we need to do some pattern matching with equation 2. It's actually easiest to rewrite equation 2, renaming the indices to match up with the above expression. (This sort of thing is a nuisance we will be able to avoid with the graphical method.)

$$\varepsilon_{ijk}\varepsilon^{lmi} = \delta^m_j\delta^i_k - \delta^i_j\delta^m_k$$

Stuff in the deltas for the product of the epsilons and you get

$$A_iB^jC^k\left(\delta^m_j\delta^i_k - \delta^i_j\delta^m_k\right)$$

Multiply out and apply several identities of the form

$$A_i\delta^i_k = A_k$$

You get

$$A_kB^mC^k - A_jB^jC^m$$

which, in old-style vector notation, is

$$(A\cdot C)B - (A\cdot B)C$$

Ta daa . . .

A geometric interpretation of this algebra appears in Figure 10.1. It's a two-dimensional version of the perspective shadow calculation I described in Chapter 6 of *A Trip Down the Grapics Pipeline*. Think of B as a light source casting the shadow of point C onto the ground, line A. The two sides of the equation are two ways of thinking about calculating the shadow location. You can think of it as finding the line through B and C, (B × C), and intersecting that line with line A, (A × (B × C)). Alternatively, you can parameterize the line through B and C as a linear combination of the vectors B and C:

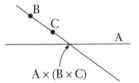

Figure 10.1 *Point B casts the shadow of C onto line A*

$$\alpha B + \beta C$$

The α,β pair forms a one-dimensional homogeneous coordinate for points on the line. Force this point to be on the line A by

$$A\cdot(\alpha B + \beta C) = 0$$

or

$$\alpha(A\cdot B) + \beta(A\cdot C) = 0$$

A solution to this equation is

$$\alpha = A\cdot C$$
$$\beta = -A\cdot B$$

so the intersection is

$$(A\cdot C)B - (A\cdot B)C$$

Quadric Line Tangency

Here's another use for the epsilon-delta rule.

In the previous chapter I noted that a symmetric 3×3 covariant tensor, **Q**, represents a second-order curve (conic sections and the like). For points on the curve,

$$PQP^T = 0$$

Then I baldly stated that a line, L, is tangent to the curve if

$$L^TQ^*L = 0$$

where **Q*** is the adjoint of **Q**. Why should you believe me (other than the fact that I am extremely trustworthy)? We need to express the fact that L and **Q** have exactly one point in common. To do this, we write an arbitrary point of L in the same way as mentioned above—as the weighted sum of two distinct points of L.

$$P = \alpha R + \beta S$$

How, you might ask, do we decide what to use for R and S? Well, it doesn't matter. It's one of the funny things that often happens in mathematical proofs. We never actually have to know explicit coordinates for R or S; we just have to know that they exist and that

$$L = R \times S$$

The points of L that intersect **Q** have

$$PQP^T = 0$$

or

$$(\alpha R + \beta S)Q(\alpha R + \beta S)^T = 0$$

Multiplying this out and remembering that **Q** is symmetric gives

$$\alpha^2(RQR^T) + 2\alpha\beta(RQS^T) + \beta^2(SQS^T) = 0$$

This is a homogeneous quadratic equation in (α, β) of the form

$$\alpha^2 a + \alpha\beta b + \beta^2 c = 0$$

If L is tangent to **Q**, this equation should have exactly one solution. Remembering our high school algebra, this condition is

$$b^2 - 4ac = 0$$

For our particular quadratic equation this translates to

$$4(RQS^T)^2 - 4(RQR^T)(SQS^T) = 0$$

We want to show that this condition is the same as

$$L^T Q^* L = (R \times S)^T Q^*(R \times S) = 0$$

At this point, with conventional vector-matrix notation, we're stuck. There's no convenient way to use the commonality between cross products and matrix adjoints.

Einstein to the rescue. Write the two expressions in Einstein index notation. The first is

$$R^i Q_{ij} S^j R^k Q_{kl} S^l - R^i Q_{ij} R^j S^k Q_{kl} S^l$$

and the second is

$$\left(R^i S^j \varepsilon_{ijm} \right) \left(\frac{1}{2} \varepsilon^{m\alpha\beta} \varepsilon^{n\gamma\delta} Q_{\alpha\gamma} Q_{\beta\delta} \right) \left(R^k S^l \varepsilon_{kln} \right)$$

You can then show that these two expressions are equal by doing a lot of renaming of indices and using the epsilon-delta rule twice. It works, but you have to be careful to keep all 10 index names straight. We want a still simpler scheme.

Diagram Notation

Back in 1949, physicist Richard Feynman began using a diagrammatic technique to express equations in high-energy physics. A vastly simplified form of these Feynman diagrams can help us out here too. The following is adapted from a book called *Diagram Techniques in Group Theory.*[1]

We represent the product of a bunch of tensors in diagram form as a directed graph. The encoding is as follows:

- Each tensor in the product is a node in the graph.
- Each index is an arc. A contravariant index is directed away from the node, a covariant index is directed toward the node.

---

1 G. E. Stedman, *Diagram Techniques in Group Theory* (Cambridge, England: Cambridge University Press, 1990).

- Bound indices (those that are summed over) are arcs connecting two nodes. The directedness of the arc represents the fact that you can sum only over a contravariant-covariant pair of indices.
- Free indices are "dangling" arcs.

The nice thing about this is that bound indices don't need to be named (although I will sometimes do so here to more easily relate the Einstein index notation to the diagram notation). Only the topology of this diagram is important. Any rearranging that preserves topology is OK, except for mirror reflections. These are not allowed since they imply transposition of some of the tensors. This is simply a sign flip for epsilon but might change the value of a non-symmetric tensor.

Here are some examples:

A point is P^i

A line is L_i

The dot product of a point and a line is $P^\alpha L_\alpha$

which is topologically equivalent to

A transformation matrix is T^i_j

and a transformed point is $P^\alpha T^i_\alpha$

We write the special tensor epsilon (in either its covariant or contravariant forms), using a dot for the node and labeling index arcs counterclockwise around the node:

ε^{ijk}

ε^{ijk}

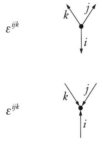

The cross product of two vectors is

$$P^\alpha R^\beta \varepsilon_{\alpha\beta i}$$

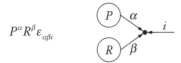

Note that mirroring this flips the sign.

Equation 1 for the adjoint of a matrix appears in diagram form as

$$\frac{1}{2}\varepsilon^{j\alpha\beta}\varepsilon^{i\gamma\delta}M_{\alpha\gamma}M_{\beta\delta}$$

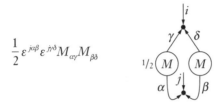

This is a bit clumsy. We can flip the lower epsilon over to make it a bit prettier but must compensate by prefixing with a minus sign.

$$-\frac{1}{2}\varepsilon^{i\alpha\beta}\varepsilon^{j\gamma\delta}M_{\alpha\gamma}M_{\beta\delta}$$

If we multiply the adjoint by the original matrix, we get the identity matrix times the determinant of the original matrix. The trace (sum of the diagonal elements) of this 3×3 matrix is then three times the determinant. I'll leave it for you to verify that, graphically, the determinant of a matrix is proportional to

Since we are not concerned with scale factors, the only interesting feature of a determinant is whether it's zero or not. In other words, if the above diagram (which evaluates to a scalar) is zero, then the matrix is singular.

The other special symbol, delta, is just written as an arc (when necessary, I will label it with two labels):

$$\delta^i_j \qquad \underrightarrow{\quad j \quad i \quad}$$

The Diagram for Epsilon-Delta

Now we get to the interesting part: the epsilon-delta rule in diagram notation. Compare this with equation 2 to see how the index names work. Note especially that the arcs are carefully labeled counterclockwise around both epsilon nodes.

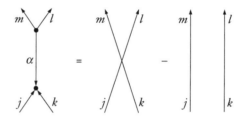

As an example, our proof of the vector identity of equation 3 in diagram notation looks like

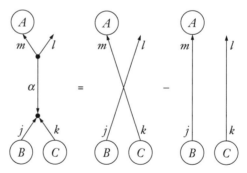

When I used this to calculate the perspective shadow, I was primarily interested in finding a transformation matrix to apply to arbitrary points C. In diagram notation, this transformation is just

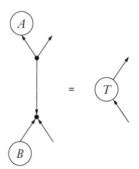

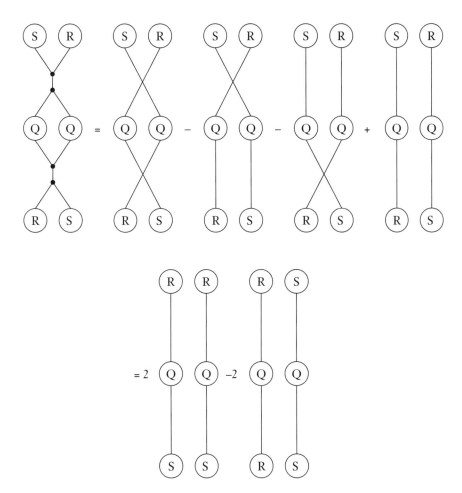

Figure 10.2 *Line tangency proof*

Note that this diagram has one covariant and one contravariant free index and thus qualifies as a transformation matrix.

Now we can do the line tangency proof diagrammatically. To show the essence of the proof, I've left out the cluttering index names, a few global scale factors, and even the arrows. This diagram appears in Figure 10.2.

The 4D (3DH) Epsilon-Delta Rule

The somewhat imposing 4D version of the epsilon-delta rule is

$$\varepsilon_{aijk}\varepsilon^{almn} = \delta_i^l\delta_j^m\delta_k^n + \delta_i^m\delta_j^n\delta_k^l + \delta_i^n\delta_j^l\delta_k^m$$
$$-\delta_i^l\delta_j^n\delta_k^m - \delta_i^m\delta_j^l\delta_k^n - \delta_i^n\delta_j^m\delta_k^l$$

(4)

This is what you must use if you are solving problems in 3D homogeneous coordinates. Note that all the delta terms have the same subscripts, but they just have even or odd permutations of the (*lmn*) letters in their superscripts.

I haven't found this directly useful yet, but it lets us evaluate another useful identity. Form the double summation by setting $i = 1$ above. When you simplify, remember that a delta summed with itself is the trace of the identity—in 4D, this would be the constant 4. That is,

$$\delta_i^i = 4$$

When you work this out, it looks a lot like our old friend, the 3D (2DH) rule:

$$\varepsilon_{\alpha ijk}\varepsilon^{\alpha imn} = 2\left(\delta_j^m\delta_k^n - \delta_j^n\delta_k^m\right)$$

4D Diagram Notation

In diagram notation, the 4D epsilon would simply be a four-pronged node. We have to be careful, however. We want to make sure that allowable diagram rearrangements do not permute the indices of the epsilons in such a manner that the sign changes. In three dimensions (with a three-pronged epsilon) this means that mirror reflections are disallowed, as they are equivalent to an odd permutation of indices. This, however, doesn't work so neatly for four-pronged epsilon diagrams drawn in a flat plane; odd permutations of four indices don't necessarily look like mirror reflections of a four-pronged planar epsilon diagram. Whenever signs matter, we can keep things straight by simply expressing four-index tensor multiplication as a three-dimensional diagram. The four-pronged epsilon would then have arcs directed to the vertices of a tetrahedron as follows:

$$\varepsilon^{ijkl}$$

Even permutations of the indices become simple three-dimensional rotations of the epsilon tensor diagram. Odd permutations become three-dimensional mirror reflections, so mirroring is disallowed just as in two-dimensional diagrams.

The 3DH homogeneous line between two points is

$$P^\alpha R^\beta \varepsilon_{\alpha\beta ij} = L_{ij}$$

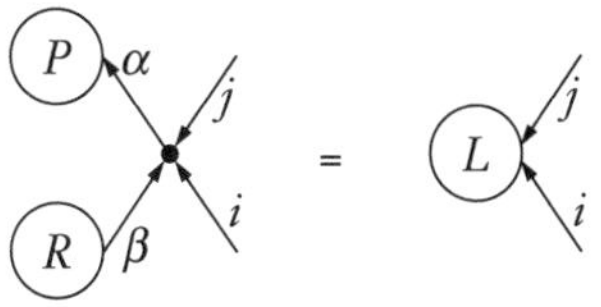

Note that this tensor has two covariant indices. The contravariant form is

$$L_{\alpha\beta} \varepsilon^{\alpha\beta ij} = L^{ij}$$

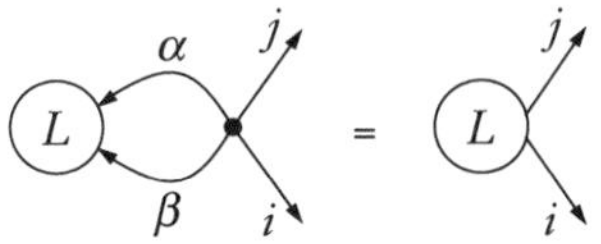

The 4D epsilon-delta rule, equation 4, appears in Figure 10.3. Keep in mind that this diagram is three dimensional; the two joined epsilons look sort of like an ethane molecule. A mnemonic to help remember this diagram is to note that the positive terms each have one pair of arcs crossing in three dimensions. (The first of the terms looks like it has three arcs crossing, but the horizontal one is actually closer to you than the other two.) The negative terms have arcs that do not cross in three dimensions. (The apparent crossings in the left two negative terms do not actually cross in three dimensions; they are a sort of twisted version of the straight-through rightmost negative term.)

The double summation can be found graphically by connecting the i and l branch together. This gives the graphic in Figure 10.4. Note that a closed loop is the graphical representation of δ^i_i and is equal to 4. This all simplifies to the graphic in Figure 10.5.

An Application

A sample application of this technique appears in Figure 10.6. This figure shows the 4D (3DH) perspective shadow calculation.

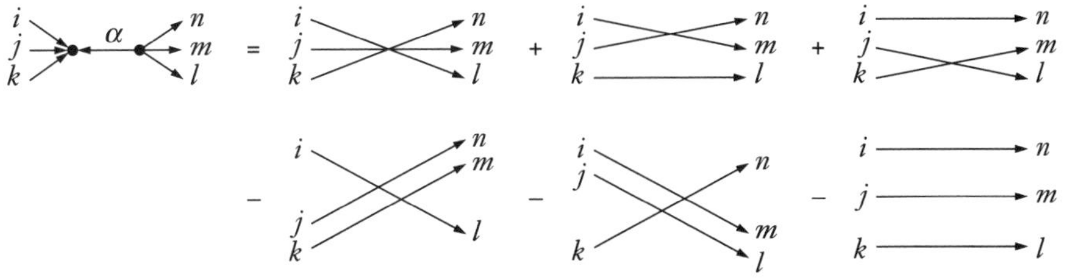

Figure 10.3 *The 4D epsilon-delta rule*

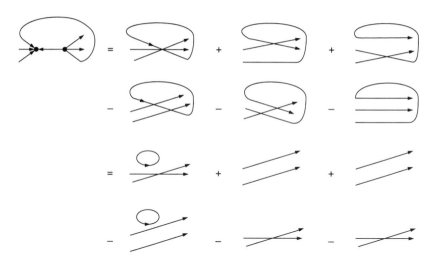

Figure 10.4 *Summing the 4D epsilon-delta rule over an additional index*

Figure 10.5 *The doubly summed 4D epsilon*

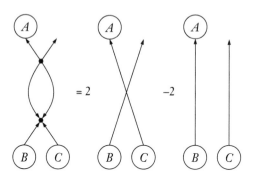

Figure 10.6 *Point B casts the shadow of point C onto point A*

Whew

The epsilon-delta rule and the nifty diagrammatic technique make a lot of pretty complicated derivations easy. I expect they will be useful in a lot of other problems too.

The observant reader will note that I've played a bit fast and loose with some global scale factors and sign changes. And that's . . . OK, 'cause, gosh darn it, we're homogeneous.

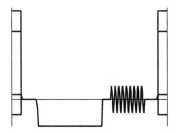

CHAPTER ELEVEN

The World of Digital Video

W e live in wonderful times. The slow elimination of all evil analog circuitry is progressing nicely. Along this line, various committees have
adopted several standards for digital video. In this chapter, I'm going to
talk about the two standards that relate most closely to the NTSC broadcast standard used in North America and Japan. Both standards were first
devised as recording technologies, but they also define byte stream signal
formats for transferring video images over serial or parallel digital cables.

The Analog World

F irst, let's review what the analog NTSC signal looks like. The basic timing of the digital byte stream must still conform to this standard. In both
the horizontal and vertical structure, there is an active video portion and a
blanked portion. A (vertical or horizontal) synch pulse is planted inside the
blanking region.

NTSC's Vertical Structure

An NTSC signal consists of 525 scan lines repeated 29.97 times per second. You can whimper about the low frame rate, but this standard is perva-
sive enough that we have to pay attention to it.

Table 11.1 *NTSC scan line numbering*

Line number	Field	Blanked	Content
1–3	1	Yes	Preequalization pulses
4–6	1	Yes	Vertical synch pulse
7–9	1	Yes	Postequalization pulses
10–20	1	Yes	Vertical retrace settling time
21–262, 263′	1	No	Visible video lines for field 1 (242.5 in all)
263″, 264–265, 266′	2	Yes	Preequalization pulses
266″, 267–268, 269′	2	Yes	Vertical synch pulse
269″, 270–271	2	Yes	Postequalization pulses
272–282, 283′	2	Yes	Vertical retrace settling time
284–525	2	No	Visible video lines for field 2 (242.5 in all)

Scan lines are interlaced, so the image is divided into two fields, each having 262.5 lines. Since there is an odd number of scan lines (the standards committee did this on purpose), the vertical synch happens in the middle of a scan line for every other field. The whole thing looks like Table 11.1. (In the table, the notation 263′ stands for the first half of line 263, and 263″ stands for the second half of line 263.)

Figure 11.1 shows the visual effect of interlace. Lines in field 1 are black and are labeled down the left side. Field 2 lines are gray and are labeled down the right side. Note that the *y* coordinate of the beginning of line 21 is the same as the *y* coordinate of the midpoint of line 283 (the point where it becomes visible, or "unblanked"). Likewise, the *y* coordinate of the midpoint of line 263 is the same as the *y* coordinate of the endpoint of line 525.

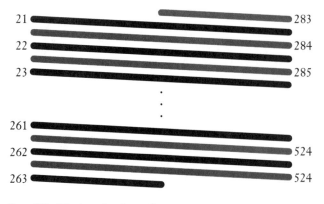

Figure 11.1 *The interlaced scan line structure*

NTSC Horizontal Timing

Figure 11.2 shows the timing of each line for which there is visible video. The line is blanked for 10.9 μs, and then visible video information occurs for about 52.7 μs. The official starting point of the line is 1.5 μs into the blanked region, on the leading edge of the synch pulse. More precisely, the starting point occurs at the instant the pulse passes the half-

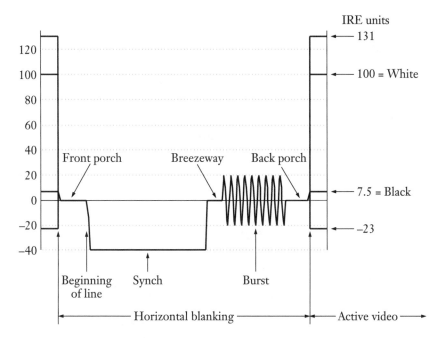

Figure 11.2 *Horizontal timing*

way point in falling to the lower level. Planted later in the blanked region is a color burst, about nine cycles of a sine wave at the color carrier frequency of $F_{sc} = 3.579545\,\text{MHz}$. The remaining portions of the blanked region have the traditionally colorful names *front porch*, *back porch*, and *breezeway*. The duration of each of these events can vary by about $\pm 0.1\,\mu\text{s}$. In addition, the transition from one voltage to another can take a few tenths of a microsecond. The total duration of a scan line, however, must equal exactly $227.5\,/\,F_{sc} = 63.55556\,\mu\text{s}$. (See Table 11.2.)

Voltage Levels

Video engineers measure voltage levels for these various events on a quaint scale called IRE units (the IRE was an early name for the IEEE). There are 140 IRE units per volt (of course). This unit was created by typical historical precedent setting. Originally, video was distributed on two wires, a

Table 11.2 *NTSC analog timings*

	Synch	Breezeway	Burst	Back porch	Video	Front porch
Duration (μs)	4.7	.6	2.5	1.6	52.65556	1.5

1-volt signal for video and a −4-volt signal for synch. When engineers merged this into one signal, they shrank the synch to −.4 volts. Then they shrank this uniformly to fit into 1 volt peak-to-peak. The IRE unit is a convenient subdivision of the volt that puts the video blanking level at the integer value of 0 IRE, with maximum video (white) at 100 IRE (.714 volts) and synch at −40 IRE (−.286 volts). They later added a bias of 7.5 IRE to the black level to make it more easily distinguishable from blanking. Therefore, the video signal ranges from 7.5 IRE (representing black) to 100 IRE (representing white).

When color was introduced, engineers encoded it by converting the (R,G,B) primaries into a more convenient space by the three relations

$$Y = .299R + .587G + .114B$$
$$I = .596R - .275G - .321B$$
$$Q = .212R - .523G + .311B$$

The letter Y is not supposed to mean "yellow"; it comes from the CIE (X, Y,Z) color space and is called *luminance*. It represents the black-and-white brightness. The letter I stands for *intermodulation* and Q stands for *quadrature*; these two represent the color part of the signal. These signals are then converted to a *composite* video signal by the following relation:

$$V = Y + I\cos(F_{sc}t) + Q\sin(F_{sc}t)$$

I will dwell on the amusing implications of this color encoding process at length in Chapter 13. For now we'll just accept it. Note that there is an implicit factor of 2π in the angles above since F_{sc} is measured in cycles per second and there are 2π radians per cycle.

There is one interesting effect to note here. A color with high luminance, Y, and high saturation might cause the V value to shoot beyond the value 1.0. For example, the color yellow with $[R \quad G \quad B] = [1 \quad 1 \quad 0]$ has $[Y \quad I \quad Q] = [0.886 \quad 0.321 \quad -0.311]$. The net video signal is

$$V = 0.886 + 0.321\cos(F_{sc}t) - 0.311\sin(F_{sc}t)$$
$$= 0.886 + 0.447\sin(F_{sc}t + 135°)$$

In other words, the V value can swing up as high as $0.886 + 0.447 = 1.333$. Likewise, for the color blue, a similar derivation shows that V can swing as low as −.333. In fact, the coefficients in the definition of I and Q were picked to keep the overflow within this range.

Finally, we stretch the composite video signal to the 7.5-to-100 IRE range by

$$IRE = 95.5V + 7.5$$

Color Plates

Figure 1.2a *Folding pattern of flat sheet*

Figure 1.2b *Folded sheet in three dimensions*

Figure 1.8 *Completed egg with equilateral triangles colored yellow*

Figure 1.9 *Completed egg with final color scheme*

Figure 1.10 *The real life egg—if you look closely, you can see Queen Elizabeth II at the base of the egg during a dedication ceremony (courtesy Ron Resch; reprinted, with permission, © Vegreville Chamber of Commerce, Alberta, Canada)*

Figure 5.6d *The quilted version of Figure 5.6c*

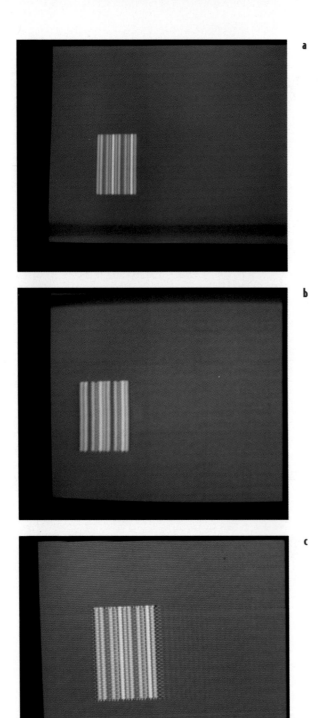

Figure 13.12 *The test pattern on three monitors: a, an RGB monitor; b, a low-pass filter monitor; c, a line-rate comb filter monitor*

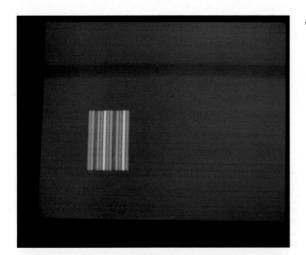

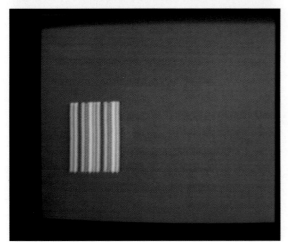

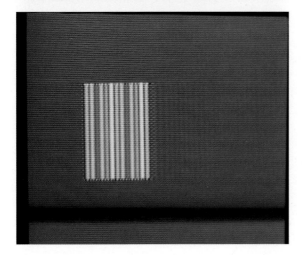

Figure 13.13 *The test pattern filtered horizontally and displayed on three monitors: a, an RGB monitor; b, a low-pass filter monitor; c, a line-rate comb filter monitor*

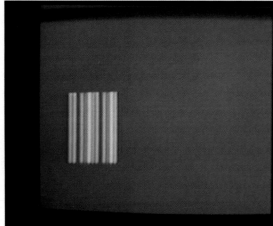

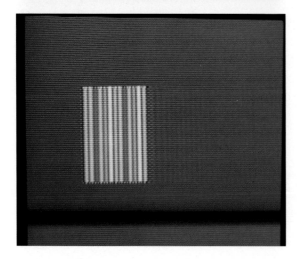

Figure 13.14 *The test pattern filtered horizontally and vertically and displayed on three monitors: a, an RGB monitor; b, a low-pass filter monitor; c, a line-rate comb filter monitor*

Table 11.3 *NTSC analog levels*

	Synch	Breezeway	Burst	Back porch	Video	Front porch
IRE level	−40	0	−20 … 20	0	B/w: 7.5…100 Color: −23…131	0

and then plop this value down into the horizontal synch framework. This means that, for saturated colors, the active video portion of the signal can swing between a maximum IRE value of $92.5 \times 1.333 + 7.5 = 131$ and a minimum of $92.5 \times -0.333 + 7.5 = -23.3$. This means that a color signal has a greater than one volt peak-to-peak swing. (See Table 11.3.)

Digital Video

As of this writing, the main use of digital video is as a recording technology. Within digital video cassette recorders, a whole lot of shenanigans are going on concerning error correction and concealment. I'm not going to talk about that part. I'm only going to discuss the external form of the digital signals. A good general reference on digital video is Watkinson's book.[1]

There are two digital standards that describe a signal with the same net timing of line rates and frame rate as analog NTSC; they are called *composite* and *component*. Both share some attributes. Both come in versions having either 8-bit samples or 10-bit samples, although early video recorders only used the 8-bit version. Both also come in serial and parallel versions. The parallel interface uses DB25 connectors. The serial interface uses coaxial cable with BNC connectors (just like analog video) but typically uses blue cable to distinguish it from cables carrying analog video. The serial version can come in one of two bit rates, but in either case the bytes are transmitted synchronously (without start or stop bits). For this reason, both formats disallow the hex byte values 00 and FF in the data stream, reserving them as synchronization codes.

The Composite Digital Standard

The first digital format I'll discuss is the most direct transfer of the composite NTSC signal but was actually devised more recently. The byte sequencing, quantization levels, and timing for the digital cabling is de-

---

1 John Watkinson, *The Art of Digital Video* (London/Boston: Focal Press, 1990).

Table 11.4 *SMPTE 244M digital timings*

	Synch	Breezeway	Burst	Back porch	Video	Front porch
Duration (μs)	4.7	.6	2.5	1.6	52.65556	1.5
Theoretical duration (clocks)	67.30	8.59	35.80	22.91	753.93	21.48
Actual duration (clocks)	67	9	36	13	768	17

fined as SMPTE standard 244M.[2] Its basic pixel clock runs at four times the F_{sc} color carrier, which comes out to 14.31818 MHz. (This is the number of samples per second that continuously stream out of the digital cable.) The vertical timing and line naming remain the same as with the analog form.

Horizontal Timing

The pixel clock gives 910 clock periods per scan line. (I'll call these periods, variously, *pixels* or *samples* or *clocks*.) By multiplying the horizontal timings by 14.31818 to get the number of clocks, we get the second row of Table 11.4. Just rounding these numbers to the nearest integer should give the number of pixels allocated to each function. But it's not quite so simple. The analog NTSC signal has a limited bandwidth, so the voltage levels for the various functions cannot transition arbitrarily in one clock time; instead, a large swing takes about four clock times.

Furthermore, the committee that specified the signal did two somewhat odd things. First, they stretched the video pixel count from 754 to 768. Converted to analog, this would provide an active video duration that is too long by 2%. The other odd thing the committee did was to name the pixels starting with 0 for the first pixel of active video rather than at the beginning of synch. This means that pixels 0 . . . 767 are active video and pixels 768 . . . 909 are the horizontal blanking interval (containing the front porch for this line, and the synch, breezeway, burst, and back porch of the next line).

Another important thing to note about horizontal timing is the exact time when the digital pixels are supposed to occur with respect to the horizontal synch pulse. The designers of the system decided to make the pixel

---

2 *Representation of NTSC Encoded (System M) Video Signal—Active Video Portion*, SMPTE standard 244M, Society of Motion Picture and Television Engineers, White Plains, N.Y.

timings coincide with the local minima and maxima of the modulated I and Q signals. This makes it easy to synthesize a composite signal. Sequential samples would look like

$$Y_0 + I_0, \quad Y_1 + Q_1, \quad Y_2 - I_2, \quad Y_3 - Q_3, \quad Y_4 + I_4, \quad Y_5 + Q_5, \ldots$$

Since there are 227.5 cycles of the color carrier per scan line, the next scan line starts with the color carrier 180 degrees offset from this one. The encoding of the pixels would look like

$$Y_0 - I_0, \quad Y_1 - Q_1, \quad Y_2 + I_2, \quad Y_3 + Q_3, \quad Y_4 - I_4, \quad Y_5 - Q_5, \ldots$$

These two line encodings alternate throughout the picture.

Now, in analog video, the relative timings of the subcarrier phase to the horizontal synch pulse are carefully defined; the zero point of the subcarrier phase must occur at the instant the horizontal synch pulse crosses the 50% point of its falling edge. This is called *maintaining proper SCH phase*. For the digital version, it works out that horizontal synch occurs exactly 33/90 of the way between samples 784 and 785. The value 33 comes from the fact that, while horizontal synch occurs in phase with the color burst, the I signal is rotated 33 degrees with respect to it. The denominator of 90 comes from 90 degrees of subcarrier phase per pixel time.

Quantization

Since we can't use the byte values 00 and FF, the remaining hex range 01 to FE covers the 140 IRE voltage range with a bit of slop at each end. Specifically, the byte value encodes an IRE value according to the equation

$$\text{ByteValue} = \text{IRE} \times 1.4 + 60$$

This gives a blanking (0 IRE) value of 60, a black level (7.5 IRE) of 70.5, and a white level of 200. This means that, for the 8-bit version, there are only 130 quantization levels—not really enough to avoid quantization artifacts. The 10-bit version gives four times as many levels (520), which is adequate. (See Table 11.5.) Digital recorders can get away with using 8 bits since analog noise generally masks the artifacts with dithering.

The phase shift between burst and the pixel centers means that the digitized values of the burst itself do not simply come out to $60 \pm (20 \times 1.4)$. The actual byte sequence is a digitized sine wave offset by 33 degrees from the zero crossings. This gives values of 83, 74, 37, 46, 83 . . . (or four times these values for the 10-bit version).

We can ensure correct SCH phase by the following calculation. First, recall I said that, because of frequency limits on NTSC, the synch pulse cannot transition from 60 (blanking) to 4 (synch) in one clock time. A rea-

Table 11.5 *SMPTE 244M digital values*

	Synch	Breezeway	Burst	Back porch	Video	Front porch
IRE level	−40	0	−20 ... 20	0	B/w: 7.5 ... 100 Color: −23 ... 131	0
8-bit value	4	60	37 ... 83	60	B/w: 70 ... 200 Color: 28 ... 243	60
10-bit value	16	240	148 ... 332	240	B/w: 280 ... 800 Color: 112 ... 972	240

sonable maximum slew rate for this pulse works out to be about 24 quantization levels per clock period. The 50% point (the exact point of horizontal synch) would occur at the quantization level 32, the average of 60 and 4. But we don't have a sample here; we have one (pixel 784) at 33/90 of a clock period before and another (pixel 785) at 57/90 of a clock period after. Now calculate that 33/90 of 24 is about 9 and 57/90 of 24 is about 15. So, to ensure SCH phase digitally, we simply give pixel 784 the value $32 + 9 = 41$ and give pixel 785 the value $32 − 15 = 17$. These are things that analog designers go into agonies over, but we can digitally synthesize them with ease.

TRS-ID

When the signal travels on a synchronous serial line, there needs to be a special byte pattern to achieve byte framing. This is called *TRS-ID* and appears just after the leading edge of the horizontal synch pulse, specifically at pixels 790 . . . 794. Since serial transmission implies 10-bit bytes, I'll switch to the appropriate 10-bit values in the following discussion. The five TRS-ID bytes have the (hex) values

3FF 000 000 000 xxx

The final byte encodes the field number and line number. The low two bits are field number, the next bit is skipped, and the next 5 bits encode the line number for lines 1 . . . 31. Lines above 31 have the value 31 here. The next bit is an even parity bit, and the high bit is the inverse of the parity bit.

More Data

Pixels 795 . . . 849 lie at the bottom of the horizontal synch pulse. Instead of merely stuffing the (10-bit) value 16 here, users have the option of inserting arbitrary auxiliary data. This data can encode the full scan line number, digital audio, or any number of other things. These bursts of data must have the format

3FC *id cnt . . . cksum*

The second byte is a data type identification code, and the third byte is a count of following bytes. The last byte is a checksum. The data ID for digital audio, for example, is 3FF. The encoding of digital audio within the data field is similar to that of the AES/EBU standard (the interchange standard for digital audio), with each sample packed into three data bytes.

Composite Recording Technologies

The composite digital format was pioneered by Sony in its D2 recorders, which use ¾-inch video tape cassettes. Later, Panasonic introduced a line of recorders called D3, which accept the same digital signal but record it on ½-inch tape. The D3 recorders might be better for editing and animation recording because they record with guard bands or gaps between the tracks, as opposed to the D2 technique in which the tracks overlap slightly.

The Component Digital Standard

Coming from an international standards effort, the component digital video standard is somewhat of an improvement over the composite one. The component standard is variously called CCIR601,[3] 4:2:2,[4] or SMPTE RP125.[5] The basic pixel clock is 13.5 MHz, which is, by design, exactly 33/35 times the NTSC clock, giving a total of 858 pixel times per line. For this standard, however, the sampling event is defined so that horizontal synch coincides with a sample, rather than having it fall between two samples as with the composite standard.

As we'll see below, there are two bytes per pixel, which gives a byte rate of 27 MB/s. In this section, therefore, I make an important distinction between pixels (858 per line, with 720 being visible) and bytes (1716 per line). Again, the time duration implied by 720 pixels at 13.5 MHz is longer than the legal analog active video duration. Analogwise, only about 711 pixels should be visible. The standards committee chose 720 to ease conversion between NTSC, PAL, and SECAM formats. The digital versions

---

3 *Encoding Parameters of Digital Television for Studios*, CCIR recommendation 601 (mod F), Comite Consultatif Internationale des Radiocommunications, 1985.

4 Glen Pensinger, editor, *4:2:2 Digital Video: Background and Implementation* (White Plains, N.Y.: Society of Motion Picture and Television Engineers, 1989).

5 *Bit-Parallel Digital Interface for Component Video Signals*, SMPTE recommended practice RP125, Society of Motion Picture and Television Engineers, White Plains, N.Y., 1984.

of all three of these have been carefully crafted to contain 720 pixels in the active video portion of the scan line.

Vertical Renaming

For the component standard, the omnipotent ones have redefined the line numbers that appear in the two fields. Digital field 1 consists of scan lines 4 . . . 265 (262 lines total) and digital field 2 consists of lines 266 . . . 525 and 1 . . . 3 (263 lines total). Go figure. Vertical blanking takes place during lines 1 . . . 9 and 264 . . . 272 but is optional on lines 10 . . . 19 and lines 273 . . . 282.

Scan Line Timing

A scan line consists of 122 blank pixels, 720 visible pixels, and 16 more blank pixels. The byte numbering, though, starts with the beginning of active video, just like the composite format. Here, however, there is no attempt to synthesize the timings of synch, blanking, and color burst. The start (and end) of the active video is denoted by a special byte sequence. Altogether, the 1716 digital samples of a single scan line have the functions listed in Table 11.6. The synchronizing sequences for start-of-active video (SAV) and end-of-active video (EAV) use the forbidden (8-bit) byte values of FF and 00. The four bytes of these sequences are

$$FF\ 00\ 00\ vv$$

A receiver of the digital signal must continuously monitor for this byte sequence and resynchronize itself appropriately whenever it sees it. The vv byte can take on eight different values indicating the conditions in Table 11.7 (the bit patterns are coded for redundancy).

Table 11.6 *CCIR 601 digital scan line*

Byte number	Contents
0 ... 1439	Active video (see below)
1440 ... 1443	End-of-active-video code
1471	The leading edge (at the half amplitude point) of the analog horizontal synch pulse coincides with this sample
1712 ... 1715	Start-of-active-video code (for next line)

Table 11.7 *vv byte meaning*

Binary value	Field	Vertical blank	Start/end
1000 0000	1	No	SAV
1001 1101	1	No	EAV
1010 1011	1	Yes	SAV
1011 0110	1	Yes	EAV
1100 0111	2	No	SAV
1101 1010	2	No	EAV
1110 1100	2	Yes	SAV
1111 0001	2	Yes	EAV

Pixel Value Quantizing

We calculate the luminance Y in the same way as with composite video. We then encode it into a byte value from 16 (black) to 235 (white). That is,

$$IY = 219Y + 16$$

This uses only 220 out of the 256 possible quantization steps. Again, this is not really enough for good images. The 10-bit version, having 880 quantization levels, is much better.

The color encoding for this format is somewhat different from the NTSC I and Q values. The so-called chrominance values are

$$C_R = 0.713(R - Y)$$
$$C_B = 0.564(B - Y)$$

The scale factors were picked to keep the C_R and C_B values in the range −0.5 to +0.5. These are then encoded into byte values 16 . . . 240 (using 225 out of the 256 quantization steps) by

$$IC_R = 224C_R + 128$$
$$IC_B = 224C_B + 128$$

We, as computer graphicists, usually encode our RGB values into the range 0 . . . 255, but if you have (IR, IG, IB) encoded into the range 16 . . . 226, the CCIR recommends that you convert these RGB values to the proper integer byte values by the following equations.

$$IY = (77\,IR + 150\,IG + 29\,IB) / 256$$
$$IC_R = (131\,IR - 110\,IG - 21\,IB) / 256 + 128$$
$$IC_B = (44\,IR - 87\,IG + 131\,IB) / 256 + 128$$

It seems to me that they should recommend that you add 128 to the values just before dividing by 256 in order to provide for rounding, but the standards committee doesn't see it that way. Anyway, for speed, you can do the multiplications of this conversion with a table lookup.

Why Is It 4:2:2?

Once you get the digital luminance and chrominance values, there is one final thing to do. The chrominance is only transmitted on every other pixel. This assumes you have (digitally or otherwise) downsampled the C_R and C_B signals to 360 samples per active video line. Thus the sampling rates for Y, C_R, C_B are in the ratios 4:2:2. (Why this isn't called 2:1:1 has to do with the mixed metaphor of the $4 \times F_{sc}$ sampling rate for composite video.) Anyway, a Y value appears for each pixel, but C_R and C_B values only appear at the even-numbered pixels. Naming the pixels with subscripts 0 . . . 719, the active video portion of the line starts out with byte 0 and looks like

$$C_{B0}, Y_0, C_{R0}, Y_1, C_{B2}, Y_2, C_{R2}, Y_3, \ldots$$

and continues up to byte 1439

$$\ldots, C_{B718}, Y_{718}, C_{R718}, Y_{719}$$

Still More Data

Just as with the digital composite signal, unused regions of the component byte stream can contain auxiliary data. Such data bursts (in 8-bit versions) should look like

$$00\ FF\ FF\ tt\ mm\ ll$$

where tt is a data identification code in the range 01 to FE. There are codes defined for line number, digital audio, teletext, and so on. mm and ll encode a 12-bit number in the range 1 to 1440, with the high bits in mm and the low bits in ll. The low bit of each of these is an odd parity bit. The six data bits occupy bits 1 . . . 6. If the identification code indicates "line number," it appears here as bytes mm and ll. Otherwise, mm and ll are byte counts for the number of bytes to follow. This data can appear anywhere within the horizontal blanking region (between the EAV and SAV codes), which that has room for 268 bytes, or it can appear in the active video region (1440 bytes long) for scan lines during vertical blanking. This will be lines 1 . . . 9 and 264 . . . 282. It can optionally be on lines 10 . . . 19 and 273 . . . 282. Whether these latter lines contain picture or data is indicated by the vertical blank status in the EAV and SAV codes surrounding the line.

Component Recording Technologies

The component digital format was originally identified with the Sony D1 recorder, which uses ¾-inch cassettes. Later, Ampex introduced a system called DCT, which also uses ¾-inch tape. Finally, Panasonic has developed something called D5 that uses ½-inch tape and can record 10-bit bytes and play D3 tapes.[6] Sounds great. Apparently, there is no such thing as D4, since "4" is an unlucky number in Asia.

I Have a Dream

I don't know why, but even though I have no intention of designing video hardware, I find these numbers fascinating. What I am really hoping for, though, is for hardware manufacturers to make frame buffers that generate the digital byte streams directly. The first thing they need to understand is the number of bytes per scan line. A lot of digital video boards have 640 pixels per active line in order to make the pixels square. This really does us no good at all with respect to the composite and component standards discussed here, which require 768 or 720 pixels and no arguments. It's important to note that this implies non-square pixel spacing. But that's all right. We just have to build a scale factor into our transformation from normalized device coordinates to pixel coordinates.

I'm not sure how to handle the inconvenient number of bits per pixel, though. Using an 8-bit byte gives too few quantization levels. Using a 10-bit byte doesn't fit very nicely into computer word lengths. What would be really neat would be to have a frame buffer that, on the computer end, looks like a standard RGB buffer. Then, on the output end, instead of having a conventional refresh controller driving DACs, there would be an on-the-fly color converter and chroma filter driving a parallel digital video connector. This would be software configurable for the component or composite encoding standard. I understand certain new video cards are beginning to do some of this.

The ideal digital frame buffer would, of course, plug directly into the various digital tape recorders for animation recording without the worries of analog noise and 60-cycle hum. Then there would be purely digital monitors that accept digital cables, do digital conversion to RGB internally, and only go to analog at the last possible moment before driving the electron guns. Ahhh . . .

---

6 B. McKernan and M. Grotticelli, D more D better, *Videography* 17(13): 28–32, March 1992.

Addendum–1998

Over the past few years, the usefulness of the NTSC composite digital video format has diminished. It was, after all, invented primarily as a recording technology that would fit easily into existing analog NTSC production facilities and provide noise-free duplication of tapes. Performing any processing on these signals still requires decoding from, and encoding to, the NTSC format with its attendant errors. See Chapter 13 for more on this.

The component digital format has become more and more popular and has spawned several new variants with different pixel/line counts and different color subsampling rates. The book *Video Demystified*[7] goes into these formats in great detail.

Both the composite and component formats described here, however, are rather wasteful in bit bandwidth. They were designed to be real-time systems, where the digital bit stream is synchronized with the scanning out of the image on the CRT. This means that they had to devote pixels to the time intervals for horizontal and vertical retrace. When you realize that only $(485/525) \times (720/858) = .775$ of the pixel time slots contain actual image information, this becomes rather painful.

More modern digital video formats do not have this waste. In addition, they apply various forms of image compression to the video itself. These typically are based on the discrete cosine transformation (DCT) described in Chapter 14. For example, a new generation of home digital video recorders is becoming popular that employs a 4:1:1 color/luminance encoding ratio. (This means that the sample rate of color information is one-quarter that of the luminance sample rate.) The format then performs some DCT-based compression on the frames to give a net bandwidth of 25 Mb/s. The frame rates, scan line count, and interlace are otherwise the same as those for NTSC.

Finally, part of my dream has been realized. It is now possible to get an RGB frame buffer with circuitry to automatically generate a component digital video signal. This allows computer animation to be recorded on digital video recorders without needing to do any analog conversion. My dreams are now moving in the direction of the elimination of interlace.

---

7 Keith Jack, *Video Demystified* (San Diego, Calif.: High Text Interactive, 1996).

NYIT

CHAPTER TWELVE

How I Spent My Summer Vacation, 1976

NOVEMBER 1992

Memories

The recent demise of the New York Institute of Technology Computer Graphics marks, as they say, an end of an era. I worked for the NYIT computer graphics lab for three months during the summer of 1976 while I was a graduate student at the University of Utah, so I thought I'd jot down some recollections about the experience. These reminiscences are just what remains in my mind 16 years later and haven't been thoroughly researched for accuracy. I just want to give you a flavor of the mood and environment of one of the early significant research institutions in computer animation. (I'll try to refrain from too many comments like, "Back in my day we had to walk five miles to the frame buffer.")

Dr. Alexander Schure, then head of NYIT, founded the lab in 1975. He had been a fan of hand-drawn animation for some time and had visions of starting his own animation department. When he set up a conventional animation studio, however, he was horrified at the slowness and expense of conventional techniques. He thought that using computers could make the whole process cheaper and faster. All of us at Utah, of course, thought so too, but it was, in fact, a radical notion at the time. Maybe someday it'll even be true.

Alex (we all called him Alex, much to the consternation of all the rest of the institute's employees, who only referred to him as Dr. Schure) hired Ed Catmull, a recent Utah graduate, to head up the lab. Ed (we called him Ed, much to the consternation of no one) then built a staff consisting of Alvy Ray Smith, David DiFrancisco, Christie Barton, Malcom Blanchard, and Bruce Laskin. The other Utah graduate students that came out with me for the summer were Lance Williams and Garland Stern.

Living Environment

So much for the characters. Now the setting: NYIT is situated in a rather posh section of Long Island, out in the middle of the woods (in fact, you can't see one building from another because of the trees). As a result, there wasn't much cheap housing for itinerant graduate students. Alex had worked out a deal with the neighboring college for me to stay in one of their dorms, but I still had to go crashing through the woods and across a main road to get to the lab.

Once, during my "commute," I was pulled over by the police since I looked suspicious coming out of the woods. After all, I had a scruffy beard and my hair was down to my shoulders. I tried to explain my somewhat unusual circumstance, but the policeman wasn't buying it. Then, as luck would have it, Alex himself happened to drive by and verified my story. I don't know what would have happened otherwise. After that, I made a nest for myself out of foam packing material under one of the workstations and began sleeping at the lab.

Since I had elected not to have a car for the brief time I was there, I was sort of at the mercy of the other, more mobile, members of the lab for food excursions. Since we also had no refrigerator, I stocked up on non-perishable items when we went to the grocery store. That's how I got my (um, totally undeserved) reputation as being a junk food junkie.

Hardware

The computing hardware we were using, while generous for that time, was of course laughably small by today's standards. The lab had two main computers, a PDP-11/45 and a PDP-11/70. These drove multiple workstations based on Tektronix storage tube terminals. The interesting part was the frame buffer situation. Alex had bought one of the new Evans & Sutherland frame buffers, which had 512×480 pixels with 1 byte per pixel and cost about $80,000. Shortly after I arrived, he placed an order with E&S of unprecedented proportions. He wanted six more buffers with the idea of ganging two sets of three of them together to make two *full color* frame buffers. We were stunned. That was 768 K of memory per full color buffer, more memory than any of us had ever seen in one place and about six times bigger than the main memory of the computer itself. The total cost (with a volume discount) was something on the order of $150,000 per frame buffer. All for one workstation. But we would have *full color*. We could do arbitrary arithmetic on the color values of the pixels for blending and antialiasing and whatever other image processing we could dream up. We no longer had to design programs around a limited palette of 256 colors with a color lookup table. The possibilities were staggering.

Today this seems quaint. I recently bought a full color frame buffer (1 MB of memory, 640×480×3 bytes per pixel) for my PC clone for $185. That's a drop in price of over a *factor of 800* in the last 16 years—the difference in cost between an 18-wheeler and a bicycle. In fact, I didn't really need the new card. I was just so amazed by the cost that I couldn't pass up the opportunity to have it. (And as I edit this article in 1998 for the book version, I note that similar cards cost about $32, a factor of almost 4700 over 22 years.)

Software

My summer at NYIT was also my first introduction to UNIX and C programming. I was not impressed.

The very first C program I wrote broke the compiler. It generated invalid code, something about a loop branch instruction that tried to jump farther than the maximum displacement that would fit in the instruction. All was not lost, however. Since UNIX came with full source code, Malcom was able to find the offending section within the compiler code and fix it. I *was* impressed by this.

The other irritation (or rather one other irritation; there were lots) was the fact that the designers of UNIX didn't believe in nine-track magnetic tape. They indicated this by punishing you for using it. Every time you tried to rewind the tape, the system would crash. And a crashed UNIX system was a pitiful thing because the file system was so fragile. Some of the staff spent much of their time "repairing I-nodes."

Work Environment

One of the most progressive things about NYIT was the physical environment. All the computers, disk drives, and other noise-producing electronics were on the first floor. The workstations were on the second floor, where it was carpeted and *quiet*. This was at a time when most computer labs placed the humans in the machine room with hard, raised floors and lots of noisy cooling fans. You could actually think in the workroom at NYIT.

The typical workday ran something like this: People wandered in about noon, as is usual in most computer installations, and gathered to go out for breakfast. We then came back, turned the track lighting down low so most of the room was dark (which we referred to as submarine lighting), played soft music (I particularly remember a jazz vibraphone record), and worked till 3 or 4 A.M. My main recollection is of people working at their terminals and every so often you'd hear someone say "Oh wow," and everybody would rush over to see what they had just done.

I was originally hired for the summer to get a special-purpose floating-point processor integrated into UNIX. That never got very far. Instead, I tinkered together two programs called m (for model) and p (for patch). The p program rendered textured patches using Ed's z-buffer algorithm. The m program implemented nested transformations and generated patch control points according to some higher-level instructions. By piping these together, I generated frames of various simple animations. Bruce Laskin had modified the lab's video recorder so that it could record single frames, so I used that to record the movie. These were some of the first animations ever produced of textured patches. The ultimate result was a scene of a running mannequin using joint-angle data taken from some early Eadweard Muybridge photographs.

Other Activities

Ed had a family to go home to each night, but the rest of us were single and usually ate and recreated together. It was sort of like summer camp, with Alvy as the head counselor. We made the summer into an animation study course. That summer, Disney had a special series of brief re-releases of most of their animated features. We dutifully attended. We also took a course taught by Leonard Maltin on the history of animation. This occurred at an odd place in New York City called the New School for Social Research, where tuition was paid at the beginning of each class meeting, like going to a movie. We'd all ride in with Alvy because he had lived in New York and knew where to find parking places.

1976 was the year of the Mars landing of the Viking spacecraft, controlled by the Jet Propulsion Laboratory. Christie and I made a trip to NASA headquarters in Washington to stock up on photos that the spacecraft returned. Little did I know that a year later I would be working at JPL myself.

1976 was also the year of the third SIGGRAPH conference, held in Philadelphia, where I gave the teapot paper with Martin Newell. We all piled into cars to drive there from Long Island. Just before we left, I videotaped a quick demo of the p program in operation to show at the conference film and video show. This was a time when the show consisted of anything anybody happened to bring with them since there wasn't enough computer animation in existence for the conference to need to be picky. When my tape played, I jumped up on stage and narrated it live.

Where Are They Now—1998

Ed and Alvy went off to Lucasfilm and then ultimately founded Pixar. David and Malcom eventually followed them. All of them but Alvy are still there. Alvy started a new company making image processing software that was ultimately bought by Microsoft. He and I now have lunch together about once a week. Lance went to Apple for a while and is now at Dreamworks. The last I heard, Christie is working at a financial institution and Bruce is in business somewhere.

The summer of '76 at NYIT was a magical time. But then if you run your life right, and have a little luck, all times are magical.

CHAPTER THIRTEEN

NTSC: Nice Technology, Super Color

MARCH 1993

NTSC, the color TV encoding scheme used in the United States, has gotten a bad rap. Everybody seems to hate it. But in my opinion the NTSC encoding scheme is one of the most amazing technical achievements of our time. Admittedly, NTSC does reduce the resolution of an image, but not as much as most people think. Done well, it can look really good, as you can see when looking at a laser video disk. Computer graphics images, though, often look messy when converted to NTSC video, even more so than the same image created with a TV camera. Why is this? In this chapter, I'll talk about the theory of NTSC, describe some ways we as computer graphicists can cooperate with NTSC hardware encoders and decoders to make better-quality images, and show the result of some semiscientific experiments on the signal. There are still a few things that puzzle me about the system, though, and I'll mention them too.

NTSC History

The main problem with the invention of color television is the same one that plagues us in computerland—downward compatibility. The color encoding system had to work transparently with existing black-and-white televisions. That means that a color signal fed to an existing black-and-white set (built before the color system was invented) had to produce a black-and-white version of the picture. Furthermore, a black-and-white signal fed to a color set had to come out as a black-and-white image. And the signal had to fit into about the same bandwidth that the original black-and-white signal took up. (Perhaps NTSC can get more respect by describing itself as an early form of lossy data compression.) To make this happen, the design engineers applied some clever frequency domain encoding as well as some knowledge of the human visual system.

Fourier Transform Theory

Before diving in and showing signals, let's review a little signal processing theory. I'm going to look at the NTSC waveform in three different ways:

1. In the time domain (the signal waveform itself)
2. In the space domain (as the interpretation of the waveform according to the raster scan)
3. In the frequency domain (as the Fourier transform of the signal)

Just as a reminder, the Fourier transform of a signal is a complex-valued function (generally interpreted as a magnitude and phase for each frequency). I will typically only show the magnitude of the transform and simply call it the frequency spectrum. Just be aware that the phase information exists but is not shown in these plots.

As shown in Figure 13.1, to do filtering operations on the spectrum, we multiply the spectrum by some desired frequency response function. In the time domain, this translates into an operation called *convolution* (a sort

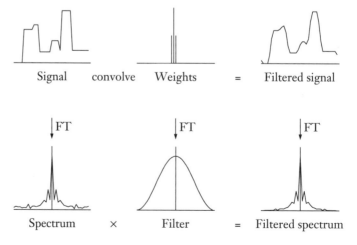

Figure 13.1 *Filtering in time and frequency domains*

of sliding weighted average). The inverse Fourier transform of the frequency response gives us the weight values. When I refer to this in the space domain, I'll usually just list these weight values. For example, a "(1,2,1) filter" means to take 2 times the current sample and add it to 1 times the previous and subsequent samples. Divide by the sum of all the weights, and the result is the output value at the current sample.

The Black-and-White Signal in Frequency Space

First, let's look at the signal for a black-and-white image scanned with a TV raster and see what its frequency spectrum looks like. In Table 13.1, I've cataloged several useful frequencies that I'll be dealing with in this chapter. Notice that I've chosen a frequency of 14.31818 MHz to define the smallest time unit. This is the pixel rate for the digital version of NTSC. Even though I'm not explicitly talking about digital video here, this clock rate is a convenient one to use. It is four times the frequency of the color subcarrier (the use of which I will define shortly), and it means that, theoretically, we can represent frequencies of up to twice the subcarrier frequency. There must be 227.5 cycles of subcarrier per horizontal line. There are 525 lines per frame, but the frame is divided into fields of 262.5 lines each. The designers of the NTSC system chose these frequency ratios very carefully, for reasons I'll describe below.

One Line

Consider a single scan line. Its intensity profile and frequency spectrum might look like the two left-hand plots of Figure 13.1. Note that the image is all positive and the DC (or zero frequency) component is just the inte-

Table 13.1 *Useful frequencies*

Event	Symbol	Frequency	
		Hz	Events/line
Pixel clock	F_p	14.31818 M	910
Subcarrier cycle	F_{sc}	3.579545 M	227.5
Scan line	F_h	15.73426 K	1
Field	F_{fld}	59.94	1/262.5
Frame	F_{frm}	29.97	1/525

grated intensity over the whole line. The magnitude of the frequencies dies down as the frequency gets higher. Since such a spectrum is symmetric about frequency 0, I'll usually only plot the right half of it.

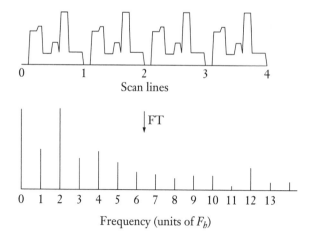

Figure 13.2 *The spectrum of a repeated scan line*

Many Lines

If this scan line is repeated over and over, the signal becomes periodic and has a discrete Fourier transform, as shown in Figure 13.2. Note that the frequency components are spaced at intervals of the horizontal line frequency F_h. In addition, in this and later figures, I have truncated the spike at frequency 0 so that I could scale up the rest of the frequency amplitudes to be visible.

Non-Interlaced Image

If the scan lines are not all the same, the signal will still be periodic, but it will repeat at the frame rate. (This assumes the image isn't moving, an assumption I will stick to for the time being.) The Fourier transform of the signal is still discrete, but it's just more finely divided, with frequency components spaced at intervals of F_{frm}. In a typical image, the scan lines do not change radically from one to the next, so there are still peaks in the spectrum at multiples of the line frequency (see Figure 13.3).

Let's take time out for a visualization discussion. In the actual NTSC signal, there are 525 gaps of width F_{frm} between every integer multiple of F_h. If I draw all of these, the diagrams would look solid black. To make details more visible, I have created Figures 13.3 through 13.11 with a sort of abbreviated NTSC signal. I've eliminated horizontal and vertical blanking (although that doesn't change the signal much), and I've used 15 lines per frame and 9.5 subcarrier cycles per line. In the text of this chapter, however, I'll always use the true values of 525 and 227.5. In the figures, whenever you see something happening at a frequency of $9.5F_h$, remember that in the actual signal it happens at the frequency $227.5F_h$.

Notice that there are two levels of detail in Figure 13.3. The peaks at integer multiples of the line rate, F_h, the

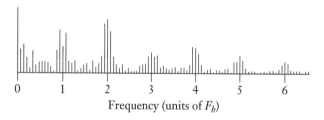

Figure 13.3 *The spectrum of a whole frame*

"macrostructure," represent the horizontal detail in the image. Between each pair of line rate peaks is a "microstructure" of 525 frequencies spaced at the frame rate (since $F_b = 525F_{frm}$). These represent the vertical detail of the image. In fact, if the microstructure had zero amplitude, we would be back to the case of identical scan lines with no vertical detail. If the image were simply blurred vertically, the microstructure amplitudes would be very small at frequencies halfway between the line rate frequencies.

As an exercise, let's examine these two levels of detail as filtering problems. A filter that will set the microstructure values to 0 will have value 1 at multiples of the line rate and will be 0 everywhere else. A plot of this filter would look like a comb, so it's called a *comb filter* (aren't engineers clever?). The inverse Fourier transform of the comb filter is another comb with teeth separated by the duration of one scan line. That is, the weights look like (. . . ,0,1,0, . . . ,0,1,0, . . . ,0,1,0, . . .) where there are enough 0s between the 1s to make up one scan line duration. Interpreting this according to the raster, we see that the unit weight values all line up vertically. We therefore have a (. . . ,1,1,1, . . .) filter that runs vertically. In other words, we must replace each pixel by the average of the entire column that it's in. Voila, we have an image with identical scan lines.

If we wanted to blur just a little bit, we might instead use a (1,2,1) filter vertically. The Fourier transform of this looks like a comb with fat teeth. It has value 1 at multiples of the frame rate (and so keeps them intact), has value 0 halfway between (and so eliminates them), and smoothly varies between. We'll have more use for this filter later.

Interlaced Image

Television signals are not scanned out simply from left to right and top to bottom, because the 29.97-Hz frame rate would look too flickery. To minimize flicker, the signal is interlaced. This means that the odd-numbered lines are scanned first, followed by the even-numbered ones. The vertical retrace rate is twice the frame rate, giving the visual impression of 59.94 flashes per second. This does not in fact make a radical difference on the frequency spectrum; there are still 525 lines per image, and the frequency spectrum is still discrete with a spacing of the frame rate. The values at integer multiples of the line rate are even the same. (Remember that these values stay intact if we vertically blur completely. It wouldn't matter if we started with a normal or an interlaced raster.)

Interlacing just changes the values at the microstructure frequencies. An easy way to think of this is to "unwrap the interlacing" and consider it as a non-interlaced image with the top and bottom halves almost identical. This introduces a strong bias toward components at 2, 4, 6, etc., times the

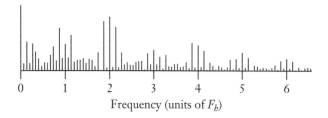

Figure 13.4 *The spectrum of an interlaced image*

frame rate. A slight complicating factor comes from the fact that there are an odd number of total lines and thus a half-integer number of lines per field. This complication makes the microstructure of the spectrum look something like Figure 13.4. Note that the first non-zero frequency (29.97 Hz) has a very small value in Figure 13.4 but a large value in Figure 13.3; that's the flicker that interlacing is designed to eliminate.

Putting Three Pounds in a One-Pound Sack

A color image has separate red, green, and blue components, each with a frequency spectrum similar to the preceding. Now, how do we combine these three components into one signal with about the same total bandwidth? The NTSC designers utilized two tricks. They first converted RGB to a color space that is based on human perception and requires less bandwidth. Second, they used the cracks in the spectrum of the signal.

Chroma Space

The human eye can perceive abrupt transitions in brightness much more readily than in hue. Furthermore, the eye is more sensitive to transitions in the orange-blue color range (where flesh tones lie) than in the purple-green range. Since NTSC takes advantage of this, the first operation is to transform RGB into a color space whose axes align with these visual ranges. The transformation is

$$Y = .229R + .587G + .114B$$
$$I = .596R - .275G - .321B$$
$$Q = .212R - .523G + .311B$$

In Chapter 8, I gave some of the motivation for the numerical coefficients used here. I just want to add a few other points. The Y signal represents the brightness, technically called *yluminance* (the *y* is silent), of the image. This is the only signal that a black-and-white TV needs. The conversion coefficients are based on the relative brightness response of the human eye to red, green, and blue. (OK, there's no such word as yluminance—that was a joke.) Given Y, we need two color coordinates that evaluate to zero when $R = G = B$. The simplest such are $R - Y$ and $B - Y$, but these values don't align with the desired color sensitivities. The I (which is the orange-blue axis) and Q (which is the purple-green axis) are simply a scaling and rotation of $R - Y$ and $B - Y$ by 33 degrees.

$$I = \frac{R - Y}{1.14} \cos 33 - \frac{B - Y}{2.03} \sin 33$$
$$Q = \frac{R - Y}{1.14} \sin 33 + \frac{B - Y}{2.03} \cos 33$$

Band-Limiting the NTSC Primaries

Just changing coordinate systems from RGB to YIQ doesn't do any data compression. Now it's time to compress. We band-limit the Y, I, and Q signals according to the NTSC broadcast standard shown in Table 13.2. The limitations on I and Q may seem extreme, but they were determined by measurements on what the human visual system can detect when viewing the screen from a typical viewing distance.

By the way, to cram six hours of video onto one teeny tape, VHS video recorders further cut the Y signal down to about 3.2 MHz and the I signal to 0.63 MHz. So VHS is considerably fuzzier than broadcast standard NTSC.

As you might expect, computer-generated images can, and often do, greatly exceed these bandwidth limitations. A typical video frame buffer has a pixel rate of $4 \times F_{sc}$. Since we can put any values we like in the pixels, we can easily generate frequencies of $2 \times F_{sc} = 7.16$ MHz by simply alternating black and white pixels or purple and green pixels. I will describe the visual results of this extreme behavior in the next section. The main punchline of this chapter is that we can't get away with this. An NTSC image will only look good if we filter these three signals (Y, I, and Q) before combining them into one composite signal.

Incidentally, it's interesting to work out how many pixels are actually necessary (in the information-theoretic sense) per scan line to represent

Table 13.2 *Bandwidth of NTSC primaries*

Signal	Maximum frequency		
	MHz	**Cycles/pixel**	**Cycles/line**
Y	4.2	1/3.4	267
I	1.5	1/9.5	96
Q	0.55	1/26	35

these signals, for example, for archiving purposes. If you downsample each signal (with proper filtering), you would need a minimum of two times as many pixels as the maximum allowed frequency. (Actually, it's best to use somewhat more than this, but we'll see what happens using just the absolute minimum number.) Next, you must take into account that only about 85% of a scan line contains image information; the rest is devoted to horizontal blanking. So we multiply the last column of Table 13.2 by 2 and by .85 and get the minimum number of image pixels needed per scan line for *Y*, *I*, and *Q* of 454, 163, and 60. These surprisingly small values are all the pixels necessary to represent a line of the best broadcast-quality video.

Combining *I* with *Q*

The NTSC process combines *I* and *Q* into one signal, called *chroma*, by a technique called *quadrature modulation*. The modulated signal is basically a sine wave of frequency F_{sc}, called the *color subcarrier*, whose amplitude, $\sqrt{I^2 + Q^2}$, is the saturation of the color and whose phase, $\tan^{-1}(Q / I)$, is the hue. Mathematically, it's simply

$$C = I \cos(F_{sc}t) + Q \sin(F_{sc}t)$$

Multiplying the *I* and *Q* signals in the time domain by a sine wave of frequency F_{sc} is the same as convolving its Fourier transform in the frequency domain with two impulses at frequencies $\pm F_{sc}$. This simply makes copies of *I* and *Q* centered around $\pm F_{sc}$. A plot of the positive copy appears in Figure 13.5. Notice that the frequencies don't line up exactly with the line rate; they're shifted by $\frac{1}{2} F_{frm}$. In addition, even though the *I* and *Q* signals are symmetric about frequency 0, the *C* spectrum is not symmetric about the subcarrier frequency because of the different phases applied when modulating *I* and *Q*. This is a case where the magnitude plots I'm using don't tell the whole story.

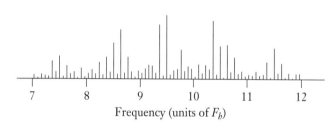

Figure 13.5 *The spectrum of modulated I and Q*

Now, how about the reverse process? In order to later extract the *I* signal from the *C* signal—that is, to demodulate it—you simply multiply by $2\cos(F_{sc}t)$, which gives

$$2C \cos(F_{sc}t) = 2I \cos^2(F_{sc}t) + 2Q \sin(F_{sc}t)\cos(F_{sc}t)$$
$$= I + I \cos(2F_{sc}t) + Q \sin(2F_{sc}t)$$

You then apply a low-pass filter to remove the last two double-frequency terms. You can get Q back similarly by multiplying by $2\sin(F_{sc}t)$ and filtering.

Now wait a minute. There's something fishy going on here. We've taken two signals, crammed them together onto one wire, and been able to separate them back out again. It looks like we're getting something for nothing. Well . . . we're not. One way to see why is to look in the time domain. Pretend for a moment that we have a digital pixel stream. The value of $\sin(F_{sc}t)$ for successive pixels has the values $0,1,0,-1,0,\ldots$ and $\cos(F_{sc}t)$ has the values $1,0,-1,0,1,\ldots$. Multiplying the I_i and Q_i samples by these values and adding the result gives us

$$+I_0 \quad +Q_1 \quad -I_2 \quad -Q_3 \quad +I_4\ldots$$

In other words, quadrature encoding basically samples I and Q at half the pixel frequency (which is twice the subcarrier frequency F_{sc}), fiddles the signs, and interleaves the samples. The whole trick is to realize that this works only if the I and Q signals don't violate the sampling theorem; that is, if they don't contain frequencies above half the sampling rate. This means that we must lop off any frequencies in I and Q that are above F_{sc}. What we've really done is take two signals, each with a bandwidth of F_{sc}, and combine them into a signal that has a bandwidth of $2 \times F_{sc}$. No magic after all. In fact, the previous section shows that I and Q are supposed to be filtered quite a bit below this limit. But, you guessed it: computer-generated signals can easily violate this, effectively giving you aliasing in the chroma signal.

Combining Chroma with Y

A recent invention called S-Video stops at this point and provides the two signals Y and C on two separate wires. But that's not good enough for broadcast video. We must combine them into one signal, and we do this by simply adding Y and C together.

Again we must ask ourselves, "Why do we think the signals are separable after simply adding them?" Here's where the cleverness of the frequency choices pays off. Look back at Figure 13.4. The Y, I, and Q signals have discrete frequency spectra (for frames that don't change in time) with spacing of F_{frm}. We formed the C signal by shifting I and Q by F_{sc}, which happens to equal $119,437.5 \times F_{frm}$. This means that the frequency spectrum of C (Figure 13.5) fits within the cracks of the frequency spectrum of Y (Figure 13.4). The result is Figure 13.6. For clarity, I've shown the frequency components due to the Y signal in gray.

Notice that there are two levels of interleaving going on here: the microstructure (representing vertical detail) and the macrostructure (representing horizontal detail). The macrostructure (which is usually all that is shown in descriptions of NTSC) consists of the line rate peaks in the spectrum. Here the C signal is shifted by $F_{sc} = 227.5F_h$ and so fits in the line rate cracks. The microstructure interleaves because the odd number of scan lines forces the $227.5F_h$ frequency point *not* to land on a microstructure frequency.

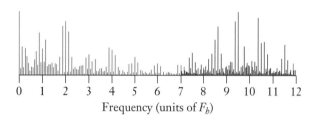

Frequency (units of F_h)

Figure 13.6 *The spectrum of the full NTSC signal*

NTSC Decoders

Now that we have the Y and C signals crammed together, let's see how a TV receiver can pull them apart again. There are several degrees of sophistication in NTSC decoders, which vary in expense and quality. We can evaluate them according to how well they separate Y from C. Errors will consist of some of the C signal remaining in the separated Y and vice versa. C remaining in Y visually looks like dots crawling up vertical edges in the image, the so-called chroma crawl. Parts of the Y signal remaining in the separated C signal visually look like rainbows superimposed on what should be a monochromatic image. In the discussions that follow, I'll describe how excessively high frequencies from a digitally generated signal can exacerbate these problems.

I'll deal with just the problem of extracting Y from $Y + C$. Once we do this, the best decoders recover the C signal by subtracting Y from the composite. Others cop out and just demodulate the whole composite signal to get I and Q, keeping the interleaved components of Y. This sort of works because the sizes of the Y signal near the color carrier frequency are typically small.

Low-Pass Filter

Older and cheaper receivers simply used a low-pass filter with cutoff at about 3 MHz to get rid of chroma. (Older black-and-white TVs do this implicitly because of their limited high-frequency sensitivity.) In Figure 13.7, I've plotted a low-pass filtered version of Figure 13.6 with the frequency filter function plotted on top of it. You can see that a bit of the C signal remains but not a lot. This technique also makes the image somewhat blurry since the high frequencies of Y are removed.

Computer-generated signals with excessive bandwidth in *C* exaggerate the chroma crawl problems with this type of decoder since the *C* signal sticks out further into the cutoff region of *Y*. For example, first note that the signal in Figures 13.6 and 13.7 has a *C* component that was band limited to the proper small range near the color carrier. Figure 13.8 is the same as Figure 13.7, except I started with *I* and *Q* signals that were not band limited. You can see that there are significant components of *C* at frequencies far from the subcarrier (at about $6.5 F_b$ in this figure) that the filter doesn't get rid of.

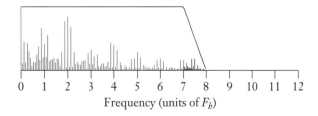

Figure 13.7 *Separating Y and Q with a low-pass filter*

Notch Filter

A somewhat more modern approach is to use a notch filter centered at F_{sc} to remove the chroma from *Y*. This retains higher frequencies above F_{sc} and thus makes for a sharper image. But notch filters still remove some of the good *Y* frequencies and have the same problems with excessive bandwidth in *C*.

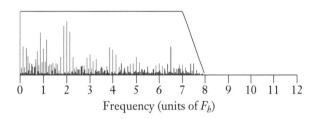

Figure 13.8 *Improper separation resulting from too much bandwidth in C*

Comb Filter at Line Rate

The interleaving of frequencies for *Y* and *C* makes their separation an ideal job for a comb filter. Let's start out by trying at a comb with fat teeth spaced at the line rate. We've seen this before. It's a (1,2,1) filter vertically. In practice, comb filter decoders usually use just a single line delay so the filter effectively has weights (1,1,0). That is, each scan line is averaged with the preceding one.

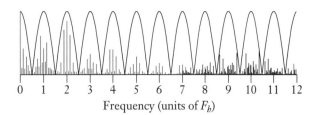

Figure 13.9 *Comb filter separation of Y and C*

The single line delay is not as good as a (1,2,1) filter, but it's cheaper. Figure 13.9 shows the effect of this filter on Figure 13.6. Here I've also plotted the filter function on top of the filtered signal. Notice that the frequency components at half-integer multiples of the line rate have been stamped out.

We can understand the scan line averaging approach in the spatial domain by noting that the chroma signal switches signs from one scan line to the next, a consequence of the half-integer (227.5) number of color carrier cycles per scan line. As long as the image doesn't change color drastically from one line to the next, the color portions of the signal cancel out. For example, a pixel might have the value $Y_{i,j} + I_{i,j}$ while the one below it would be $Y_{i,j+1} - I_{i,j+1}$. As long as $I_{i,j+1} \approx I_{i,j+1}$, the cancellation works.

The problem with the comb filter is that it can generate horizontal chroma crawl dots. This occurs when the color *does* change quickly from one scan line to the next. Look at Figure 13.10, a zoomed-in version of Figure 13.6 near the color carrier frequency. The comb filter is going to keep frequencies that are near to integer multiples of the line rate. The Y components near these frequencies represent horizontal detail. The C components near these frequencies lie in the microstructure portion of C and thus represent vertical chroma detail. Even though they have much smaller magnitudes than the macrostructure frequencies of C (which the comb filter gets rid of), the magnitudes can still be greater than those of the Y signal. In other words, vertical chroma detail comes out of the comb filter interpreted as horizontal brightness detail and actually overshadows legitimate horizontal brightness detail. Sure enough, computer images tend to do this too.

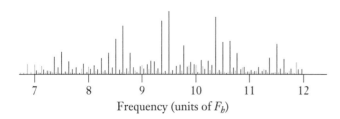

Frequency (units of F_b)

Figure 13.10 *Comb filter problems*

Comb Filter at Frame Rate

We can separate the Y and C signals more perfectly by using a finer comb filter, one whose teeth are spaced at the frame frequency. A plot of the signal subjected to this filter looks exactly like Figure 13.4. In the spatial domain, the finer comb filter translates into averaging each pixel with the same pixel from the previous and subsequent frames. (The eye does some of this implicitly—another reason for the selection of frequencies like this.) The finer filter works because the chroma changes sign not only from one line to the next but also from one frame to the next, a consequence of the $227.5 \times 525 + 119{,}437.5$ cycles of color carrier per frame. Only the most expensive monitors use this type of filter. The only problem now is if there is motion in the image. If they detect motion, very fancy monitors switch automatically between line and frame rate combs. I don't have any experience with how good this looks since Santa didn't bring me one of these monitors for Christmas. And for my purposes, that's OK. I'm really most concerned with how my images are going to look on cheap monitors since that's my primary distribution medium.

How to Cooperate with the Decoder

As mentioned previously, the way to improve the quality of the NTSC images is to filter the Y, I, and Q signals to the appropriate frequencies before passing them to an NTSC encoder. This will minimize the chroma that erroneously sticks out into the Y if you are using a low-pass filter receiver.

Then, to help with comb filter decoders, you should also filter the chroma in the vertical direction (TV cameras do this implicitly because of the focusing of their optics). A vertical $(1,2,1)$ filter applied to I and Q before modulating (leaving the Y unfiltered) should work fine. There is some trickiness here, though. The filter must act on three temporally adjacent scan lines. However, because of the interlacing, these three lines will not be visually adjacent. If you address your scan lines according to visual sequencing, your filter should be more like $(1,0,2,0,1)$. The result is the spectrum in Figure 13.11. Note that the microstructure frequencies of C from Figure 13.10 are considerably attenuated. When we apply a line rate comb filter later, there won't be any chroma here to leak through.

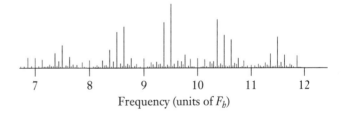

Figure 13.11 *The vertical filter applied to YIQ before encoding*

Some Experiments

OK, that's the theory. Now for some practice. My video setup consists of an RGB frame buffer feeding a transcoder that converts it to the color space $(Y, R-Y, B-Y)$. This is the color space used internally by Sony Betacam video cassette recorders. The Betacam machine has an NTSC encoder for output. Some encoders have the proper bandpass filters built in for Y, I, and Q, but apparently this one doesn't. It is, after all, designed to work mostly with signals that come from a camera and that have been filtered already.

I created a test pattern with a lot of high frequencies in *I* and *Q* and viewed it on three different monitors: an RGB monitor, a low-pass filter monitor, and a line rate comb filter monitor. The results are shown in Figure 13.12 (Color Plates). Each colored bar is six pixels wide, and there are two pixels between each bar. These eight pixels represent two cycles of the color carrier. To make problems more visible, I photographed this and the two subsequent figures with an exposure of $\frac{1}{60}$ second, so what you are seeing is only one field of the image. Note the vertical dots on both of the NTSC monitors. This is chroma crawl. Note also the horizontal dots on the comb filter monitor, especially along the bottom edge of the colored region. I am puzzled by one thing, though. Why are there vertical dots on the comb filter monitor? Shouldn't these cancel out more perfectly?

The next experiment is to do the proper filtering. Ideally, we should filter *Y*, *I*, and *Q* at three different cutoff frequencies. I shortcut a bit and did the following: I took each RGB scan line and converted the pixels to *Y*, *R* − *Y*, and *B* − *Y*. Then I filtered *Y* at a 4.2-MHz cutoff using a 9-pixel-wide filter with weights (0.0295, −0.0524, −0.118, 0.472, 1, 0.472, −0.118, −0.0524, 0.0295). Then I filtered both *R* − *Y* and *B* − *Y* with a 1.5-MHz cutoff (this is the same as filtering *I* and *Q* at 1.5 MHz). This required a filter that was 29 pixels wide. Like the previous filter, it's symmetric, and the first half has weights (0.00474, 0.01739, 0.0295, 0.02743, 0, −0.0524, −0.1123, −0.1467, −0.118, 0, 0.20746, 0.4720, 0.73489, 0.92867, 1.0, . . .). Finally, I converted the filtered values back to RGB and returned them to the frame buffer. The result is Figure 13.13 (Color Plates). Note that the vertical chroma crawl is reduced greatly, though not entirely gone. Maybe filtering *Q* further would help, but I doubt it. I do want to point out that this figure is a particularly violent test case. More typical images benefit more noticeably from filtering.

A possible problem with this technique is that filtering in the *Y*, *R* − *Y*, *B* − *Y* space might generate negative values or overflow values in the RGB space. None of the pixels in the test pattern hit these limits. If they had, I would have had to clamp them between 0 and 255. I don't know how big a problem this would be.

Finally, in an attempt to remove the horizontal chroma dots, I filtered the image vertically. I first tried a (1,0,2,0,1) filter, but it didn't look too great. Instead, I found good results by using the same spatial filter vertically as I used horizontally. After all, you don't really need any more resolution vertically than you have horizontally. Besides, filtering *Y* vertically helps get rid of 29.97-Hz flicker. The result appears in Figure 13.14 (Color Plates). Again, Figure 13.14c shows an improvement, though the dots aren't entirely gone.

Parting Thoughts

Generating a proper NTSC signal has a lot in common with the aliasing problem in computer graphics. High frequencies that the system was not designed to handle can show up as undesirable artifacts in the image. The solution is the same: Filter out the high frequencies before encoding. At first, you might say, "Ooh, ick. We're giving up high resolution." But if the high resolution just turns around and bites you with chroma crawl or rainbows, you're better off without it.

Often, people who complain about not enough pixels are not using the ones they've got effectively (a theme I will return to in the future). I think it's amusing that many feature films with computer-generated images were generated at thousands of pixels per scan line and, if they weren't very successful at the box office, have been seen on VHS tape (with its 350-pixel resolution) by more people than ever saw them in a movie theater. They almost might as well have generated them at 350 pixels in the first place.

Each of the decoders removes C from the composite signal by averaging a pixel with its neighbors. This causes blurring. The low-pass filter decoder blurs horizontally. The line rate comb filter blurs vertically. The frame rate comb filter blurs in time. Maybe it's possible to make a decoder that distributes the blur equally over all the three axes. This is something for the hardware people to look into.

And wouldn't you know it? Now that we're just figuring out how to do NTSC right, the Federal Communications Commission is going to take it away from us. Current plans call for the FCC to adopt a new high definition television standard sometime this year. The FCC will then strongly encourage all broadcasters to switch over as soon as possible. By the year 2007, the FCC wants this conversion to be complete. Broadcasters will no longer be allowed to use NTSC. Boo hoo.

Addendum—1998

Looking back on this chapter from the perspective of 1998 I find there are three things I want to add.

The Hardware Three-Axis Decoder

I speculate, in the chapter, about an NTSC decoder that would adjust its filtering across the three axes of horizontal, vertical, and time. In fact, three-axis decoders do exist but are included primarily in expensive professional video equipment. The requirement of a full frame buffer for the temporal filtering still makes them a bit pricey for home units. And by the time they are cheap enough, NTSC will have gone away anyway.

An Alternative Derivation of RGB to NTSC

In June of 1994 I received an email message from an engineer named David J. Carlstrom, who pointed out an alternative derivation of the NTSC encoding. He wrote:

> *Are you also aware that NTSC can be construed as time division multiplex, switching RGBRGB at 3.579545 MHz? I learned this is how RCA originally conceived it from a book by an RCA engineer, Brown. They originally tried to do it at about 3.9 MHz! They called it dot sequential in contrast to CBS's field sequential. Brown claims the first RCA switching receivers would receive the final form of NTSC with no modifications.*

After thinking about this for a while, I realized why this works. Using the definition of *YIQ* and the NTSC composite signal we can write

$$\text{NTSC} = Y + I\cos(F_{sc}t) + Q\sin(F_{sc}t)$$
$$= R(.299 + .596\cos(F_{sc}t) + .212\sin(F_{sc}t))$$
$$+ \ G(.587 - .275\cos(F_{sc}t) - .523\sin(F_{sc}t))$$
$$+ \ B(.114 - .321\cos(F_{sc}t) + .311\sin(F_{sc}t))$$

A little trigonometry turns this into

$$\text{NTSC} = R(.299 + .633\cos(F_{sc}t - 19.6°))$$
$$+ \ G(.587 + .591\cos(F_{sc}t + 117.7°))$$
$$+ \ B(.114 + .447\cos(F_{sc}t - 135.9°))$$

This is almost like multiplying *R*, *G*, and *B* by raised cosine waves out of phase by about 120 degrees and adding them up. This is made even more obvious by writing it in terms of a gating function that is phase-aligned with the red signal:

$$F(\varphi) = .5\cos(F_{sc}t - 19.6° + \varphi) + .5$$

Giving

$$\text{NTSC} = R(1.266\,F(\ \ \ 0° \ \ \ ) - .334)$$
$$+ \ G(1.182\,F(\ 137.3° \ \ ) - .004)$$
$$+ \ B(0.894\,F(-116.3°) - .333)$$

This actually generates the sequence *RBGRBG* rather than *RGBRGB* since the peak contribution of *B* comes before that of *G*. So . . . we could imagine a digital frame buffer that had a pixel clock at three times the subcarrier frequency with *RBGRBG* stored in successive pixels. Instant (almost) NTSC! (Well, there is the problem of the required phase reversal on alternate lines.)

HDTV Update

Finally, it's amusing to note that the comments about the FCC replacing NTSC with HDTV are as accurate today in 1998 as they were when this was originally written in 1993. Current plans call for initial broadcasts of digital HDTV in November of 1998. (Really, this time for sure.) How this will ultimately resolve itself is anybody's guess.

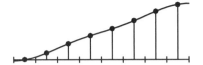

CHAPTER FOURTEEN

What's the Deal with the DCT?

J U L Y   1 9 9 3

Image compression is all the rage these days, and many popular techniques are based on a gimmick called the discrete cosine transform (DCT). It shows up in JPEG and MPEG compression schemes, in techniques for picture phone transmission, and in all of the proposals the FCC is considering as high-definition television standards to replace NTSC. Why is the DCT so wonderful and, in particular, why is it better than the easier-to-compute discrete Fourier transform (DFT)? In this chapter, I'm going to play around with both of these transforms, review their properties, and show an interesting way of thinking about them.

What Are We Talking About?

A function is a little machine that turns numbers into other numbers. You feed a number in, you get another number out. A transform is a somewhat bigger machine that turns functions into other functions. For example, the Fourier transform takes a continuous function of time (like a sound wave) or space (like an image), which we'll call $s(x)$, and turns it into a continuous function of frequency, $F(f)$. The *discrete* Fourier transform takes a list of samples of a function (indexed by discrete time or space steps), s_x, and changes it into a list of samples of another function (indexed by discrete frequency steps), F_f.

The general DFT and DCT equations have lots of variables and subscripts that make them a bit confusing to understand. Fortunately, I can simplify this a bit. All of the preceding image compression techniques divide an image into 8×8 pixel blocks and perform two-dimensional, eight-element DCTs on the blocks. For this reason, we only need to discuss eight-element transforms. This lets me explicitly write out some formulas instead of getting buried in subscripts.

For the purposes of this chapter, I will describe all frequencies in units of "cycles per eight samples." Thus, a frequency of 1 will be a sine or cosine wave with one cycle across the eight samples. According to the sampling theorem, we can't expect to represent anything higher than a frequency of 4, called the Nyquist rate.

The Discrete Fourier Transform

Let's start by considering only one-dimensional transforms. We'll first look at an eight-element DFT. The official definition is

$$F_f = \sum_{x=0}^{7} s_x e^{-2\pi i f x / 8}$$

This takes a list of eight pixel values, s_x, and generates a list of eight complex numbers, F_f. (Note that the i is not an index; it's the square root of −1.) A more edifying way of writing this is in terms of trigonometric functions, separating the real and imaginary parts of the result as follows:

$$F_f = \sum_{x=0}^{7} s_x \cos\left(\frac{2\pi f x}{8}\right) - i \sum_{x=0}^{7} s_x \sin\left(\frac{2\pi f x}{8}\right)$$

It'll be useful to give names to the separate real and imaginary parts of the F values, so

$$F_{Rf} = \sum_{x=0}^{7} s_x \cos\left(\frac{2\pi f x}{8}\right)$$

$$F_{If} = \sum_{x=0}^{7} s_x \cos\left(\frac{2\pi f x}{8}\right)$$

Now, let's admire these equations a bit. See the summation? See the product of two values under the sum? What does this remind us of? Hmm . . . yes! It's a matrix product. We can write the Fourier transform as a matrix of cosines and sines times a vector of samples, s_x. What's more, since we only evaluate the sine and cosine at integer multiples of $2\pi / 8 = 45°$, the actual values in the sine and cosine matrices are particularly simple.

Let's give a name to $\sin(45°) = \cos(45°) = \sqrt{2}/2 \equiv r$. Explicitly calculating the cosines, we can write the real part of the transform as

$$
\begin{bmatrix} F_{R0} \\ F_{R1} \\ F_{R2} \\ F_{R3} \\ F_{R4} \\ F_{R5} \\ F_{R6} \\ F_{R7} \end{bmatrix} =
\begin{bmatrix}
1 & 1 & 1 & 1 & 1 & 1 & 1 & 1 \\
1 & r & 0 & -r & -1 & -r & 0 & r \\
1 & 0 & -1 & 0 & 1 & 0 & -1 & 0 \\
1 & -r & 0 & r & -1 & r & 0 & -r \\
1 & -1 & 1 & -1 & 1 & -1 & 1 & -1 \\
1 & -r & 0 & r & -1 & r & 0 & -r \\
1 & 0 & -1 & 0 & 1 & 0 & -1 & 0 \\
1 & r & 0 & -r & -1 & -r & 0 & r
\end{bmatrix}
\begin{bmatrix} s_0 \\ s_1 \\ s_2 \\ s_3 \\ s_4 \\ s_5 \\ s_6 \\ s_7 \end{bmatrix}
$$

Giving roman letter names to vectors and boldface names to matrices, we can condense this to

$$F_R = \mathbf{R}s$$

I really wanted to write the matrix equation transposed, as a row vector times the matrix. That would make the condensed version look more like the summation version. But two eight-element row vectors don't fit on the page very well, so we'll have to use the column-vector notation.

Anyway, now let's write the imaginary part of the DFT as a matrix

$$
\begin{bmatrix} F_{I0} \\ F_{I1} \\ F_{I2} \\ F_{I3} \\ F_{I4} \\ F_{I5} \\ F_{I6} \\ F_{I7} \end{bmatrix} =
\begin{bmatrix}
0 & 0 & 0 & 0 & 0 & 0 & 0 & 0 \\
0 & r & 1 & r & 0 & -r & -1 & -r \\
0 & 1 & 0 & -1 & 0 & 1 & 0 & -1 \\
0 & r & -1 & r & 0 & -r & 1 & -r \\
0 & 0 & 0 & 0 & 0 & 0 & 0 & 0 \\
0 & -r & 1 & -r & 0 & r & -1 & r \\
0 & -1 & 0 & 1 & 0 & -1 & 0 & 1 \\
0 & -r & -1 & -r & 0 & r & 1 & r
\end{bmatrix}
\begin{bmatrix} s_0 \\ s_1 \\ s_2 \\ s_3 \\ s_4 \\ s_5 \\ s_6 \\ s_7 \end{bmatrix}
$$

Naming the vectors and matrix, we get

$$F_I = \mathbf{R}s$$

Let's pause to observe some patterns in the elements of the previous two matrices. First, note that they are both symmetric and are both singular (because of repeated rows). Each row of $\mathbf{R}$ is a cosine function digitized at some sample rate, while each row of $\mathbf{S}$ is a sine function digitized at the same rate. We will call a row of such a matrix, plotted against its index, a *basis function*.

A pair of corresponding rows from $\mathbf{R}$ and $\mathbf{S}$, when dotted with the column vector of samples, gives the real and imaginary part of the frequency response for that frequency: Row 0 (the top row) gives the amount of frequency 0 (also called the DC component), row 1 gives the amount of frequency 1, and so forth.

Note that there are lots of common terms in the arithmetic for computing the matrix products. For example the product rs_1 shows up in rows 1, 3, 5, and 7. The fast Fourier transform (FFT) is simply an organized way of exploiting these common computations.

The Inverse DFT

The inverse transform is defined as

$$s_x = \frac{1}{8} \sum_{f=0}^{7} F_f \cos\left(\frac{2\pi fx}{8}\right) - i\frac{1}{8} \sum_{f=0}^{7} F_f \sin\left(\frac{2\pi fx}{8}\right)$$

The reason this works can be easily seen in terms of matrix products. The forward transform is the matrix

$$\mathbf{R} - i\mathbf{S}$$

The matrix form of the inverse is

$$\frac{1}{8}(\mathbf{R} + i\mathbf{S})$$

Multiplying these two matrices gives

$$\frac{1}{8}((\mathbf{RR} + \mathbf{SS}) + i(\mathbf{SR} - \mathbf{RS}))$$

The basis functions for the Fourier transform (the rows of the matrix) are *orthogonal*. That means that if you take the dot product of any two different rows, you get zero. This makes the product of $\mathbf{R}$ times $\mathbf{R}$ and of $\mathbf{S}$ times $\mathbf{S}$ easy to calculate (recall that they're symmetrical). The result is quite pretty.

$$\mathbf{RR} = \begin{bmatrix} 8 & 0 & 0 & 0 & 0 & 0 & 0 & 0 \\ 0 & 4 & 0 & 0 & 0 & 0 & 0 & 4 \\ 0 & 0 & 4 & 0 & 0 & 0 & 4 & 0 \\ 0 & 0 & 0 & 4 & 0 & 4 & 0 & 0 \\ 0 & 0 & 0 & 0 & 8 & 0 & 0 & 0 \\ 0 & 0 & 0 & 4 & 0 & 4 & 0 & 0 \\ 0 & 0 & 4 & 0 & 0 & 0 & 4 & 0 \\ 0 & 4 & 0 & 0 & 0 & 0 & 0 & 4 \end{bmatrix}$$

The square of the **S** matrix is

$$
\mathbf{SS} =
\begin{bmatrix}
0 & 0 & 0 & 0 & 0 & 0 & 0 & 0 \\
0 & 4 & 0 & 0 & 0 & 0 & 0 & -4 \\
0 & 0 & 4 & 0 & 0 & 0 & -4 & 0 \\
0 & 0 & 0 & 4 & 0 & -4 & 0 & 0 \\
0 & 0 & 0 & 0 & 0 & 0 & 0 & 0 \\
0 & 0 & 0 & -4 & 0 & 4 & 0 & 0 \\
0 & 0 & -4 & 0 & 0 & 0 & 4 & 0 \\
0 & -4 & 0 & 0 & 0 & 0 & 0 & 4
\end{bmatrix}
$$

Note that some rows of **R** and **S** are identical, otherwise their squares would be diagonal matrices. Anyway, add these matrices, divide by 8, and voila—an identity matrix.

Now how about the imaginary component? Well, the product of **R** and **S** is all zeros since you always get different rows when picking one each from **R** and **S.**

A More Compact Form

The eight-element DFT takes a list of eight numbers and produces 16 numbers (eight real and eight imaginary coefficients). This seems to violate the law of conservation of information. We expect to shove eight numbers into the DFT and get eight independent numbers out. And that's really what happens. In matrix **R**, note that row 3 equals row 5, row 2 equals row 6, and row 1 equals row 7 (we start numbering from 0). In other words rows 5, 6, and 7 give redundant information; there are only five independent rows. Likewise in matrix **S,** row 0 and row 4 are really boring, row 3 equals minus row 5, row 2 equals minus row 6, and row 1 equals minus row 7; so only rows 1, 2, and 3 give interesting information.

Let's formulate a transformation matrix that just generates the interesting information from the DFT. We can define a new output vector containing just the unique elements of F: F_0, the real and imaginary parts of F_1, F_2, and F_3, and the real part of F_4. This gives us

$$
\begin{bmatrix}
F_{R0} \\
F_{R1} \\
F_{I1} \\
F_{R2} \\
F_{I2} \\
F_{R3} \\
F_{I3} \\
F_{R4}
\end{bmatrix}
=
\begin{bmatrix}
1 & 1 & 1 & 1 & 1 & 1 & 1 & 1 \\
1 & r & 0 & -r & -1 & -r & 0 & r \\
0 & r & 1 & r & 0 & -r & -1 & -r \\
1 & 0 & -1 & 0 & 1 & 0 & -1 & 0 \\
0 & 1 & 0 & -1 & 0 & 1 & 0 & -1 \\
1 & -r & 0 & r & -1 & r & 0 & -r \\
0 & r & -1 & r & 0 & -r & 1 & -r \\
1 & -1 & 1 & -1 & 1 & -1 & 1 & -1
\end{bmatrix}
\begin{bmatrix}
s_0 \\
s_1 \\
s_2 \\
s_3 \\
s_4 \\
s_5 \\
s_6 \\
s_7
\end{bmatrix}
$$

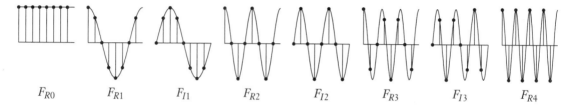

F_{R0} F_{R1} F_{I1} F_{R2} F_{I2} F_{R3} F_{I3} F_{R4}

Figure 14.1 *Basis functions for the discrete Fourier transform (labeled with the coefficients they generate)*

Let's call this gigantic matrix **F**. Row 0 gives the DC component. Rows 1 and 2 are digitized cosine and sine at frequency 1. Rows 3 and 4 are digitized cosine and sine at frequency 2. Rows 5 and 6 are digitized cosine and sine at frequency 3. Row 7 is a cosine at frequency 4. Figure 14.1 shows a plot of all eight of these basis functions. In these plots, I've overlaid the curve of the continuous sines and cosines for reference.

We can also think of the results of this transform in terms of magnitudes and phase angles. We get a magnitude for frequencies 0, 1, 2, 3, and 4, and we get phase angles for frequencies 1, 2, and 3. The phase angles of frequencies 0 and 4 are implicitly zero.

There's something special about this matrix. Can you find it? It's based on the orthogonality property of the basis vectors. Orthogonality implies that multiplying **F** times the transpose of **F** gives you something that's almost an identity matrix. In particular, you get a diagonal matrix with the diagonal elements having values (8, 4, 4, 4, 4, 4, 4, 8). I'll let you ponder this a bit while I proceed to the DCT.

The Discrete Cosine Transform

As I've indicated, the discrete Fourier transform generates a complex-valued result. We use the discrete *cosine* transform as a way of doing frequency analysis without needing complex numbers. There are two ways of thinking about how the DCT does this: We either modify the signal or we modify the basis functions.

The signal modification approach works as follows. First, note that all imaginary components of the Fourier transform come from multiplication by a digitized sine wave (an antisymmetric function) at some frequency. Specifically, each row of matrix **S** is antisymmetric about column 4. If the signal happened to be symmetric, that is, if $s_1 = s_7, s_2 = s_6,$ and $s_3 = s_5,$ then all the terms would cancel out and all the imaginary components would be zero. The DCT builds on this concept with a few modifications. An eight-element DCT generates an artificial symmetric 16-element signal by appending a reversed copy of the signal to itself. It then performs a variant of a 16-element DFT on the symmetric signal. The variation, as illustrated in Figure 14.2, centers the 16-element signal within the cosine or sine wave. The result is eight unique non-zero terms from the cosines and eight zero terms from the sines.

In the basis function interpretation, we simply use basis functions that are only cosines, but we also allow half-integer frequencies. That is, instead of using frequencies 0, 1, 2, 3, and 4, we use frequencies 0, 0.5, 1, 1.5, 2, 2.5, 3, and 3.5. Again, for symmetry, we don't start digitizing the cosine basis functions at zero degrees but at an offset of one-half the pixel spacing.

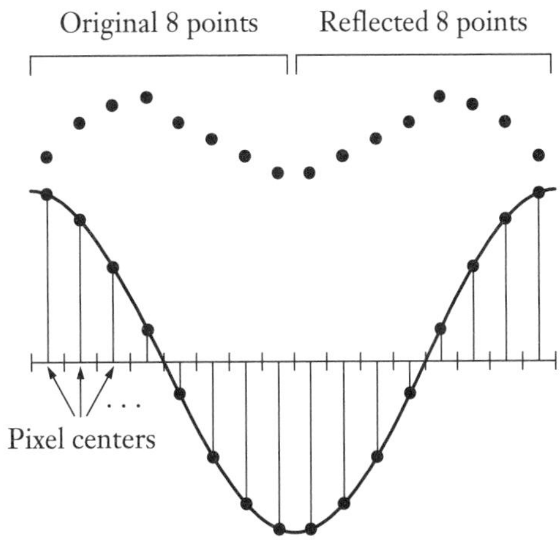

This all boils down to an official definition of the DCT as

Figure 14.2 *Centering of the discrete cosine transform basis function* $G_{\frac{1}{2}}$

$$G_{u/2} = \frac{1}{2} K_u \sum_{x=0}^{7} s_x \cos\left(\frac{(2x+1)u\pi}{16}\right)$$

where $K_0 = \sqrt{2}/2$ and $K_u = 1$ for $u \neq 0$.

Now let's discuss some of the details of this definition. First, note the somewhat funny "subscripting" of the output elements, $G_{u/2}$. I did this to label each output coefficient with the frequency it stands for. I'll tell you the reason for the K_u factor in a minute.

The DCT formula only uses samples of the cosine function spaced at integer multiples of $\pi/16$, so we can see what is going on a bit more easily by defining the function

$$c_j \equiv \cos\left(\frac{j\pi}{16}\right)$$

You really only need to know the values from the first quadrant of the cosine function, $c_0, \ldots, c_7$, since you can get the cosine of all other angles by shifting and reflecting them back to the first quadrant. I've listed these eight values in Table 14.1.

Since the c_i values are cosines, you can use various trigonometric identities to establish a whole catalog of relationships between their values. In particular, the equation for the cosine of the sum of two angles turns into

$$c_{i+j} = c_i c_j - c_{8-i} c_{8-j}$$

Given this, I entertained myself for a weekend by plugging in all permutations of i and j, shifting and reflecting the c_j's to only use subscripts from 0 to 7, and eliminating duplicates. The resultant collection of identities is

Table 14.1 *Values of c_j*

| | Angle | | Value | |
	Radians	Degrees	Precise	Numeric
c_0	0	0	1	1
c_1	$\pi/16$	11.25	$\frac{1}{2}\sqrt{2+\sqrt{2+\sqrt{2}}}$	0.9807853
c_2	$2\pi/16$	22.50	$\frac{1}{2}\sqrt{2+\sqrt{2}}$	0.9238794
c_3	$3\pi/16$	33.75	$\frac{1}{2}\sqrt{2+\sqrt{2-\sqrt{2}}}$	0.8314695
c_4	$4\pi/16$	45.00	$\frac{1}{2}\sqrt{2}$	0.7071065
c_5	$5\pi/16$	56.25	$\frac{1}{2}\sqrt{2-\sqrt{2-\sqrt{2}}}$	0.5555699
c_6	$6\pi/16$	67.50	$\frac{1}{2}\sqrt{2-\sqrt{2}}$	0.3826829
c_7	$7\pi/16$	78.75	$\frac{1}{2}\sqrt{2-\sqrt{2+\sqrt{2}}}$	0.1950897

$$1 = c_1^2 + c_7^2 = c_2^2 + c_6^2 = c_3^2 + c_5^2 = 2c_4^2$$
$$c_1 = c_1c_2 + c_7c_6 = c_2c_3 + c_6c_5 = c_4(c_3 + c_5)$$
$$c_2 = c_1c_3 + c_7c_5 = 2c_3c_5 = c_1^2 - c_7^2 = c_4(c_2 + c_6)$$
$$c_3 = c_1c_2 - c_7c_6 = c_2c_5 + c_6c_3 = c_4(c_1 + c_7)$$
$$c_4 = c_1c_3 - c_7c_5 = c_1c_5 + c_7c_3 = 2c_2c_6 = c_2^2 - c_6^2)$$
$$c_5 = c_1c_6 + c_7c_2 = c_3c_2 - c_5c_6 = c_4(c_1 - c_7)$$
$$c_6 = c_1c_5 - c_3c_7 = c_3^2 - c_5^2 = 2c_1c_7 = c_4(c_2 - c_6)$$
$$c_7 = c_1c_6 - c_2c_7 = c_5c_2 - c_3c_6 = c_4(c_3 - c_5)$$

You can generate another glob of identities by looking at the "Precise" column in Table 14.1. Some fiddling gives

$$c_1 = \tfrac{1}{2}\sqrt{2+2c_2} \qquad c_7 = \tfrac{1}{2}\sqrt{2-2c_2}$$
$$c_2 = \tfrac{1}{2}\sqrt{2+2c_4} \qquad c_6 = \tfrac{1}{2}\sqrt{2-2c_4}$$
$$c_3 = \tfrac{1}{2}\sqrt{2+2c_6} \qquad c_5 = \tfrac{1}{2}\sqrt{2-2c_6}$$

I haven't yet determined whether these observations are particularly useful.

Anyway, finally writing the definition of the DCT as a matrix gives us

$$
\begin{bmatrix} G_0 \\ G_{1/2} \\ G_1 \\ G_{3/2} \\ G_2 \\ G_{5/2} \\ G_3 \\ G_{7/2} \end{bmatrix} = \frac{1}{2} \begin{bmatrix} c_4 & c_4 & c_4 & c_4 & c_4 & c_4 & c_4 & c_4 \\ c_1 & c_3 & c_5 & c_7 & -c_7 & -c_5 & -c_3 & -c_1 \\ c_2 & c_6 & -c_6 & -c_2 & -c_2 & -c_6 & c_6 & c_2 \\ c_3 & -c_7 & -c_1 & -c_5 & c_5 & c_1 & c_7 & -c_3 \\ c_4 & -c_4 & -c_4 & c_4 & c_4 & -c_4 & -c_4 & c_4 \\ c_5 & -c_1 & c_7 & c_3 & -c_3 & -c_7 & c_1 & -c_5 \\ c_6 & -c_2 & c_2 & -c_6 & -c_6 & c_2 & -c_2 & c_6 \\ c_7 & -c_5 & c_3 & -c_1 & c_1 & -c_3 & c_5 & -c_7 \end{bmatrix} \begin{bmatrix} s_0 \\ s_1 \\ s_2 \\ s_3 \\ s_4 \\ s_5 \\ s_6 \\ s_7 \end{bmatrix}
$$

We'll name the vector and matrix as follows:

$$G = \mathbf{C}s$$

A few notes: The factor $\frac{1}{2}$ is built into the matrix **C**. I left it outside for neatness when I wrote the explicit matrix. Also, note that, according to the formula, the top row of the matrix should be a row of the values $K_0 c_0$. Since $K_0 = c_4$ and $c_0 = 1$, I just used c_4 for the top row.

Perusing the matrix, we can see various patterns. For example, if we ignore signs and treat the top row c_4 as a disguised c_0, we see that each column contains each value of c_j exactly once. Each row of the matrix is a digitized cosine of frequencies 0, 0.5, 1, 1.5, 2, 2.5, 3, and 3.5. There is no wave at the Nyquist rate of 4. Note that row 1 has one sign change, row 2 has two sign changes, and so forth. A plot of these basis functions appears as Figure 14.3.

This matrix **C** is not symmetric, but it does have the orthogonality property. In addition, each row of the matrix dotted with itself gives the value 1. (We invented the factor of K_0 to make this true for the top row too.) In other words, matrix **F** times the transpose of matrix **F** gives an identity matrix; the transpose is the inverse. And what does this mean? *The DCT matrix is a rotation matrix in 8-dimensional space.*

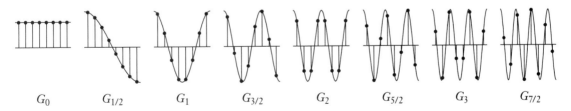

G_0 $\qquad$ $G_{1/2}$ $\qquad$ G_1 $\qquad$ $G_{3/2}$ $\qquad$ G_2 $\qquad$ $G_{5/2}$ $\qquad$ G_3 $\qquad$ $G_{7/2}$

Figure 14.3 *Basis functions for the discrete cosine transform (labeled with the coefficients they generate)*

Among other things, this means that the Euclidean length of a sample vector remains unchanged after rotation. So

$$\sum G_{j/2}^2 = \sum s_j^2$$

This quantity is sometimes referred to as the energy of the signal. The nice thing about both the DFT and DCT is that they pack more of the energy into the lower-order coefficients, so we don't lose energy by dropping some of the high-order coefficients.

Comparing the DFT with the DCT

Our compact form of the DFT—the matrix $\mathbf{F}$—was almost a rotation matrix. We could modify it a bit to make it exactly a rotation by scaling the top and bottom rows by $\sqrt{1/8}$ and the inside rows by $\sqrt{1/4}$. We would then have to define some scaled frequency components, like $\tilde{F}_{R0} \equiv \sqrt{1/8}\,F_{R0}$, $\tilde{F}_{R1} \equiv \sqrt{1/4}\,F_{R1}$, and so forth, as results of the transform. I won't explicitly rewrite the matrix equation for this, but I will use the pure rotation version in the example later.

The main point of comparing the DFT with the DCT is the amount of arithmetic necessary. Note that, with the DFT, all the multiplications involve the rather simple numbers 0, 1, -1, r and $-r$. In fact, you can perform the compact DFT with only four multiplications of r by s_1, s_3, s_5, and s_7 and a handful of additions and subtractions. On the other hand, examining the DCT matrix product reveals that we must calculate all possible permutations of products of c_j with s_x. That, on the surface of it, would look like 64 multiplications. Fortunately, there is a whole raft of fast DCT algorithms that take advantage of various symmetries in the calculation. A nice introduction to these algorithms appears in Pennebaker and Mitchell's *JPEG Still Image Data Compression Standard*.[1] None of them, however, is as fast as an eight-element DFT.

Why Is the DCT Better?

The DCT is harder to compute, so there must be some good reason for using it. The reason can be most simply stated as follows: *We need fewer DCT coefficients than DFT coefficients to get a good approximation to a typical signal.* Remember, the whole reason for performing a transform is that we

---

1   William B. Pennebaker and Joan L. Mitchell, *JPEG Still Image Data Compression Standard* (New York: Van Nostrand Reinhold, 1993).

expect that the higher-frequency coefficients are small in magnitude and can be more crudely quantized than the low-frequency coefficients.

For example, consider a simple ramp function, shown in Figure 14.4a. The DCT coefficients and the DFT coefficients appear in Table 14.2. Now suppose, for compression purposes, that we keep only the three largest coefficients of each of these transforms and then perform the inverse transform. The result appears in Table 14.3 and is plotted in Figure 14.4b and 14.4c. You can see that the DCT result is much better. This is basically because the DFT approximation is trying to model a repeated ramp, or sawtooth wave. It has to devote a lot of high-frequency coefficients to approximate the (actually spurious) discontinuities from one copy of the wave to the next. The DCT, on the other hand, is effectively operating on a triangle wave, one formed from the ramp alternating with its reflection. There is no discontinuity and therefore less need for high frequency coefficients to model one. The DCT is thus better equipped to model finite-length pieces of a function (eight samples' worth in our examples) that have fairly different values on their right and left sides. In fact, you can do approximate linear interpolation between any two endpoint values of a pixel row by using just the two lowest-frequency DCT basis functions.

Figure 14.4a *Original ramp*

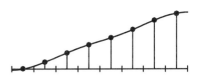

Figure 14.4b *Reconstruction from truncated DCT*

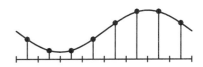

Figure 14.4c *Reconstruction from truncated DFT*

The 2D DCT

Image compression uses a two-dimensional DCT applied to blocks of 8×8 pixels. The 2D DCT consists of taking a one-dimensional DCT of each column of pixels followed by a one-dimensional DCT of each row of the result. This gives an 8×8 matrix, **G.** In matrix terms, this is simply

$$\mathbf{G = FsF^t}$$

where each item in the above equation is an 8×8 matrix.

Table 14.2 *Transforms of ramp function*

s_x	DCT	DFT
0	356.38	356.38
36	−213.92	−72.00
72	0.00	−173.82
108	−24.24	−72.00
144	0.00	−72.00
180	−7.23	−72.00
216	0.00	−29.82
252	−1.83	−50.91

Table 14.3 *Accuracy of truncated transforms*

Truncated DCT	IDCT	Truncated DFT	IDFT
356.38	2.19	356.38	90.00
−213.92	31.95	−72.00	39.09
0.00	73.46	−173.82	39.09
−24.24	110.11	0.00	90.00
0.00	141.89	0.00	162.00
0.00	178.54	0.00	212.91
0.00	220.05	0.00	212.91
0.00	249.81	0.00	162.00

Why Is This Interesting?

DCT-based image compression takes advantage of the fact that most images don't have much energy in the high-frequency coefficients. Thinking of the DCT as an eight-dimensional rotation gives us another way to look at this. Let's go back to one-dimensional transformations and consider a row of eight pixels as a point in eight-dimensional space. Various rows of eight pixels from various images would make a cluster of points in this space. For typical images, this cluster is not uniformly dispersed; it is squashed fairly flat in some directions. The eight-element DCT rotates this cluster so that the flat directions line up along some of the coordinate axes. You can then get away with representing the points of the cluster (each of which represents a row of eight pixels) in a lower-dimensional space. The DCT doesn't always find the flattest direction, though. In fact, analyzing images for the direction (in eight-space) where the cluster is flattest corresponds to looking for other sets of basis vectors to use for a transformation. This is the idea behind a transformation called the Karhunen-Loéve transform.[2] The DCT comes pretty close to the Karhunen-Loéve, though.

Finally, the representation of the DCT or DFT as a matrix and the inverse transform as a matrix inversion bolsters my claim: *All problems in computer graphics can be solved with a matrix inversion.*

---

2 R. J. Clarke, Orthogonal transforms for image coding (Chapter 3), in *Transform Coding of Images* (San Diego, Calif.: Academic Press, 1985).

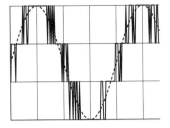

CHAPTER FIFTEEN

Quantization Error and Dithering

We all love the digital world of the future. Digital storage and transmission promise noise-free images, but it's important to keep in mind that even digital isn't perfect. Digital images have their own sources of noise: roundoff error and quantization error. Whenever you do any sort of image arithmetic, such as contrast enhancement or compositing, you get roundoff error. In fact, since the arithmetic is often done in only 8-bit accuracy, sometimes the roundoff error can be substantial. You get quantization error, on the other hand, whenever you go from an analog signal to a digital signal or whenever you go from a high-color-resolution signal (for example, 24 bits per pixel) to a low-resolution signal (for example, 8 bits per pixel). It's my purpose here to play around a bit with just a subset of these problems: the quantization error from analog to digital.

Input Signals

I'm going to present a series of experiments that compare various ways of quantizing analog signals. For simplicity, I'll just deal with a single monochrome scan line containing 512 pixels. All the analysis is therefore one dimensional. I'll start with 512 analog samples in the range from 0.0 (for black) to 1.0 (for white). You can think of these as coming from a cam-

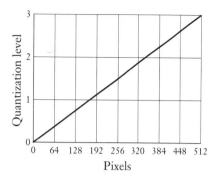

Figure 15.1a *Ramp*

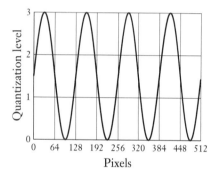

Figure 15.1b *Sine wave*

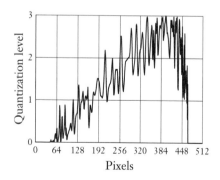

Figure 15.1c *Image*

era, or you can think of them as the floating-point results of some rendering calculation.

I'll use three analog input signals: a simple ramp (since it shows the effect of the quantization process very clearly), a pure sine wave, and a typical scan line from an image. Figure 15.1 shows these three signals.

Output Signals

Our quantized signal will have four quantization levels—from 0 (black) to 3 (full brightness). The first thing we will do, then, is scale the floating-point analog input by 3 to get it in the range 0.0 through 3.0. The main decision our quantizer must make is how to assign an integer value for a pixel with a fractional intensity value.

Discrete Quantization

The most obvious quantization technique is to approximate the analog value F by assigning it the nearest integer value I. We round to the nearest integer by adding one-half to F and truncating:

$$I = \text{floor}(F + .5)$$

First, look at how this affects the ramp signal in Figure 15.2a. It divides the analog input range into four regions and assigns a digital value to each: (0.0, 0.5) maps to 0, (0.5, 1.5) maps to 1, (1.5, 2.5) maps to 2, and (2.5, 3.0) maps to 3. This is the technique I used in Chapter 5. Figures 15.2b and 15.2c show it applied to the sine wave and image scan line.

Evaluation

How good an approximation is discrete quantization to the original signal? The most obvious comparison is just to plot the digital signal on top of the analog one and see how they differ. I've done this in Figures 15.2a, 15.2b, and 15.2c—the original signal appears as a dashed line in the background. These diagrams miss some important things, however. We all know that discrete quantization makes crummy images—all banded and posterized-looking. How can we see this mathematically?

A more revealing analysis is to compare the Fourier transforms of the original and quantized signals. There are two reasons that this visualization is interesting: the Kell factor and the spatial frequency response of the eye.

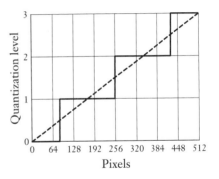

Figure 15.2a *Discrete quantization: ramp*

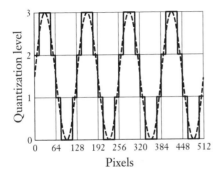

Figure 15.2b *Discrete quantization: sine wave*

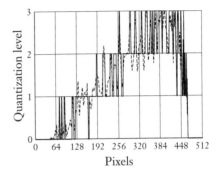

Figure 15.2c *Discrete quantization: image*

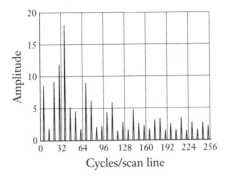

Figure 15.2d *Discrete quantization: sine wave spectrum error*

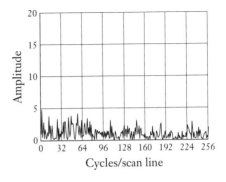

Figure 15.2e *Discrete quantization: image spectrum error*

The Kell Factor

According to the sampling theorem, a digitally sampled image can represent any frequency up to half the sampling frequency (the Nyquist rate, which would be a simple alternation of 1s and 0s). This is only a theoretical limit, however. In the real world of display technology, we're not so lucky. When we display a digital signal on a monitor, we must use what is called a *reconstruction filter*. This simply means that the analog circuits will do some sort of interpolation for intensity values between the pixels. A perfect filter, one that keeps all frequencies up to the Nyquist rate, would use a $(\sin x)/x$–shaped interpolation profile. Real-world displays, as a result of amplifier response and electron beam profile, use a more Gaussian-shaped profile.

Experimental measurements of the visibility of various sine wave frequencies have shown that, as a rule of thumb, we can expect to retain only frequencies up to about 0.7 of the Nyquist rate. This is why a Nyquist checkerboard of black and white pixels looks pretty much uniform gray on a monitor. The factor of 0.7 is called the Kell factor.[1] This works out to about 180 cycles per scan line in our examples. Any errors in the frequency spectrum above 180 cycles per scan line will be pretty much smeared out by the display.

Spatial Response of Eye

The eye also acts as a filter—a bandpass filter. The most sensitive frequency is approximately 2 cycles per degree of angle subtended at the eye.[2] Frequencies lower and higher than this are attenuated. What does this mean for a typical computer graphics viewing situation? Well, viewing a 14-inch monitor from 36 inches away gives a viewing angle of $2 \arctan(\tfrac{7}{36}) = 22$ degrees across a scan line. This means that the eye's most sensitive frequency is about 44 cycles per scan line.

Comparisons

To see how well (or how poorly, actually) uniform quantization does, let's compare the frequency spectrum of the original signals with their quantized versions. One way to do this would be to subtract the original from the quantized signal and take the Fourier transform of this error signal. I don't like this a whole lot. The eye, after all, never really subtracts images. Instead, I'm going to reverse the order and plot the difference in the (mag-

---

1 D. E. Pearson, *Transmission and Display of Pictorial Information* (New York: John Wiley & Sons, 1975), pages 94–95.

2 Pearson, page 44.

nitude of the) Fourier transforms. The absolute value of these differences appears in Figures 15.2d and 15.2e. These plots, then, show the difference between the spectral content of the signal and its approximation. Ideally, this would be zero.

For Figures 15.2d and 15.2e, we see that most of the error is in the sensitive range near 44 cycles per line, and not much is up near the higher frequencies. Uniform quantization doesn't work very well.

Random Dither

You can get a better approximation by the following realization. For an analog value some fraction of the way between 3 and 4, say, 3.25, you should not just pick 3 for your quantized version. You should probabilistically pick 3 with 75% probability and 4 with 25% probability. A way to implement this is to add random white noise of amplitude equal to the quantization step to the signal and then truncate the result.

$$I = \text{floor}(F + urand())$$

That is, instead of just adding 0.5 before truncating, we add a random number whose expected value is 0.5 (since it is uniformly distributed from 0 to 1). Figure 15.3 shows our signals quantized this way and the associated error plots. (For visibility, I expanded the horizontal axis of the graphs for the ramp and sine waves.) Note that the error noise is more evenly spread out—there is less near 44 cycles per scan line and more above 180 cycles per scan line.

Ordered Dither

Ordered dither is a simple approximation to random dither that is a lot easier to compute. For ordered dither, you add a fixed pattern (whose average is 0.5) to the analog signal and threshold that. One simple pattern is just the values ($\frac{1}{4}$, $\frac{3}{4}$) repeated over and over across the scan line. This has the effect of causing pixel values in the range ($0 \ldots \frac{1}{4}$) to round down to 0, a region with values in the range ($\frac{1}{4} \ldots \frac{3}{4}$) would generate the spatially repeating pattern (0,1,0,1,0,1, . . .). A region with values in the range ($\frac{3}{4} \ldots \frac{5}{4}$) would round up to 1.

You can generate finer divisions of intensity spread over larger regions of space with the following recursive trick: Repeat the current pattern twice, giving ($\frac{1}{4}$, $\frac{3}{4}$, $\frac{1}{4}$, $\frac{3}{4}$), then add a pattern of half the amplitude and half the frequency, i.e., ($-\frac{1}{8}$, $-\frac{1}{8}$, $+\frac{1}{8}$, $+\frac{1}{8}$). Then repeat the resultant pattern ($\frac{1}{8}$, $\frac{5}{8}$, $\frac{3}{8}$, $\frac{7}{8}$) over and over across the line. Iterate again and get

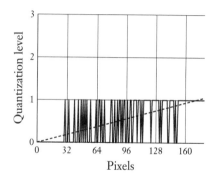

Figure 15.3a *Random dither: ramp*

$(\frac{1}{16}, \frac{9}{16}, \frac{5}{16}, \frac{13}{16}, \frac{3}{16}, \frac{11}{16}, \frac{7}{16}, \frac{15}{16})$. This is the pattern I used in Figure 15.4.

$$I = \text{floor}(F + pattern_{x \bmod 8})$$

The spectral content of this fixed pattern shows through in the final image. It has its highest amplitude at the Nyquist rate of 256 cycles per scan line (which will largely be smoothed out by the display), half that amplitude at 128 cycles per scan line, and so forth. When applied to two-dimensional images, this can create patterns that are visible to the viewer. This technique therefore represents a cheap but only partly effective solution.

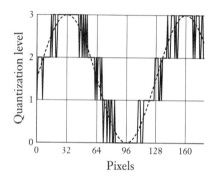

Figure 15.3b *Random dither: sine wave*

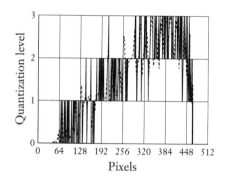

Figure 15.3c *Random dither: image*

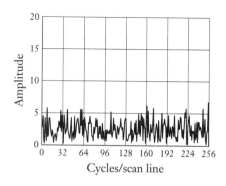

Figure 15.3d *Random dither: sine wave spectrum error*

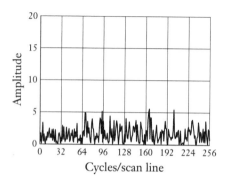

Figure 15.3e *Random dither: image spectrum error*

Error Diffusion

The idea behind error diffusion is as follows: If we have an analog value of 2.25 and we quantize it to the value 2, we have made the output picture 0.25 units too dark at that pixel. We should compensate by quantizing the next pixel as though it were 0.25 units brighter than it really is. This enhances the probability that we will quantize the next pixel to a higher value. A simple implementation keeps a running tally of the difference between our quantized brightness and the true analog brightness. We add this to each successive pixel value before thresholding. Algorithmically, this looks like

```
float error = 0.;
    for (int x=0; x<512; x++) {
    I[x] = floor(F[x]+error+.5);
    error += F[x]-I[x]; }
```

The results of this algorithm applied to our friendly signal appear in Figure 15.5. Looking at the error plots, we see that now we're really getting somewhere. Much of the error is concentrated in the highest frequencies, with relatively little at the sensitive frequency of 44 cycles per scan line. This is why images made with error diffusion look so much better than those with ordered dither.

Non-Uniform Quantization

This is all very nice, but there is a fly in the ointment. For a real display, the CRT luminance, L, does not increase linearly with the values 0, 1, 2, 3. Rather, it follows a power law:

$$L = \left(\frac{I}{3}\right)^{\gamma}$$

where γ is between 2 and 3, depending on the setting of the (poorly named) "brightness" knob. Using a value $\gamma = 2$, we find that the four possible pixel luminances are (0, ⅑, ⁴⁄₉, 1). As I described in Chapter 5, we must quantize to the available hardware luminance levels, not the integer numerical values we use to code them.

The results for non-uniform quantization appear in Figure 15.6. Here, I changed the scale on the output images to go from 0 to 1 since there is no longer an advantage in going from 0 to 3. Non-dithered quantization makes our error plots look ugly again. We must deal with this, but first there's one other thing to consider.

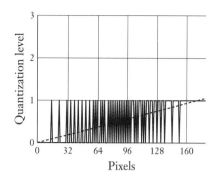

Figure 15.4a *Ordered dither: ramp*

Perception Is Reality

In Figure 15.6a, the floating-point input values are rounded to the nearest luminance output value. An input value of, say, $^2\!/_9$ rounds to the output value of $^1\!/_9$ instead of $^4\!/_9$ because it is closer to $^1\!/_9$. This might not be the best idea. The tricky part is the definition of "closer." To see why, we must consider another aspect of the eye's perception mechanism: It does not respond to light linearly. Instead, the perceived brightness, *B*, also approximately follows a power law:

$$B = L^\gamma$$

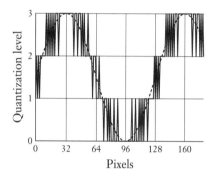

Figure 15.4b *Ordered dither: sine wave*

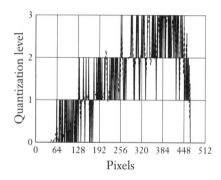

Figure 15.4c *Ordered dither: image*

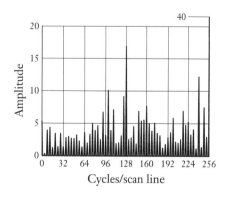

Figure 15.4d *Ordered dither: sine wave spectrum error*

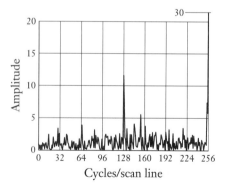

Figure 15.4e *Ordered dither: image spectrum error*

where the γ is between ½ and ⅓, depending on the brightness of the surroundings.[3] This is one reason displays are built with a power law for luminance.

Going back to the preceding numerical example, let's determine "closer" in terms of perceived brightness. We'll use ½ for the γ of the eye and so take the square root of the luminances. The input brightness value is $^{1.5}\!\%$, and we must chose between output values of ⅓ and ⅔. This time the higher value wins.

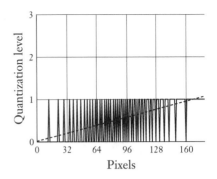

Figure 15.5a *Error diffusion: ramp*

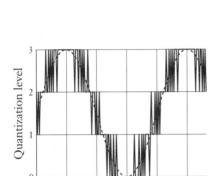

Figure 15.5b *Error diffusion: sine wave*

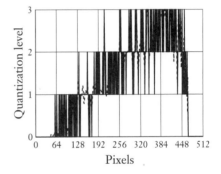

Figure 15.5c *Error diffusion: image*

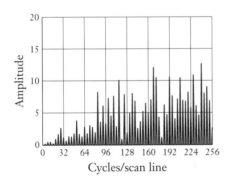

Figure 15.5d *Error diffusion: sine wave spectrum error*

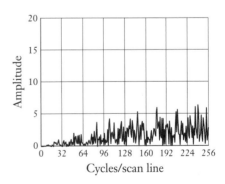

Figure 15.5e *Error diffusion: image spectrum error*

---

3 Pearson, page 41.

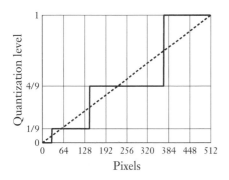

Figure 15.6a *Non-uniform quantization: ramp*

Error-Diffused Non-Uniform Quantization

Now let's put this together with error diffusion. We start with an input sample between 0 and 1. Take its square root to go to a roughly uniform perceptual space. Then quantize, using error diffusion, to the values $(0, \frac{1}{3}, \frac{2}{3}, 1)$. These match the perceived brightnesses of the hardware luminance levels. I've calculated the errors here in the square root space too. This all appears in Figure 15.7.

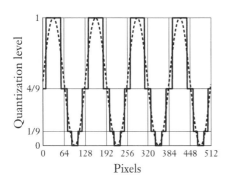

Figure 15.6b *Non-uniform quantization: sine wave*

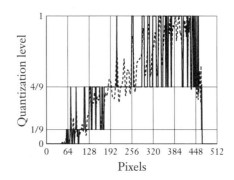

Figure 15.6c *Non-uniform quantization: image*

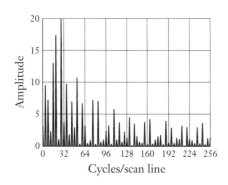

Figure 15.6d *Non-uniform quantization: sine wave spectrum error*

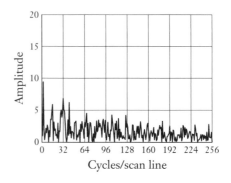

Figure 15.6e *Non-uniform quantization: image spectrum error*

So What?

As always in computer graphics, We Must Be Careful. We must take into account the operation of the human eye and the deficiencies of typical display devices. The result is better pictures for everybody.

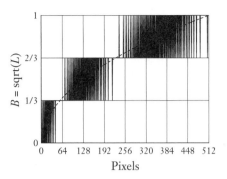

Figure 15.7a *Error diffusion in approximately uniform perceptual space: ramp*

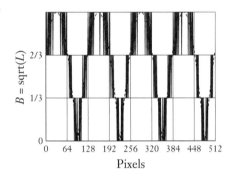

Figure 15.7b *Error diffusion in approximately uniform perceptual space: sine wave*

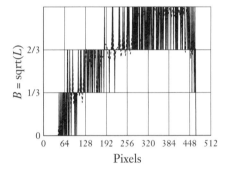

Figure 15.7c *Error diffusion in approximately uniform perceptual space: image*

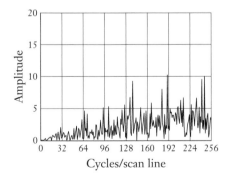

Figure 15.7d *Error diffusion in approximately uniform perceptual space: sine wave spectrum error*

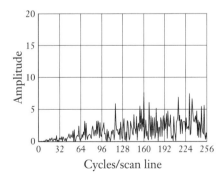

Figure 15.7e *Error diffusion in approximately uniform perceptual space: image spectrum error*

$$\tilde{\mathbf{F}} + (1-\alpha)\tilde{\mathbf{B}}$$

CHAPTER SIXTEEN

Compositing—Theory

My currently favorite journalistic quote comes from a magazine called *Morph's Outpost on the Digital Frontier*. They refer to the operation of avoiding jaggies as "antialiening." Either this was a typo or they thought of the Jaggies as aliens. This got me thinking about ways to get rid of these creatures—the offspring of 3D geometry and raster displays.

One of the most important antialiening tools in computer graphics comes from a generalization of the simple act of storing a pixel into a frame buffer. Several people simultaneously discovered the usefulness of this generalization so it goes by several names: matting, image compositing, alpha blending, overlaying, or lerping. It was most completely codified in a paper by Porter and Duff,[1] where they call it the "over" operator. In this chapter, I'm going to show a new way to derive Porter and Duff's "over" operator and describe some implementation details that I've found useful. In the next chapter, I'll go into some of the subtleties of how this operator works with integer pixel arithmetic.

The Basic Idea

The simplest form of compositing goes as follows. Say we want to overlay a foreground image on top of some background image. The foreground image covers only a part of the background; pixels inside the foreground

---

1 T. Porter and T. Duff, Compositing digital images, *SIGGRAPH '84 Conference Proceedings* (New York: ACM), pages 253–259.

shape will completely replace the corresponding background pixels, and pixels outside the shape leave the background pixels intact.

If we want antialiened edges, though, things are a bit more complicated. Pixels on the edge of the shape only partially cover the background pixels. If the shape is to be properly antialiened, we must blend the foreground color, **F**, and background color, **B**, according to the fraction α. This value represents the percentage of the pixel covered by color **F**. The standard way to calculate this is to find the geometric area covered by **F**. This implements a simple box filter for antialiening. More accurate filters can be used, but I'll stick to the box for now.

Now let's get down to algebra. **F** and **B** are each three-element vectors representing the red, green, and blue components of a pixel. Ordinary vector algebra applies. The new color in the frame buffer is

$$\mathbf{B}_{new} = (1 - \alpha)\mathbf{B}_{old} + \alpha\mathbf{F}$$

which can be more efficiently calculated as

$$\mathbf{B}_{new} = \mathbf{B}_{old} + \alpha(\mathbf{F} - \mathbf{B}_{old})$$

Actually, you can use the value of α for a variety of things. In addition to its antialiening function, it can represent transparent objects or establish a global fade amount. For this reason, the α value also goes by various names: coverage amount, opacity, or simply alpha. You can also think of it as 1 minus the transparency of the pixel. I'm going to call it *opacity* for now. If it's 0, the new pixel is transparent and does not affect the frame buffer. If it's 1, the new pixel is opaque and completely replaces the current frame buffer color.

Next, suppose that we want to layer yet another object on top of our image. We just blend in the new object's color, which I'll call **G**, on top of our current background image using its opacity, β, to get

$$\mathbf{B}_{newnew} = (1 - \beta)\mathbf{B}_{new} + \beta\mathbf{G}$$

We can keep on plastering stuff on top of our image until we are happy. This is the essence of $2\frac{1}{2}$-D rendering, also known as the painter's algorithm or temporal priority.

For most rendering purposes, I've been able to provide this as the only necessary accessing operation into the frame buffer. But it's not quite general enough.

Associativity

There is another intriguing generalization here. **F** and **G** each have an opacity, but **B** doesn't. Does it even mean anything to composite into a pixel that itself has an opacity? Yes. Consider the following scenario. Suppose we have the images **F** and **G** but haven't yet decided what to use for a background. Let's see if we can merge **F** and **G** into one image **H** that we can store away and then later overlay on top of **B** and get the same result. If we denote the compositing operation with the symbol $\oplus$, what we want is

$$\mathbf{G} \oplus (\mathbf{F} \oplus \mathbf{B}) = (\mathbf{G} \oplus \mathbf{F}) \oplus \mathbf{B}$$

In other words, we want to make compositing *associative*.

How can we define $\mathbf{H} \equiv \mathbf{G} \oplus \mathbf{F}$ to make this work out? We want to calculate a new pixel color **H** and opacity γ in terms of colors **F** and **G** and their own opacities α and β. Plug in the definitions:

$$(1-\beta)((1-\alpha)\mathbf{B}+\alpha\mathbf{F})+\beta\mathbf{G} = (1-\gamma)\mathbf{B}+\gamma\mathbf{H}$$

Rearrange the left side to get

$$(1-\alpha)(1-\beta)\mathbf{B}+(\alpha(1-\beta)\mathbf{F}+\beta\mathbf{G}) = (1-\gamma)\mathbf{B}+\gamma\mathbf{H}$$

Since we want this to work for arbitrary backgrounds **B**, we can split this into two equations by equating the **B** coefficients and the non-**B** coefficients.

$$(1-\alpha)(1-\beta) = 1-\gamma$$
$$\alpha(1-\beta)\mathbf{F} + \beta\mathbf{G} = \gamma\mathbf{H}$$

The first of these gives us γ:

$$\gamma = \alpha + \beta - \alpha\beta$$

The second equation gives us **H**:

$$\mathbf{H} = \frac{\alpha(1-\beta)\mathbf{F} + \beta\mathbf{G}}{\gamma}$$

With a little fiddling, this turns into

$$\mathbf{H} = (1-\beta/\gamma)\mathbf{F} + (\beta/\gamma)\mathbf{G}$$

This gives us a definition for how to composite two colors, each of which has its own opacity.

Let's play with this a bit. If we composite $\mathbf{G}$ over a totally opaque color $\mathbf{F}$, what is the result? Plug $\alpha = 1$ into the preceding and we get

$$\gamma = 1$$
$$\mathbf{H} = (1 - \beta)\mathbf{F} + \beta\mathbf{G}$$

In other words, our more general compositing operation boils down to the basic one if we assume our background has its own opacity value, which happens to be 1.

Now let's try overlaying a completely opaque color $\mathbf{G}$ on top of $\mathbf{F}$. Plug in $\beta = 1$ with an arbitrary α and we discover

$$\gamma = 1$$
$$\mathbf{H} = \mathbf{G}$$

independent of α, as we expect.

Another Form of Association

The preceding definition of $\mathbf{H}$ is a bit complicated. Fortunately, there is a better way. One of the key insights in the Porter and Duff paper is that $\mathbf{F}$ shows up in the compositing formula only when multiplied by α, and $\mathbf{G}$ appears only when multiplied by β. Why not simply represent the pixel with the colors already multiplied by their opacity? This representation is usually referred to as having the opacity *associated* with the color, or as having the color *premultiplied* by its alpha value. I'll write (for the time being) an associated pixel color with a tilde over it. We have

$$\tilde{\mathbf{F}} = \alpha\mathbf{F}$$
$$\tilde{\mathbf{G}} = \beta\mathbf{G}$$
$$\tilde{\mathbf{H}} = \gamma\mathbf{H}$$

An associated color is just a regular color composited onto black—that is, if you displayed it directly by itself, you would get the correct antialiened image. (Is the joke worn out now? OK, I'll use the real word again.) Note that if the opacity equals 1, an associated color is the same as an unassociated color.

Using these definitions in the general compositing function and doing a bit of algebraic fiddling, we get

$$\tilde{\mathbf{H}} = (1 - \beta)\tilde{\mathbf{F}} + \tilde{\mathbf{G}}$$
$$\gamma = (1 - \beta)\alpha + \beta$$

This is a bit less arithmetic than our earlier definition, but what makes it particularly pretty is that we are now doing exactly the same arithmetic on the opacity components of a pixel as we are doing on the (associated) color components. This is simple, elegant, and general.

More Reasons to Associate

It turns out that there are more reasons to store associated pixel colors than mere prettiness of the compositing formula. For one thing, some intensity calculation algorithms directly generate associated pixel colors. Additionally, we must use associated colors for any filtering or interpolation operations. Let's see why.

Antialiasing by Subsampling

One typical way to do antialiasing is by subsampling. You calculate an image using point sampling at, say, four times your final resolution in x and y and then downsample to get your final result. There are still aliases, but you have pushed them up into higher frequencies.

How does this work with our scheme here? You can consider each final pixel as broken into a 4×4 grid of subpixel cells, each containing a color and an opacity flag. Initialize all these to zero. Then, whenever your renderer writes a color to a subpixel cell, have it also set the opacity flag to 1. After rendering, sum up the 16 opacity flags within the pixel and call the result N. The net opacity for the pixel is $N/16$. Next, sum up the 16 color cells in the pixel. The average color of the pixel is this sum divided by N, the number of cells colored. But the *associated* color is even more simply calculated as the color sum divided by 16, $(\text{sum}/N)*(N/16) = \text{sum}/16$. You can then composite this associated color using the calculated opacity, $N/16$. In other words, the net associated pixel color and opacity is the sum of the subpixels divided by 16.

This works even better if your renderer is scan line oriented—that is, it visits each pixel once in order, left to right, top to bottom. You don't need individual subpixel cells. Just accumulate the color and opacity into a single pixel cell and divide by 16. In practice, I implement this with a scan line buffer of pixel cells of length equal to the output picture. During scan line processing, each generated high-resolution pixel simply adds its value to cell number $x/4$. Then, every four scan lines, I purge this buffer by dividing its contents by 16 and compositing it with the background using the associated compositing formula. Then I zero the buffer in preparation for the next four scan lines.

Clouds

The cloud simulation I used for Saturn's rings[2] generates a pixel's brightness as a product of the *color* of a cloud particle times the *probability* of a particle being both present and illuminated in the pixel. We can now recognize this as being an associated color. The Saturn ring simulation also generates a transparency value based on probabilities of blocking particles. The compositing I described for the simulation is just the associated compositing operator, but I didn't recognize it as such at first. Originally, I actually divided the color by the opacity before passing it to an *un*associated compositing routine. Live and learn.

Filtering

Suppose we want to filter an image that has opacities at each pixel. Do we filter the unassociated colors, $\mathbf{F}$ (this was my first thought), or do we filter the associated colors, $\tilde{\mathbf{F}}$? To find out, consider the following thought experiment.

Let's downsample a scan line by a factor of two in the x direction by simply averaging successive pairs of pixels. Then let's overlay the result over an opaque background $\mathbf{B}$. We want to arrange things so that downsampling and overlaying generates the same color as overlaying and downsampling. Let's follow the adventures of a typical pixel pair $\mathbf{F}$ (with opacity α) and $\mathbf{G}$ (with opacity β). Note that $\mathbf{F}$ and $\mathbf{G}$ are side by side here, not on top of each other as in our earlier examples.

First, try overlaying, then downsampling. Overlay $(\mathbf{F}, \alpha)$ on $\mathbf{B}$ getting $\alpha\mathbf{F} + (1-\alpha)\mathbf{B}$. Overlay $(\mathbf{G}, \beta)$ on $\mathbf{B}$ getting $\beta\mathbf{G} + (1-\beta)\mathbf{B}$. These two pixels are now opaque. Now downsample by averaging these results. The color will be

$$\frac{\alpha}{2}\mathbf{F} + \frac{\beta}{2}\mathbf{G} + \frac{2-\alpha-\beta}{2}\mathbf{B}$$

As long as you composite first, it actually doesn't matter if you do it associated or *un*associated.

Next, let's do this in the other order: downsampling first, then overlaying. Downsampling the *un*associated colors and opacity, we get

$$\text{color} = \frac{\mathbf{F} + \mathbf{G}}{2}, \quad \text{opacity} = \frac{\alpha + \beta}{2}$$

---

2 J. Blinn, Light reflection functions for simulation of clouds and dusty surfaces, *SIGGRAPH '82 Conference Proceedings* (New York: ACM), pages 21–29.

Now we overlay this on top of **B** using the unassociated color compositing function to get

$$\left(1 - \frac{\alpha + \beta}{2}\right)\mathbf{B} + \left(\frac{\alpha + \beta}{2}\right)\frac{\mathbf{F} + \mathbf{G}}{2} = \frac{\alpha + \beta}{4}\mathbf{F} + \frac{\alpha + \beta}{4}\mathbf{G} + \frac{2 - \alpha - \beta}{2}\mathbf{B}$$

—the wrong answer.

Now let's do this with associated colors. We downsample $\alpha\mathbf{F}$ and $\beta\mathbf{G}$:

$$\text{color} = \frac{\alpha\mathbf{F} + \beta\mathbf{G}}{2}, \quad \text{opacity} = \frac{\alpha + \beta}{2}$$

Now we overlay this on top of **B** using the associated compositing function to get

$$\left(1 - \frac{\alpha + \beta}{2}\right)\mathbf{B} + \frac{\alpha\mathbf{F} + \beta\mathbf{G}}{2} = \frac{\alpha}{2}\mathbf{F} + \frac{\beta}{2}\mathbf{G} + \frac{2 - \alpha - \beta}{2}\mathbf{B}$$

—the right answer.

To reiterate, downsampling and, in fact, *all* filtering operations should operate on arrays of associated pixel colors as well as, of course, on the array of opacity values.

Interpolation

Here's another example. Suppose we are doing Gouraud interpolation across a polygon. Each vertex has a color, and we do the standard interpolation of vertex colors to get the colors inside the polygon. Now, what if the vertices have opacities as well? We simply interpolate them in a similar manner. But should we interpolate unassociated colors or associated colors? (I'll bet you can guess.)

Actually, this might seem a little open to interpretation. After all, Gouraud interpolation is itself an approximation to a more accurate curved-surface-shading function. Who's to say what the correct interpolation amount is? Well, consider the following: Interpolation is another form of filtering. Suppose we wanted to expand an image two times by interpolating between each pixel pair. We would again like this to look the same if we interpolated and then overlaid on a background or if we overlaid first and interpolated second.

Going back to polygons, we might have a scan line with the colors $(\mathbf{F}, \alpha)$ on one end and $(\mathbf{G}, \beta)$ on the other. We want the inside colors to look the same when overlaid onto a background. We want to interpolate and then overlay over **B**, and we want to make this the same as overlaying and then interpolating.

You can do the algebra yourself. Does it look familiar? It's just the same as the filtering example, leading us to the conclusion that Gouraud interpolation should also be done on associated pixel colors.

Computer Notation

Each pixel has a red, green, and blue color and an opacity α. Since we like associated colors so much, we will henceforth represent a pixel by the quadruple

$$\mathbf{F} = [\alpha F_{red} \quad \alpha F_{green} \quad \alpha F_{blue} \quad \alpha]$$

This looks suspiciously like homogeneous coordinates. I've tried real hard, but for the life of me I can't figure out any use for this observation.

I'm going to start talking about computation now, so let's take a moment to switch from the preceding vector algebra mathematical notation to a more C-like computer data structure representation. We could represent the pixel color as a four-element vector `F[i]` with `F[0]` holding the opacity and `F[1],...,F[3]` holding the colors. Or we could define a pixel data structure containing the fields `(r,g,b,a)`. We will assume the colors to be associated, so that `F.r` $= \alpha F_{red}$, and so on.

The opacity value is more conventionally called *alpha*, which is why I've called that field a. I'll call it alpha from now on since we no longer have to worry about having a separate Greek letter for the opacity value of different pixels.

Marching in Place

I want to reformulate this a bit to return to our original operation of overlaying a foreground on top of a background stored in a frame buffer. Here, $\mathbf{H}$ and $\tilde{\mathbf{F}}$ from the compositing formula are the same storage locations: the background C language variable B. $\tilde{\mathbf{G}}$ is the new foreground image, which I'll get from a variable named F. The in-place formulations of the operation become

```
for(i=0; i<4; i++) B[i] = B[i]*(1-F[0])+F[i];
```

We could go really nuts and define a set of overloaded operators for standard four-dimensional array arithmetic. Compositing could then look something like

```
B = B*(1-F[0]) + F;
```

I'm not sure I would recommend this after seeing the sort of code some C++ compilers come up with for such things. Instead, I'll splurge on source code and write explicitly

```
transparency = 1 - F.a;
B.r = B.r*transparency + F.r;
B.g = B.g*transparency + F.g;
B.b = B.b*transparency + F.b;
B.a = B.a*transparency + F.a;
```

Again, for most rendering applications, this new formulation is the only access method you need into the frame buffer. I've resisted the temptation (barely) to overload a pixel class operator to do this.

Examples

To motivate our next bit of gimcrackery, let's look at a few examples of the types of things we might do with this.

Example 1

1. Load an opaque background into the frame buffer, one with `B.a==1` everywhere.
2. Run a rendering program that overlays its results into the frame buffer. Pixels inside the object (which is most of them) all have `F.a==1`. Only the ones on the edges have `F.a!=1`.
3. Run another rendering program that similarly overlays its results into the frame buffer. Part of the new object overlaps the first one, and part of it sticks out onto the background. Note that a rendering program doesn't need to know what's under it. The overlay operation does the correct thing.
4. Run another rendering program that places algorithmically defined shapes. These might be lines, spots, smears, and so forth with a constant color across them but whose shapes are "sculpted" by the alpha channel.
5. Save the resultant image to a file.

Example 2

1. Load the frame buffer with the transparent color (0, 0, 0, 0).
2. Render all sorts of stuff like in the previous example.

3. Save the resultant image to a file. This rectangular image will have B.a==0 for pixels that never got "hit" by any renderers (which might be a substantial portion of the image).

Example 3

1. Load an opaque background into the frame buffer.
2. Overlay the image saved from Example 2 (there it was the partially transparent background image B; now it becomes the foreground image F). Only those pixels with F.a!==0 will affect the background.

Example 4

I'll just mention here an entirely different way do this that I don't happen to use. It involves the classic engineering trick of reversing the order of loops. The preceding examples performed the operations in the order

```
for (each overlaid image)
        for (each pixel in image)
                composite with background
```

Some systems reverse this order and do

```
for (each pixel in output)
        for (each overlaid image)
                composite all together
```

This sequence allows some speedup by optimizing the (possibly complicated) algebraic expression generated by all the pixel arithmetic for one pixel.

Shortcuts

Examples 1 through 3 show that a lot of compositing arithmetic can wind up being done with alpha values of 0 and 1. This motivates us to look for a few shortcuts in our implementation. Since the arithmetic is identical for the four fields of a pixel, I'll write calculations just once using the symbol F.i (where i stands for r, g, b, or a). Table 16.1 shows possible special cases.

You might think that the case of F.a==0 necessarily implies that all the color fields F.i must be zero. After all, we are dealing with associated colors here. The first case would then just leave B.i unchanged. It turns out, however, that there are some reasons not to always make this assump-

Table 16.1 *New value of* B.i *composited with associated pixel* F.i, *where* B.i = B.i*(1-F.a) + F.i

F.a==0	B.i = B.i + F.i
F.a==1	B.i = F.i
F.a==anything else	B.i = B.i*(1-F.a) + F.i

tion. I'll go more deeply into this in the next chapter. Anyway, here's the optimized algorithm:

```
if      (F.a==0) B.i += F.i;
else if (F.a==1) B.i = F.i;
else             B.i = B.i*(1-F.a) + F.i;
```

We can do a little better with the a field in the latter case. If B.a==1, we can skip the calculation of a new B.a since it will stay 1 no matter what F.a is. Table 16.2 shows the possible values of B.a and what the calculations look like with redundant arithmetic and stores removed.

To take advantage of this, let's first note that the most likely case is B.a==1. We therefore make that the fastest test. Now turn this into an algorithm:

```
if (B.a!=1){
    if(B.a==0) B.a = F.a;
    else       B.a = B.a*(1-F.a) + F.a;}
```

There is, of course, a trade-off here between the number of tests you make versus the time to just go ahead and do the general arithmetic. On some pipelined machines, it's probably better to avoid conditional jump instructions, do the arithmetic always, and keep the pipe full. Only your profiler knows for sure. I've found the testing to be worthwhile in my situation. In general, I think it's nicest to provide one general-purpose, easy-to-remember function, then test for special cases inside the function. The special-case testing is usually negligible compared to the arithmetic you save by detecting the special case.

Table 16.2 *New value of* B.a *where* B.a = B.a*(1 - F.a) + F.a

B.a==0	B.a = F.a
B.a==1	Unchanged
B.a==anything else	B.a = B.a*(1-F.a) + F.a

Table 16.3 *Porter-Duff operators in C notation*

F over B	F.i + B.i*(1-F.a)
F in B	F.i*B.a (color of B unused)
F out B	F.i*(1-B.a) (color of B unused)
F atop B	F.i*B.a + B.i*(1-F.a)
F xor B	F.i*(1-B.a) + B.i*(1-F.a)
F plus B	F.i + B.i

Other Operators

Just for completeness, Table 16.3 lists how Porter and Duff's other operators look in my notation and what the algebra boils down to. Of these,
the "over" operator is by far the most often used. This may lead you to
wonder the following: How about storing the value (1-F.a) instead of
F.a in a pixel? That value would be the transparency rather than the
opacity of the pixel. Let's call this field t. Transparencies combine by simple multiplication. Why? Remember, in our original derivation of γ, we
had

$$(1-\alpha)(1-\beta) = 1-\gamma$$

And 1 minus opacity is transparency. The associated color compositing
operation would then be

```
B.i = B.i*F.t + F.i; // for i = r,g,b
B.t = B.t*F.t;
```

This formulation is, of course, even less arithmetic than before. The
only trouble is that most industry standard file formats and compositing
programs deal with alpha values as meaning opacity. You would have to
translate your image by storing (1-B.t) when you output your image to
a file. Since the transparency-based formulation only saves one add and
one subtract per pixel, it might not be worth it.

A Teaser

In the next chapter I'll talk about how number representations for pixels
and roundoff error affect compositing calculations. And I'll froth about
the phenomenal stupidity of compilers and why parts of this calculation
should still be done in assembly language.

"Composting"–Practice

N O V E M B E R   1 9 9 4

At this year's SIGGRAPH, Chris Wedge told the story of an audience member who once asked him about "image composting." I like this even better than the antialiening quote I mentioned in Chapter 16.

Well, anyway. Enough of this levity. This time I want to discuss the practice of image composting and, in particular, the Porter-Duff "over" operator. In the last chapter, we derived the operator for compositing a foreground pixel **F** over a background pixel **B** as

$$\mathbf{F} \text{ over } \mathbf{B} \equiv \mathbf{B}(1 - \mathbf{F}_a) + \mathbf{F}$$

where each pixel is a vector with four components—red, green, blue, and alpha (the coverage or opacity amount)—and standard vector algebra applies. I've found it most useful to provide "over" as an in-place operator; you have an image stored in a frame buffer and want to overlay another image on top of it. In other words, the result of "**F** over **B**" replaces **B.**

C Notation

In translating this vector notation to C, I'll write the components of a pixel using class member notation: (F.r, F.g, F.b, F.a). Code to implement the compositing operation is then

```
t = 1 - F.a;
B.r = B.r*t + F.r;
B.g = B.g*t + F.g;
B.b = B.b*t + F.b;
B.a = B.a*t + F.a;
```

For most rendering operations, this is the *only* access method to the frame buffer that you will need.

In what follows, I'm going to complexify this a bit, so let me make life easier and define an abbreviation. Since I will always treat the red, green, and blue components in the same way, I'll just give a single statement for color components, using the generic class member .c. Any such statement actually expands into three statements. I will sometimes do different arithmetic for the .a member, so I'll keep it separate. Using this abbreviation scheme, the preceding code would look like

```
t = 1 - F.a;
B.c = B.c*t + F.c;
B.a = B.a*t + F.a;
```

Shortcuts

In Chapter 16, I talked about some shortcuts to avoid unnecessary arithmetic whenever F.a and/or B.a are 0 or 1. The result is the code

```
if (F.a==0)
    B.c += F.c;
else if (F.a==1) {
    B.c = F.c;
    B.a = 1;}
else {
    t = 1 - F.a;
    B.c = B.c*t + F.c;
    if (B.a!=1){
        if(B.a==0) B.a = F.a;
        else       B.a = B.a*t + F.a;}}
```

Now this is, of course, more complicated than simply doing the arithmetic straightforwardly, as in the first code fragment. It might seem only barely worthwhile, but in Chapter 16 I showed that the various cases tested for are actually pretty common. They occur, for example, when you overlay or render an opaque object into the frame buffer. When this happens, you have F.a==1 almost everywhere in the object except at the antialiased edges. With the special-case testing, you can simply store the interior pixels with no arithmetic at all. In this chapter, I'll describe some even better reasons why this economization is worthwhile.

Pixel Representations

So far I haven't said anything about how to represent the numerical quantities in a pixel. Well, here's where we get real. I will represent the red, green, blue, and alpha components of a pixel in three ways.

Floating Point (float)

This is the easiest method and the one that most complex rendering algorithms generate. You don't have to worry about overflow or underflow except in extreme cases. Arithmetic with floating-point numbers is slow—but at least they take up lots of memory!

16-Bit Scaled Integers (short int)

Here, we scale the floating-point value by the quantity 16384 and round to the nearest integer. Thus the 16-bit value 0 represents the floating-point value 0.0, and the 16-bit value 16384 represents the floating-point value 1.0. (This is the system I described in Chapter 5.) Note that this choice of scale factor does not use all the possible precision of a 16-bit number; only about a quarter of the possible 16-bit values cover the range from 0.0 to 1.0. I chose to use this range so that the scale factor is a power of two (good for divisions; see following) and so that there is an explicit representation of the number 1.0. Using this scheme, the possible 16-bit integer values actually represent the floating-point quantities from −2.0 to +1.9999. This technique of giving the pixels a bit of "headroom" avoids overflow and underflow problems when doing filtering with negative lobed filters. (See Chapter 3.)

8-Bit Bytes (unsigned char)

These are the values that we actually store in the frame buffer and that the refresh hardware uses to display the image. Typical display hardware does not translate these values directly into intensity, however. Instead, the displayed brightness, D, is a power of the byte value, I:

$$D = (I / 255.)^\gamma$$

with γ typically being around 2 or 2.2. For this reason, you must calculate the inverse of this power function when you convert a desired intensity to a byte value. I also described this process in more detail in Chapter 5.

In addition to being needed for hardware display, 8-bit bytes are what you typically store if you save an image in a file (although not all image manipulation programs expect the pixels to be gamma corrected).

The alpha component of the pixel, however, doesn't need to be gamma corrected. For this component, I scale the desired alpha by 255 and round to the nearest integer. This uses the whole range of byte values. The byte value 0 represents 0.0 and the byte value 255 represents 1.0.[1]

Conversions

One of the reasons to look for economizations in the compositing calculations is that conversion between these forms is not free (timewise). If we can skip a conversion because we detect that its result is going to be multiplied by zero, we win even more than if we only avoid the multiplication.

Let me quickly list the conversions necessary. Following the conventions in Chapter 5, I will use the variable D to represent a floating-point value, J to represent a 16-bit integer, and I to represent an 8-bit byte value.

Float to 16-Bit

```
J = int(D*16384. +.5);
```

16-Bit to Float

```
D = J/16384.;
```

Float to 8-Bit

The arithmetic is different for the color components and for the alpha component because the color component is gamma corrected.

```
I.c = unsigned char(pow(D.c,1./gamma)*255. + .5);
I.a = unsigned char(      D.a          *255. + .5);
```

8-Bit to Float

```
D.c = pow(I.c/255., gamma);
D.a = I.a/255.;
```

---

1 1998 addendum: I am becoming increasingly dissatisfied with the idea of non-gamma-corrected alpha values. See my more recent article, *A ghost in a snowstorm*, in *IEEE Computer Graphics and Applications* (Jan./Feb. 1998, page 79) for more ideas on this.

8-Bit to 16-Bit

We define the result of this conversion by converting 8-bit to float and then float to 16-bit. In practice, this is too slow since you must calculate a power. But, since there are only 256 possible 8-bit patterns, you can pre-calculate all the possible values and do conversion by table lookup. I will define a routine for such a conversion as

```
J.c = cv16c(I.c);
```

The alpha value, on the other hand, is not gamma corrected, so we can convert it by direct scaling:

```
J.a = (I.a*16384 + 127)/255;
```

Again, it is usually faster to put this into a table. I will define a routine for this as

```
J.a = cv16a(I.a);
```

16-Bit to 8-Bit

Again, we define the desired result by converting 16-bit to float and then float to 8-bit. In Chapter 5, I described how to do this relatively quickly by using a simplified binary search through a table. I will hide this in the function

```
I.c = cv8c(J.c);
```

Since the alpha component is encoded linearly here too, we can convert directly

```
I.a = (J.a*255 + 8192)/16384;
```

and define the function to do this:

```
I.a = cv8a(J.a);
```

Unassociated Float to Associated 16-Bit

On some occasions, we will be given an unassociated floating-point pixel to process (one whose color components haven't been multiplied by alpha). As a happy bonus, we can combine the association operation (multiplying color by alpha) with the scaling to 16-bit integers. We first get the 16-bit value for alpha and then use that to scale the color components:

```
J.a = int(16384.*D.a + .5);
J.c = int( J.a  *D.c + .5);
```

This does have a potential roundoff problem, though, since we are multiplying D.c by an approximate version of D.a instead of the exact amount. For example, starting with (D.c,D.a) = (.5,.2), we get J.a = 3277. Converting J.c the hard but correct way gives us

```
J.c = int(.5*.2*16384.+.5) = int(1638.9) = 1638
```

Converting J.c our quicker way gives us

```
J.c = int(3277*.5 + .5) = 1639
```

This might be close enough if you are really worried about speed, but maybe the bonus isn't so happy after all. This just shows us that we have to be careful about compounding the results of rounding operations (cue the foreshadowing music).

Pixel Arithmetic

In a nutshell, I do all pixel arithmetic in 16-bit form; floating-point arithmetic is too slow and 8-bit representations are not linear. Some rendering programs generate results in floating point, but I convert the numbers to 16-bit as soon as possible. 16-bit arithmetic is plenty accurate for image compositing and filtering. If you need more accuracy, say, for Gouraud interpolation across a polygon, you can easily tack 16 bits of zeros on the right to convert it to a 32-bit fraction.

Now let's review how to do arithmetic with 16-bit scaled integers. Happily, addition and subtraction are the same as normal addition. Only multiplication is tricky. Since each factor has a built-in scale factor, the result winds up scaled twice. We must divide out the extra scale factor and round the result to get

```
(J1*J2 + 8192)/16384
```

Here's where our choice of scale factor pays off. The product of the two 16-bit numbers is a 32-bit number, and you can do the division by simply shifting this 32-bit result right by 14 bits.

At least you could if compilers were built correctly.

Unfortunately, I have yet to see a compiler that realizes that the product of two 16-bit numbers is a 32-bit number. The hardware knows it. We know it. But the four different compilers I have looked at take this perfectly natural function and make it into something dirty: They do the multiply and throw away the high-order 16 bits. To circumvent this, you have to convert the two 16-bit numbers to two 32-bit numbers and do a 32-bit multiply, giving a 64-bit result. Then, since the compiler throws away the top 32 bits of that resultant product, you're in business.

I mean, I'm not one to spend inordinate amounts of time shaving bits, but it *hurts* me to see this. I have been forced to code the scaled 16-bit multiplication operation in inline assembly language. I've currently put it into a subroutine, but apparently I need to put it in a C macro to get real inline code. (Generally speaking, C macros have been obsoleted by the C++ concept of inline functions. However, in the real world, it seems that inline functions cannot contain assembly language instructions.) The routine does a simple 16-bit multiply, adds the rounding bias, and shifts the result down. To emphasize what's going on, I'll explicitly call the routine M instead of overloading the multiplication operator in what follows.

```
J = M(J1,J2);
```

One other thing to note about M: It also works properly if one of the arguments is an 8-bit linearly scaled value (padded on the left with zeros), producing an 8-bit result. Why? The first parameter is really a fraction whose "actual" value is J1/16384. M, which then effectively multiplies the other parameter (however it may be scaled) by this fraction.

What We Want

There are two services my "over" operation supports: overlaying 16-bit pixels into the frame buffer and overlaying 8-bit pixels into the frame buffer. The frame buffer itself is always 8-bit pixels. To provide some orthogonality of functionality, the "over" routines operate on arrays of pixel values (typically, a scan line's worth). Reading and writing to the actual frame buffer is done elsewhere. I won't explicitly show the array loop below, but it's there. It's always best to make your subroutines process data in big globs to minimize the overhead of subroutine calls.

Things That Cost Time

In the code at the beginning of this article, many seemingly simple operations contained, hidden within them, a lot of conversions between types. Let's review what they are, roughly in order of nastiness.

- cv8c(J)—binary search in table
- cv8a(J)—multiply, 14 bit shift
- cv16c(I)—table lookup
- cv16a(I)—table lookup

In the code below I'll explicitly call these conversion routines to make it easier to see where time goes. Assignments will happen between like types, so no hidden conversions will be performed. Also, I'll use the variable names BJ and FJ to hold the 16-bit form of the pixels and BI and FI to hold the 8-bit form. Reference to simply B or F means the floating-point version.

16-Bit over 8-Bit

This is the workhorse routine. Generally, the results of any rendering or image processing calculation are in 16-bit form. Here is the raw code (with no special-case testing) to composite the pixel FJ over the pixel BI.

```
BJ.c = cv16c(BI.c);
BJ.c = M(BJ.c,16384-FJ.a) + FJ.c;
BI.c = cv8c(BJ.c);

BJ.a = cv16a(BI.a);
BJ.a = M(BJ.a,16384-FJ.a) + FJ.a;
BI.a = cv8a(BJ.a);
```

Alpha Calculation

Let's first see how we can improve on the calculation of B.a. The formula is

```
B.a = B.a*(1-F.a) + F.a
```

The two main special cases

```
if      (F.a==0) {/* B.a unchanged*/ }
else if (F.a==1) B.a=1;
```

are taken care of in the general shortcut scheme at the beginning of this chapter. For more general values of F.a, we actually have to do some work.

We can avoid a conversion by recalling that our M routine can multiply a 16-bit fractional number by an 8-bit number.

```
BI.a = M(BI.a,16384-FJ.a) + cv8a(FJ.a);
```

The only problem with this is that it gets the wrong answer much of the time; it's sometimes off by 1. The correct answer is defined by converting both BI.a and FJ.a to float, doing the calculation, and then converting that floating result to 8-bit. In fact, the brute-force calculation that we are trying to improve on often gets the wrong answer too. The basic reason is that both schemes contain the sum of two or more rounded calculations (either explicitly or hidden inside the M routine). If each term of the sum was, say, 2.4, then rounding first and then summing would give 4. Summing and then rounding would give 5.

In order to get the right answer and, incidentally, make the code faster, we can rewrite the mathematical definition of B.a as

```
B.a = B.a + F.a*(1-B.a);
```

We turn this into code again by using the fact that the M routine can multiply the 8-bit version of (1-B.a) by the fractional value represented by F.a:

```
BI.a += M(FJ.a,255-BI.a);
```

This formulation only rounds once, and I've verified that it always gets the "right" answer as defined previously. Faster and more correct—who could ask for anything more?

Now, to get the fastest calculation of the new BI.a, we include some tests for trivial case values of B.a. The most likely case is B.a = 1; the next most likely case is B.a = 0.

```
if(BI.a != 255) {
    if(BI.a==0)
        BI.a = M(FJ.a,255);
    else
        BI.a += M(FJ.a,255-BI.a);}
```

This is how we will calculate BI.a in both the 16-bit and 8-bit routines that follow.

Superluminous Pixels

There is another issue to discuss that relates to associated pixels with $\alpha = 0$. In an associated pixel, the color components have been multiplied by alpha. Therefore, if $\alpha = 0$, all the color components should be 0 also. When compositing such a pixel over a background, you should be able to skip pixels with F.a==0. The very first special-case test can then read

```
if (F.a==0) {}
```

There are two situations where this can cause problems.

The first is the possible use of special pixel values for unusual lighting effects. For example, an associated pixel with values (.2,.2,.2,0) effectively has some light but no "coverage." Applying it to a background pixel just adds something to the color components without changing the background pixel's coverage. This can be useful, but I haven't had occasion to use it myself. I will therefore, for illustration purposes in this code, not expect superluminous pixels. For the nonce, I'm going to assume that if F.a==0, then all the other elements of F are zero.

The second problem will only hit us when we overlay 8-bit pixels into the frame buffer, so I'll talk about it later.

Final 16-Bit Code

Note that in the following code I've also tossed in a test to skip some arithmetic if the color of B is black (another common occurrence).

```
if(FJ.a==0)
    {}        // leave B unchanged
else if (FJ.a==16384){
    BI.c = cv8c(FJ.c);
    BI.a = 255;}
else {
    if (BI.c==0)
        BJ.c = FJ.c;
    else {
        BJ.c = cv16c(BI.c);
        BJ.c = M(BJ.c,16384-FJ.a)+FJ.c;}
    BI.c = cv8c(BJ.c);
    BI.a (calculated as above)}
```

8-Bit over 8-Bit

We need this second routine when compositing a stored image over the 8-bit frame buffer. It calculates FI over BI. The naive approach is to convert all 8-bit quantities to 16-bit, do the arithmetic, then convert 16-bit to 8-bit. Here it is, with no special-case testing, but using the improved calculation of BI.a:

```
FJ.c = cv16c(FI.c);
FJ.a = cv16a(FI.a);
BJ.c = cv16c(BI.c);
BJ.c = M(16384-FJ.a,BJ.c) + FJ.c;
BI.c = cv8c(BJ.c);
BI.a+= M(FJ.a,255-BI.a);}
```

This cries out for special-case testing.

Alpha Calculation

Since we have the two alphas encoded linearly into 8 bits, we could do the arithmetic directly. Since they are scaled by 255, the formula

```
B.a = B.a*(1-F.a) + F.a;
```

translates into

```
BI.a=(BI.a*(255-FI.a)+127)/255 + FI.a;
```

We have to divide by 255. Ick. This sounds scary, but Chapter 19 presents an algorithm for doing this pretty quickly.

Superluminous Pixels and Roundoff Error

Here's where we have to face the "other" problem that occurs with $F.a==0$. It comes from the fact that, for 8-bit pixels, color components are gamma corrected but alpha components are not. For example, if you convert the very dim, very transparent 16-bit pixel (1, 1, 1, 16) to 8-bit values, you get (2, 2, 2, 0). The alpha component has rounded to 0 even though the color components haven't.

In this situation, we cannot simply ignore pixels with $F.a==0$. Consider the following scenario.

1. Clear the frame buffer to black: $BI = (0,0,0,255)$
2. Overlay $FJ = (1,1,1,16)$; giving $BJ = (1,1,1,16384)$
3. Convert to 8 bits: $BI = (2,2,2,255)$

We want this result to match the scenario that follows:

1. Clear the frame buffer to transparent: $BI = (0,0,0,0)$
2. Overlay $FJ = (1,1,1,16)$, giving $BJ = (1,1,1,16)$
3. Convert to 8 bits: $BI = (2,2,2,0)$
4. Store this in a file
5. Clear the frame buffer to black: $BI = (0,0,0,255)$
6. Overlay the file pixel: $FI = (2,2,2,0)$

If we then use the code

```
if (F.a==0) B.c += F.c
```

(with appropriate conversions), we will get the desired result:

```
BI = (2,2,2,255)
```

Final 8-Bit Code

We won't give up completely on skipping transparent foreground pixels. The first test in the code below is a test of all 32 bits of FI being zero. This handles overlaying an image with substantial transparent regions. You can often do this test in one instruction by leaning on the compiler a little.

In fact, I actually scan the F array to see if any pixels at all are non-transparent. This allows me to skip whole scan lines of transparent foreground image without even reading the frame buffer. I won't show this part explicitly.

Anyway, the code:

```
if(FI==0)  skip this mess;
if (FI.a==0){
     FJ.c = cv16c(FI.c);
     BJ.c = cv16c(BI.c);
     BI.c = cv8c(FJ.c+BJ.c);}
else if(FI.a==255){
     BI.c = FI.c;
     BI.a = 255;}
else{
     FJ.c = cv16c(FI.c);
     FJ.a = cv16a(FI.a);
     BJ.c = cv16c(BI.c);
     BJ.c = FJ.c + M(16384-FJ.a,BJ.c);
     BI.c = cv8(BJ.c);
     BI.a (calculated as above)
```

Note that if a pixel of the foreground image is opaque (i.e., if F.a==1), no conversion or arithmetic of any kind is necessary.

Another 8-Bit Possibility

$\int$ uppose we had encoded the *rgb* values linearly into 8-bit bytes in the same way that we did alpha. We could write the overlaying code to operate directly on 8-bit numbers and wouldn't need to convert up and down to the 16-bit representation. Wouldn't that be a lot faster? Well, it can be if we are careful. When scaling to 8 bits, we must use the factor 255; we don't have the bits to waste to make the factor a power of two like we did with 16-bit scaling. Therefore, we would have to divide by 255 after multiplying two scaled-by-255 byte values together. See Chapter 19 for a nice way to do this.

The Craft of Programming

Wow. Life sure can get complicated. I still have a nagging feeling that all this special-case testing still might not be worth it. But no, all the cases I added to the code were motivated by actual profiling runs showing that time was being wasted in these routines. And consider the situations that fall into the special cases:

- Opaque regions of foreground
- Transparent regions of foreground
- Opaque backgrounds
- Black backgrounds

These are all pretty common situations.

This is all part of the craft of programming—trading off special-case speed with complex code against general-case slowness with simple code. Actually, in this situation, we have the best of both worlds. There is just one general-purpose routine for each data type for the user to learn. The special cases are automatically detected internally, so that the user doesn't have to worry about a speed penalty. We get the generality of being able to overlay translucent objects onto transparent backgrounds with virtually no overhead if we don't happen to be using that generality.

What could be finer.

I HUGGED
JIM BLINN

CHAPTER EIGHTEEN

How to Attend a SIGGRAPH Conference

J U L Y   1 9 9 5

In *A Trip Down the Graphics Pipeline*, I described how to write a paper for SIGGRAPH (Chapter 5) and how to present the paper (Chapter 7). This time I'm going to describe something of more general usefulness: how to *attend* a SIGGRAPH conference. I'm one of the few people who has been to all 22 (including '95) of the SIGGRAPH annual conferences, so this might give me some perspective. They do tend to blur together a bit, though. (Looking over the past conferences, in fact, I find I remember them largely in terms of who I met at them.) So here are some historical nuggets and tips I've formulated over the years.

Tip: Bring an extra suitcase. You'll be bringing back great baskets full of proceedings, notes, and junk picked up at the toy store.

Tip: Pack munchies in your suitcase for your hotel room at night. It was very hard to find quick food at the early conferences. Later ones had fast food stands, but you never can be too careful.

Time Management

The conference is a madhouse of overlapping events occurring in parallel for six days. You'll find that your most important job during the conference is time management. The obvious thing to do is to make a time line.

Generally, the conference provides a program (usually tall and thin and impossible to keep open) that has a global time line in it. Start with this and mark off the things you want to see. I find myself continually looking at this program and saying to myself, "What's going on now? What am I missing?"

Technical Talks

The conference was founded to give researchers opportunities to present technical papers. This is still the foundation of the conference, but there are so many other activities going on that there is a tendency to skip the technical sessions. After all, you can always read the proceedings. However, since the deadline for publication is weeks before the conference, the talk that most speakers give includes refinements made since the paper was sent in. In addition, speakers often show animations with their talk that you probably won't get in the proceedings. Usually, these refinements and animations were produced the night before the speaker got on the plane for the conference. (I myself have even brought a roll of exposed film to the conference, hoping I could get it developed locally in time for my talk later in the week. Scary.)

Tip: Interesting videos are most often shown during the sessions on animation; go to these.

Panels

Let's face it, panel sessions are usually not real deep. They generally consist of such long opening comments by the panelists that there is no time for discussion and interaction between speakers. But since it's so much easier for a celebrity to prepare a panel talk than a technical talk, panel sessions are a great venue for you to see someone famous performing live.

Tip: Go early to any panel session that has the word "sex" in the title.

The Toy Store

The toy store (aka the equipment show) has become one of the most visible parts of the conference. It's a wonderland of color displays and real-time texture mapping, but a lot of the interesting exhibits have long lines. The equipment show is a good place to just hang around and meet people, though.

Tip: Allocate explicit time to see this. The equipment show closes early on Thursday and is totally gone on Friday. I have often not gotten around to visiting the toy store until late in the week, only to find it closed already.

Tip: How to predict the future: Look at manufacturers and designers of special-purpose chips, e.g., Phillips, Brooktree, etc. One or two years later the market will be flooded with cheap plug-in boards that are essentially just these chips interfaced to the computer's bus. Witness the proliferation of cheap video digitizing boards.

Electronic Theater

The ET started out as a bunch of us crowding into Dan Sandin's dorm room to watch video tapes. (The first few SIGGRAPHs were held at college campuses and everyone stayed in the dorms.) For the next few years, it consisted essentially of "open projector/VCR night." The organizer would set up a 16-mm projector and a Umatic VCR and call out, "Anybody bring anything to show?" Somebody would jump up, load the film/tape, and narrate it live. That's how I showed my first Voyager flybys and teapot rendering demos.

Nowadays, the ET is a very competitive juried show where the applicants must submit their entries months in advance, and there is only time to show about one in ten of them. The conference attendance is so big that several identical showings are spread out through the week to give everyone a chance to see it.

Tip: I usually try to get to the second night of the show. The first night often has technical problems that are worked out by the second night.

Tip: Don't even think of eating a formal dinner the night you attend. You'll get trapped in some restaurant and not get back in time to get in line.

Tip: Get in line early. I mean an *hour* early at minimum, preferably an hour and a half. The seats are first come, first served. (Some years the show will be at a site far enough away from the convention center so that shuttle buses will be used, so this advice might not apply.)

Tip: If you want to go to the ET with someone, don't meet somewhere and then get in line. Meet *in* the line. The first one there gets in line and the later arrival joins the first. Then you won't be watching the line grow exponentially while fuming over why your friend is a couple of minutes late.

In 1995, I was on the ET jury and learned a lot about what gets a film/video accepted. In 1996, my friend, colleague, and co-columnist for *IEEE*, Andrew Glassner, was on the jury. Together we wrote up our experiences and recommendations for getting your film accepted to the show.[1]

Art Show

Having an art show as part of a technical conference is an example of the confluence of art and technology that computer graphics has given us. The art show has morphed and bifurcated into a gallery show, artists' presentations, and continuous interactivity demonstrations. Like the toy store, the art show is a good place to hang out and bump into people. It's also a good place to arrange to meet someone. The early arrival then has lots of interesting things to look at while waiting for the late arrival.

Tip: If you arrange to meet someone at the art show, specify exactly where within the show to meet. Saying "meet me at the art show" is now somewhat akin to saying "meet me in New York."

Tip: Don't miss the T-shirt judging contest. Entrants in the contest display their works and give humorous presentations about how and why they were made. The contest itself is generally on Thursday at noon and is open to the public. The awards are presented during the papers/panels reception on Thursday evening.

Parties

Of course, a conference is not just the official sessions but the informal get-togethers where you can meet others in the business. This leads to lots of late-night parties all during the conference. In the early days, these just consisted of bunches of us getting together in hotel rooms. This was often a problem since a large group of elbow-to-elbow people makes a lot of noise even when they aren't trying to. Usually the parties lasted until the hotel security got too many complaints about the noise.

Nowadays, in keeping with SIGGRAPH's attempt to make itself as much like the Cannes Film Festival as possible, lavish parties are hosted in ballrooms or nightclubs by the larger and hipper of the production or hardware companies. Said companies get lots of good PR by throwing good parties, which often translates into being able to hire better people.

---

1   Check out Hey, buddy, how do I get into the SIGGRAPH electronic theater? in *IEEE Computer Graphics and Applications* (November 1996, page 72).

Tip: Be suspicious of parties held at clubs. These tend to be crowded and very noisy and often have live "entertainment," which means you won't be able to find or talk to anybody. My favorite parties have quiet rooms for discussion and relaxation as well as noisy dance rooms.

There's another unfortunate trend. Many companies give invitation-only parties as a show of exclusivity or simply because there isn't much room at their venue. My impression is that these turn into a mad scramble to scam tickets and turn a lot of people off.

Tip: You really don't want to go to exclusive parties. In fact, if you get any such invitations, protest by putting them on the SIGGRAPH message board in an envelope with the name "Jim Blinn" on it.

Ribbons

Everyone at the conference wears name badges. This is fortunate for me because I can now fake remembering everyone's names. In fact, I wish people wore name badges all the time in real life.

Tip: I have always been paranoid about my name badge falling out of its clear plastic holder. My solution is to go the booth that advertises the next year's SIGGRAPH conference (SIGGRAPH $n + 1$) and pick up one of the lapel pins they are handing out. Fasten the badge to the holder with this. You are then advertising the next year's conference as well as providing security for this year's badge.

Early on, those who helped organize the conference or were speakers, etc., were given ribbons to stick onto their badges to advertise their status—"Speaker", "Film Show Jury," etc. Then in 1983 (the tenth conference), Tom DeFanti had some extra ribbons made up for those of us who had attended the first conference, which said "SIGGRAPH '74 Attendee." Then in 1984, he gave out ribbons that said "SIGGRAPH '85–'89 Attendee." In 1985, Rob Cook was handing out ribbons that said "Party Jury." After that, everybody went crazy making and handing out ribbons with clever and/or obscure sayings. *The* thing at SIGGRAPH was to see how many fake ribbons you could collect. My favorite, of course, was in 1990 when Maxine Brown made 100 ribbons that said "I Hugged Jim Blinn" for me to hand out (but only to those who earned them).

Tip: Random strangers and old friends will run up to you and hand you fake ribbons. Smile graciously and glue them on.

Tip: Bring a roll of masking tape with you. If your ribbons collection gets too long the glue won't hold them together very well. A strip of masking tape down the back will keep you from losing some.

The fake ribbon joke might very well have run its course, however. My count has fallen from a maximum of nineteen different ribbons in 1992 down to just six ribbons in 1994. In true computer fashion, now that the fake ribbon phenomenon has been documented, it becomes obsolete.

The Summer Camp Session

The last session of the conference generally takes place just outside the lecture hall after the last technical talk. It resembles the last day of summer camp; everyone hugs goodbye, exchanges cards, promises to send each other copies of their latest papers, and promises to come to each other's institution to give a talk.

Tip: Stay until Saturday morning. Planning to leave Friday night makes Friday a very hectic day. You can't do much conferencing because you're worried about checking out of the hotel and getting to the airport on time.

Tip: Eat and sleep a lot before the conference. You won't get much of either during it because there's so much to see.

I personally think SIGGRAPH should be two weeks long, with fewer overlapping sessions, but then I'm a maniac.

Three Wrongs Make a Right

N O V E M B E R 1 9 9 5

When dealing with graphics operations that must be fast (e.g., the inner loops of rendering algorithms), I usually like to do calculations with fixed-point arithmetic (i.e., scaled integers) rather than floating-point arithmetic. The exact scaling factor used can have some interesting effects on the speed and errors in the calculation. In this chapter, I'm going to relate some tidbits on this subject that I've either discovered for myself or picked up from others. In particular, I'll talk about some of the advantages of using odd numbers of the form $2^n - 1$ as scaling factors.

The motivation for this discussion is the desire to do arithmetic on pixel values; red, green, blue, or alpha. These numbers are in the range $0 \ldots 1$, so all numbers you will see here are positive. In the discussion that follows, I'll use floating point as a test bed and as scaffolding to derive integer formulas. All final calculations will take place using only integer arithmetic.

Representation

Let's first review the process of representing a number as a scaled integer. To convert from a floating-point value, f, to the appropriate integer value, i, we multiply by the scale factor and round to the nearest integer. I'll do this by adding a bias of $\frac{1}{2}$ and truncating.

$$i = \text{int}(fs + 0.5)$$

The int function simply truncates the fractional part of a number; this is what normally happens when you convert a float to an integer. It is a potentially information-destroying operation. (Note that if the value of f is negative, this simple technique won't work. Fortunately, we are dealing with positive pixel values here so we're OK.) This operation essentially divides the continuous number line into bins, each of which is represented by an integer value:

To convert from a scaled integer to a floating-point value, just divide the integer bin number by the scale factor.

$$f = i / s$$

Multiplication

ow let's see what the arithmetic operation of multiplication looks like using this scheme. We would like an algorithm that takes two scaled integer values and produces the scaled integer that represents their product. A way to determine the "correct" result is to convert to floating point, do the arithmetic there, and then scale back to an integer. Thus, the product of two scaled integers a and b is

$$r = \text{int}[((a / s)(b / a))s + 0.5]$$

This simplifies to

$$r = \text{int}[(ab) / s + 0.5]$$

Since we are trying to avoid floating-point calculations, we'd like to scale the 0.5 too. This leads us to rearrange this into

$$r = \text{int}[(ab + s / 2) / s] \tag{1}$$

If all the quantities are integers, the preceding int function has the effect of calculating the integer quotient of $(ab + s / 2)$ and s.

Scale Factor = 2^n

If s is a power of two, this works out nicely since you can implement the division with a shift. For example, in Chapter 5, I discussed doing arithmetic on pixel values using a scaling factor of 16384. Equation 1 becomes

$$r = \text{int}[(ab+8192)/16384]$$

Turning this into C code and using a shift for the division, we get

```
r = (a*b + 8192) >> 14
```

I used a scale of 16384 because it was the largest power of two that preserves two's complement arithmetic; the high bit is still a sign bit. A 16-bit word then gives you an effective value range of $-2...1^{16383}\!/_{16384}$. This is good for some signal processing calculations where negative lobe filtering might generate intermediate values above 1 or below 0.

A possible objection to this scale factor is that it does not utilize the whole range of bit patterns. Only about one-quarter of the 65536 bit patterns in a 16-bit word represent values in the range $(0 \ldots 1)$. This isn't too bad, though; subdividing the range $(0 \ldots 1)$ into 16384 bins generally gives plenty of resolution for most purposes.

Scale Factor = $2^n - 1$

If you are storing a pixel value in 8 or fewer bits, however, you cannot afford to be so lavish. For an 8-bit value, you are best off filling up the range completely. This implies a scale factor of 255. Since s is now not a power of two, you can't do the division of equation 1 with a shift. The correct result of the product of two scaled 8-bit quantities is

$$r = \text{int}[(ab+127.5)/255]$$

We've got a problem if we want to implement this with integer arithmetic; 127.5 isn't an integer. What to do . . . we might be able to come close if we use either 127 or 128 instead. Let's try an experiment. Do a brute-force comparison, for all values of a and b from 0 to 255, between the "right" answer (found by doing the arithmetic in floating point) and those obtained using a bias of 127 and of 128. (Tick, tick, ding!) Well, I happen to have one already prepared here in the oven. We find that a bias of 128 gives an answer that is too large for several values of a and b. But using a bias of 127 always gives the right answer. So . . . use 127. Can't argue with success. The correct code is

```
r = (a*b + 127)/255;
```
(2)

Why Does This Work?

I was puzzled by this, though. I would have thought that, since a bias of 128 gives several results that are too high, a bias of 127 would have given several results that are too low. Here's what I've figured out.

Let's just look at the division and forget about rounding for a minute. When you divide an integer i by 255, you get a quotient j and a remainder k. You can write the results of the division as

$$i \, / \, 255 = j + \frac{k}{255}$$

That is, j is the whole number part, and k is the number of 255ths.

Now let's do the rounding. If k is 127 or less, we want to round down; if k is 128 or greater, we want to round up. (Notice that there is no value of k that makes the fractional part equal to $\frac{1}{2}$. This is nice because the decision of whether to round $\frac{1}{2}$ up or down is ambiguous.)

We actually do rounding by adding one-half and truncating. This is the same as adding one-half to the fractional part and seeing if it has become bigger than 1. (Even though we don't calculate the fractional part explicitly, we can see the machinery better by looking at it.) In other words, we calculate

$$r = j + \frac{k}{255} + \frac{1}{2}$$

Rounding up happens if $(k \, / \, 255 + 1 \, / \, 2) > 1$. The correct arithmetic for the two borderline cases is

$k = 127$: $r = j + \dfrac{127}{255} + \dfrac{127.5}{255} = j + \dfrac{254.5}{255}$ (round down)

$k = 128$: $r = j + \dfrac{128}{255} + \dfrac{127.5}{255} = j + \dfrac{255.5}{255}$ (round up)

In the actual integer calculation, we add one-half by adding a bias of either 128 or 127 before dividing by 255. A closer look at our experiment will show that the situations where a bias of 128 gives the wrong answer are just those where $k = 127$. We can now see why this happens.

$k = 127$: $r = j + \dfrac{127}{255} + \dfrac{128}{255} = j + \dfrac{255}{255}$ (round up; WRONG)

$k = 128$: $r = j + \dfrac{128}{255} + \dfrac{128}{255} = j + \dfrac{256}{255}$ (round up)

If we use the equally wrong bias of 127, though, we do get the right rounding for both of the borderline cases.

$$k = 127: \qquad r = j + \frac{127}{255} + \frac{127}{255} = j + \frac{254}{255} \text{ (round down)}$$

$$k = 128: \qquad r = j + \frac{128}{255} + \frac{127}{255} = j + \frac{255}{255} \text{ (round up)}$$

In fact, to get rounding up to happen at the correct value of k, we can use any value of bias p that satisfies the following:

$$\frac{127}{255} + \frac{p}{255} < 1, \quad \text{and} \quad \frac{128}{255} + \frac{p}{255} \geq 1$$

We can rearrange these to find that we can use any p that satisfies

$$127 \leq p < 128$$

A bias of 127 is the only integer that qualifies. 128 is just a scrunch too big.

Avoiding Division

O K. So the code of equation 2 works. But it has an unpleasant division in it. We don't like divisions. Divisions are slow. Divisions wear out the electrons in our computer. How can we avoid this? Use a clever trick that I learned from Alvy Ray Smith of Microsoft: Instead of dividing by 255, multiply by 1/255. You can win with this because of a nice property of fractions of the form $1 / (2^n - 1)$. The bit patterns of their binary representations are

$$(1/3)_{10} = (0.01010101\ldots)_2$$
$$(1/7)_{10} = (0.001001001001\ldots)_2$$
$$(1/15)_{10} = (0.0001000100010001\ldots)_2$$

and

$$(1/255)_{10} = (0.0000000100000001\ldots)_2 = (0.01010101\ldots)_{16}$$

Alvy's implementation used the approximation 0.0101_{16}. To divide by 255, he multiplied by 101_{16} and divided by 10000_{16}. This can be done by shifts and adds:

```
r = ( (i<<8)+i ) >> 16
```

This is sure better than doing a general division.

Now let's talk for a bit about word lengths. We are going to apply this formula to values of i that we get from the expression

```
i = a*b + 127;
```

If a and b are 8-bit unsigned integers, i will always fit into 16 bits. In fact, the maximum values of $a = b = 255$ gives the largest possible result in hexadecimal as 0xFE80.

Since the calculation contains (i<<8), it can produce intermediate results that are 24 bits long. This means that the integer word length in this calculation needs to be at least this big. This is not a problem if you have a 32-bit CPU. But you can do the same arithmetic using only 16-bit quantities with only a slight perturbation of his formula.

To see how this works, let's give names to the two bytes of our input quantity i. We'll call the high-order byte YY and the low-order byte ZZ. The 24-bit sum in the calculation is

```
YYZZ00    (i<<8)
+ YYZZ    (i)
-------
ssssss
```

The final answer is the high-order 8 bits of this sum.

Now, note that the ZZ byte in the second row is added to 00, so it never can overflow into the middle byte. So you could just as well calculate

```
YYZZ      (i)
+ YY      (i>>8)
-----
ssss
```

and take the high-order 8 bits of this 16-bit sum. Alvy's code then looks like

```
r = (i + (i>>8)) >>8;
```

This implementation generates the same result as before but requires only 16-bit arithmetic.

Does This Work?

But does this expression actually generate the same result as dividing by 255? Well, no, not always. Another quicky test program tells us that it gets the wrong answer for any i that is a multiple of 255. Why is this?

Let's look at exact division by 255 in terms of its infinite expansion $(1/255)_{10} = (0.01010101...)_{16}$. For our input YYZZ, this will be

```
YY.ZZ           (YYZZ * .01)
+ .YYZZ         (YYZZ * .0001)
+ .00YYZZ       (YYZZ * .000001)
  . . . etc.
```

The integer part of this infinite sum will simply be YY unless there is a carry from the sum ZZ + YY. In this case, the answer will be YY + 1. This works fine except in the case where YY + ZZ = 0xFF. In this case there is no carry, but the sum in hexadecimal is YY.FFFFF . . . . Mathematically, this equals YY + 1, but simply truncating the digits to the right of the radix point won't tell us so.

By the way, it's an interesting exercise to show that YY + ZZ = 0xFF is the same as saying that YYZZ is a multiple of 255.

How to Fix It
We can make this work correctly by the following logic. If YY + ZZ > 0xFF, the sum generates a carry and we get the right answer. If YY + ZZ < 0xFF, we don't get a carry; still correct. But if YY + ZZ = 0xFF, we don't get a carry, but we'd like to. We can make the carry happen for exactly the right cases (YY + ZZ ≥ 0xFF) by simply adding 1 to the sum.

```
  YYZZ (i)
+ YY (i>>8)
  + 1
  ----
  ssss
```

In code, this is

```
r = ( i + (i>>8) + 1 ) >> 8;
```

Try this out and you will see that it gets the right answer for any value of i from 0 to 65534.

The Final Formula
One last little decoration. The preceding calculation also works if you add 1 to both i values.

```
r = ( (i+1) + ((i+1) >> 8) ) >> 8;
```

This makes it easy to merge the addition of 1 to the value of i with the addition of the rounding bias of 127.

The final quick, accurate, and wonderful code is

```
i = a*b + 128;
r = ( i + (i >> 8) ) >> 8;
```

This generates the correct result for all possible 8-bit input values a and b and only requires 16-bit arithmetic.

Really Turning the Screws

Since the only shifts in our final calculation are by 8 bits, we can perform them by addressing the bytes directly. The Intel 80x86 architecture is ideal for this. It has a 16-bit register called ax, and you can access the high byte as register ah (containing YY) and the low byte as al (containing ZZ). (You say you don't use the 80x86 architecture? Well, sooner or later . . . *you will.*)

Here's the most streamlined assembly code I've been able to come up with to do our scaled integer multiplication.

```
mov al,a      ;load a
mul b         ;multiply by b
add ax,0x80   ;add bias
add al,ah     ;add YY to ZZ
adc ah,0      ;carry into YY
mov r,ah      ;store answer
```

The multiply operation here is an 8-bit multiply. It takes two 8-bit inputs and generates a 16-bit result. Getting this to work with 16-bit arithmetic also turns out to be useful with the new generation of Intel processors with MMX instructions that can do several 16-bit operations in parallel.[1]

Wrong, Wrong, Wrong = Right

We wanted to divide a number by 255 and round the result. We did this by doing three seemingly wrong things: We added one to the input, added a rounding bias that was too small, and then multiplied by an approximation to 1/255 that was too small. But we still got the right result!

---

1 Take a look at Fugue for MMX in *IEEE Computer Graphics and Applications* (Mar./Apr. 1997, page 88) for more on this.

The reason that we got away with this is that, over the range of i we are interested in,

$$\text{int}\left[\frac{i}{255}+0.5\right]=\text{int}\left[(i+128)\frac{257}{65536}\right]$$

And the right-hand side of this equation is, believe it or not, easier to calculate than the left-hand side.

The lesson from this is that three wrongs make a right. Computers are sometimes more forgiving than real life.

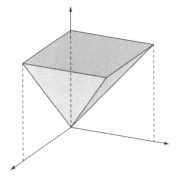

CHAPTER TWENTY

Fun with Premultiplied Alpha

SEPTEMBER 1996

The computer graphics universe consist of pixels. Pixels, in turn, consist of components: red, green, blue, and the coverage or opacity value alpha. For various reasons, it is convenient to store and process a given $rgb\alpha$ quadruple with the rgb values already multiplied by α. This was originally pointed out in the Porter-Duff compositing paper,[1] and I presented some further justifications in Chapter 16. This premultiplication has some other interesting implications; that's what I'll talk about here.

A Pyramid on Its Nose

Before premultiplication, the four pixel components would have values from 0 to 1. After premultiplication, the rgb values must all be less than or equal to the α value. (You can create some interesting effects with pixels that have a premultiplied color value greater than its alpha value, but I will assume we aren't doing that here.) The range of valid $rgb\alpha$ values gives pixel color space a characteristic shape. To visualize this, it's usually only necessary to consider a two- or a three-dimensional subset of color space, as long as one of the dimensions we use is the special alpha component.

---

1 T. Porter and T. Duff, Compositing digital images, *SIGGRAPH '84 Conference Proceedings* (New York: ACM), pages 253–259.

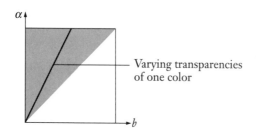

Figure 20.1 *Valid color space in two dimensions*

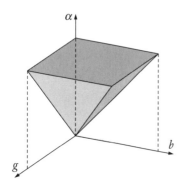

Figure 20.2 *Valid color space in three dimensions*

In two dimensions, plotting, say, just b and α, the space of valid values is the triangle shown in Figure 20.1. Only the points on the top of the triangle, on the $\alpha = 1$ line, represent the space of opaque colors. The points in the body of the gray triangle represent various transparencies of the top surface color space. In particular, all points on a ray from the origin through a particular (b,α) point represent the same color—just different transparencies of it.

In three dimensions, the total color space would be a quarter of an inverted Egyptian pyramid on its nose, as in Figure 20.2. Here the top surface of the pyramid represents the entire opaque color space. Pixel colors within the body of the pyramid are varying transparencies of these.

In four dimensions, you might be able to visualize the space as a series of solid cubes, one for each alpha value. The largest (unit) cube, at $\alpha = 1$, represents the entire opaque color space.

Shave and a Haircut, 1.9887 Bits

If you look at the pyramid of validity, you will notice one interesting thing: lots of empty space surrounds it. One implication is that, if you store *rgba* pixels as four 8-bit bytes, a lot of the bit patterns never get used (having *r*, *g*, or *b* greater than α). In fact, it turns out that almost three-fourths of the 2^{32} possible bit patterns represent invalid pixel values.

How did I figure this out? Well, for each valid value of α, there are $(\alpha + 1)^3$ valid *rgb* combinations. To get the total number of valid values, we want to calculate

$$\sum_{\alpha=0}^{255}(\alpha+1)^3$$

A quicky program can show that this value is 1,082,146,816. This, unfortunately, is a *little* bit larger than 2^{30} (which equals 1,073,741,824). In other words, we could *almost* encode all valid pixel values into 30 bits, giving us two free bits in a 32-bit word for other information. In reality, though, we only get to free up $32 - \log_2(1{,}082{,}146{,}816) \approx 1.9887$ bits.

If we were really desperate, though, we could at least use this to compress 32-bit *rgba* values into 31 bits. One way to do this is to sequentially number the valid *rgba* values: for $\alpha = 0$ there is one valid value, which we'll encode as 0; for $\alpha = 1$ there are eight valid values, which we'll encode as 1 through 8; for $\alpha = 2$ there are 27 *rgb*'s, which we'll encode as 9 through 35, etc. Basically, the encoded value is $r(\alpha + 1)^2 + g(\alpha + 1) + b$ plus the number of encodings used up for alpha values from 0 to $\alpha - 1$. This number is

$$\sum_{k=0}^{\alpha-1}(k+1)^3 = \sum_{m=1}^{\alpha} m^3 = \frac{1}{4}\alpha^2(\alpha+1)^2$$

Where did this come from? Well, there's probably some fancy proof, but I intuited that the sum of cubes was likely to be some fourth-order polynomial. I evaluated the function manually for $\alpha = 0, 1, 2, 3, 4$ and fit a fourth-order polynomial to it. To check that this worked, I evaluated the polynomial for all values of alpha and compared it against an explicitly calculated sum. Sometimes brute force works. Let's store the values of this function in a table:

```
long table[256];
for (long a=0; a<256; a++) {
    long t=a*(a+1)/2;
    table[a]= t*t; }
```

You could then do the encoding as follows:

```
struct pixel (unsigned char r,g,b,a;);

long Encode(pixel P)
{
    long k = P.a+1;
    return (P.r*k + P.g)*k + P.b + table[P.a];
}
```

Decoding is only slightly trickier. Given an encoding e, we look up the largest table entry that is less than or equal to e. The index is our alpha value, P.a. Since the table is monotonic, we can use a binary search. I mentioned an extremely streamlined binary search for this type of purpose in Chapter 5; I'll express it here in a highly condensed and slightly obfuscated fashion. Finally, once we have P.a, we just reverse the preceding *rgb* encoding.

```
#define T(bit) if (e>=table[P.a+bit]) P.a+=bit;

void Decode(long e, pixel& P)
{
P.a = 0;
T(128) T(64) T(32) T(16) T(8) T(4) T(2) T(1)
long t = e-table[P.a];
long k = P.a+1;
P.b = t % k; t = t/k;
P.g = t % k; t = t/k;
P.r = t % k;
}
```

This code is primarily an existence proof. Some tinkering with it might do the encoding or decoding faster. For example, table lookups are dangerous on modern CPUs since they bother cache coherence. In addition, I find it a bit offensive to have to do two divisions to get both the quotient and the remainder of a single division.

Alternatively, there might be entirely different encoding schemes that make encoding or decoding easier. But, really, all this fuss and bother is probably not worth it just to save one bit out of 32.

The Geometry of "Over"

Now that I've gotten that off my chest, let's look at something more consequential. In what follows, I'll write the four-dimensional pixel color vectors in boldface, with the elements named as follows:

$$\mathbf{F} = [F_r \quad F_g \quad F_b \quad F_\alpha]$$

One of the motivations for premultiplied pixels is that it makes many of the basic image compositing operations more convenient. The particular compositing operation that I use most often was given the name "over" in the original Porter-Duff paper. It, not too surprisingly, expresses the result of placing one semitransparent image over another one. Algebraically, given a foreground pixel color $\mathbf{F}$ and a background color $\mathbf{B}$, the pixel color formed by placing $\mathbf{F}$ in front of $\mathbf{B}$ (i.e., "over" it) is

$$\mathbf{C} = \mathbf{F} + (1 - F_\alpha)\,\mathbf{B}$$

Whenever I see an algebraic equation, I like to be able to visualize it geometrically. So here's the basic exercise: Given $\mathbf{F}$ and $\mathbf{B}$ as points in $rgb\alpha$ space, how can you geometrically construct $\mathbf{F}$ over $\mathbf{B}$? I'll work up to this by first thinking of the **B** value as constant and see how the valid color region of **F** distorts when matted over it. Then I'll treat the **F** value as constant and see how the valid color region of **B** distorts when matted under it. Finally, I'll merge these into a general geometric construction of **F** over **B**.

Varying F over Constant B

We must be able to drag matrices in here somewhere. I know. Thinking of **B** as a constant, let's write the "over" operation as

$$
\mathbf{C} = \mathbf{F}
\begin{bmatrix}
1 & 0 & 0 & 0 \\
0 & 1 & 0 & 0 \\
0 & 0 & 1 & 0 \\
-B_r & -B_g & -B_b & 1-B_\alpha
\end{bmatrix}
+ \mathbf{B}
$$

This means that "over" is an affine mapping of **F** onto **C**. The matrix has **B** as an eigenvector, with eigenvalue $(1 - B_\alpha)$. How can we visualize this geometrically? One way is just to look at where the corners of **F** space go and imagine a shear that moves the rest of the space in the same way. Key transformed points are

$$
[0,0,0,0] \mapsto \mathbf{B}
$$
$$
[r, g, b, 1] \mapsto [r, g, b, 1]
$$

In other words, points on the $\alpha = 1$ surface don't move, and the [0, 0, 0, 0] point moves up to the point **B**. The pyramid of valid values squishes so that its apex aligns with the background point **B**. In two dimensions this looks like Figure 20.3.

This is good, but there is a little more intuition we can squeeze out of it. Let's look at the "path" of each **F** value as it composites. If we connect each original value with its transformed value, we see that the displacement is always parallel to the vector **B**. (This is pretty obvious if we note that $\mathbf{C} - \mathbf{F} = (1 - F_\alpha)\mathbf{B}$.) We can visualize this by thinking of a bunch of

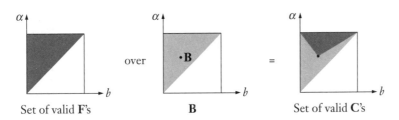

Figure 20.3 *How the valid region of* **F** *transforms*

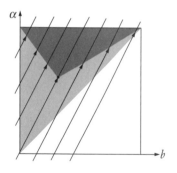

Figure 20.4 *Each **F** transforms to a **C** on the same diagonal line*

lines, parallel to the direction of **B,** overlaid on the diagram. Each point on such a line will transform to another point on the same line, as shown in Figure 20.4.

Visualizing Unmatting

The construction in Figure 20.4 gives an interesting insight into the process of blue screen matte extraction. In this common special effects technique, we photograph some object in front of a blue screen and later wish to composite it over some different background. What does this look like in premultiplied *rgba* space?

When we photograph an object in front of a blue screen, we produce pixels of the object **F** composited over a constant blue background **B.** Since, in the real world, the background has an alpha value of 1, the "over" transformation is singular. All **F** colors on a given line parallel to **B** will be squashed onto the same point in the $\alpha = 1$ plane, as shown in Figure 20.5a. For comparison, if the backing screen were black, we would have Figure 20.5b. This shows that matting a premultiplied color over black is the same as just setting its alpha values to 1 with the *rgb* values unchanged.

Now we would like to matte the object over some other background. In order to do this, we need the original **F** colors (with their alphas), but we only have pixels from the blue screen shot. Information has been lost. We do know the global color of the blue background, however. Each pixel color of the blue screen shot could have come from any point in *rgba* space lying on a line parallel to the blue background color vector, Figure 20.6a. Various commercial matting processes solve this problem by allowing operators to select the opaque colors $\tilde{\mathbf{F}}$ that make up the foreground object. The various transparencies of those colors (due to actual transparency or

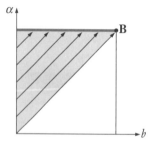

Figure 20.5a **F** *over opaque pure blue*

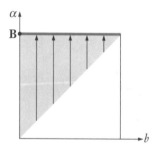

Figure 20.5b **F** *over opaque black*

to antialiased edges) will then lie on lines through the origin as shown in Figure 20.1. The intersection of these two lines then gives the uncomposited color $\mathbf{F}$, Figure 20.6b.

This technique is not perfect, however. If there are two foreground colors $\tilde{\mathbf{F}}_1$ and $\tilde{\mathbf{F}}_2$ that are colinear with $\mathbf{B}$, there is an unresolvable ambiguity, Figure 20.6c. (This is rather trivial in our two-dimensional diagrams, but imagine Figure 20.6c embedded into Figure 20.2. There, each $\tilde{\mathbf{F}}$ would be a line or perhaps even a polygon in the $\alpha = 1$ plane, and all the lines through the origin would become planes through the origin.) Alvy Ray Smith and I published a paper that goes into this in more detail.[2]

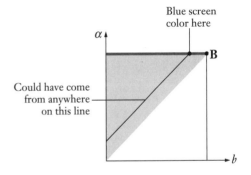

Figure 20.6a *Unknown inverse matting*

Constant F over Varying B

OK. So much for matte extraction. Now let's look at the general $\mathbf{F}$ over $\mathbf{B}$ construction another way. Let's let $\mathbf{F}$ be constant and see how the range of valid $\mathbf{B}$ values changes. Matrixwise, we have

$$\mathbf{C} = \mathbf{B}\begin{bmatrix} 1-F_\alpha & 0 & 0 & 0 \\ 0 & 1-F_\alpha & 0 & 0 \\ 0 & 0 & 1-F_\alpha & 0 \\ 0 & 0 & 0 & 1-F_\alpha \end{bmatrix} + \mathbf{F}$$

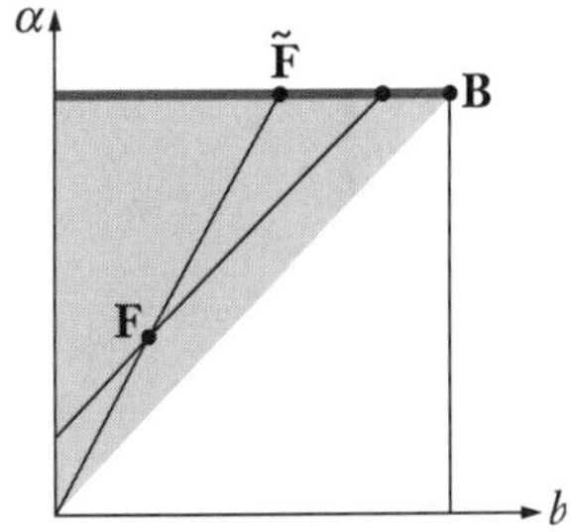

Geometrically, this just scales the triangular valid $\mathbf{B}$ region by a uniform factor and translates the origin up to coincide with $\mathbf{F}$, as shown in Figure 20.7. One interpretation of this is that, if you overlay a transparent polygon of color $\mathbf{F}$ over a general background, the color space of the final image must be inside the valid $\mathbf{C}$ region in Figure 20.7.

Once again, let's look at the "path" that colors take when being overlaid by the color $\mathbf{F}$. We start by finding the particular background color $\tilde{\mathbf{B}}$ that remains unchanged by the transformation. That is, we want

$$\mathbf{F} + (1 - F_\alpha)\tilde{\mathbf{B}} = \tilde{\mathbf{B}}$$

A quick solve gives us

$$\tilde{\mathbf{B}} = \mathbf{F} / F_\alpha$$

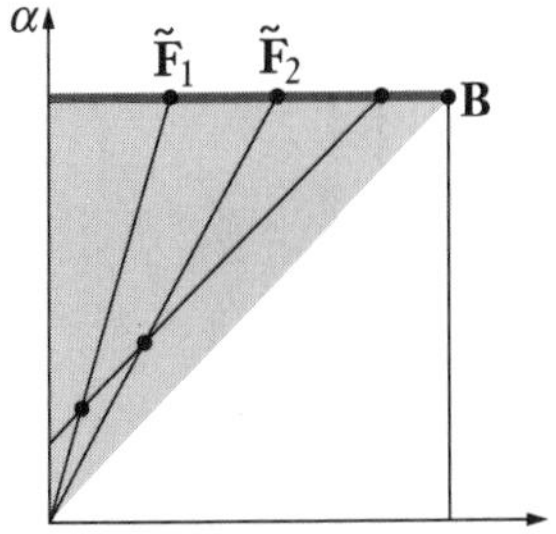

In other words, the valid $\mathbf{B}$ range scales around the point found by extending the vector $\mathbf{F}$ until it hits the $\alpha = 1$ plane. It shrinks about that point until the original origin, $[0, 0, 0, 0]$, coincides with $\mathbf{F}$. See Figure 20.8.

Figure 20.6b *Inverse matting constrained to plane*

Figure 20.6c *Ambiguity in inverse matting*

---

2 A. R. Smith and J. Blinn, Blue screen matting, *SIGGRAPH '96 Conference Proceedings* (New York: ACM), pages 259–268.

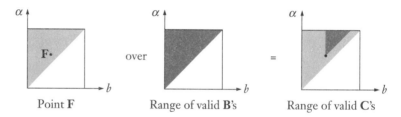

Figure 20.7 *Constant* **F** *over variable* **B**

Full-Tilt Boogie

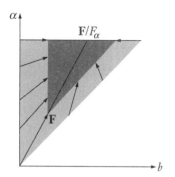

Figure 20.8 *Path of transformed points*

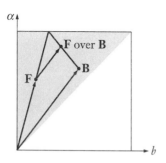

Figure 20.9 *General construction of* **F** *over* **B**

Finally, here's the general geometric construction of **F** over **B**. Follow along on Figure 20.9 while I describe it in words. First, extend the vector through **F** until it hits the $\alpha = 1$ plane. Draw a line from that point, $\mathbf{F}/F_\alpha$, to the point **B**. Now go back and draw a vector from **F** parallel to the vector **B** and extend it until it hits the line. This shorter vector is $(1 - F_\alpha)$ times the **B** vector, so the intersection is **F** over **B**.

Now here's a great exercise in visualization. Look at Figure 20.9 and imagine that point **B** is nailed down and that you can grab point **F** and wiggle it around while the construction of **F** over **B** dynamically updates. You should be able to convince yourself that the point **F** over **B** always stays inside the valid **C** region from Figure 20.3. Now imagine **F** being nailed down and grabbing point **B** and moving it. You should be able to see that point **F** over **B** always stays inside the valid **C** region of Figure 20.7. Got it? Congratulations, you've just graduated from the Jim Blinn School of Visualization.

Graduate School

So far I've shown this primarily in two dimensions. Try to imagine all the preceding diagrams generalized to the 3D *rgbα* space of Figure 20.2. The shear lines of Figure 20.4, for example, become a forest of lines, all parallel to the **B** vector. The case of ambiguous matte extraction of Figure 20.6c would, as I mentioned, become less trivial. The geometric construction of **F** over **B** still remains a 2D problem, however, lying in the plane formed by **F** and **B**. With full *rgbα* color, these diagrams must generalize to four dimensions. Good luck.

Transformation Notation

Reprinted below is the notation for transformations that I defined in *Jim Blinn's Corner: A Trip Down the Graphics Pipeline.*

The Language

The notational scheme I will use is not just a theoretical construct, it's what I actually use to do all my animations. It admittedly has a few quirks, but I'm not going to try to sanitize them because I want to be able to use databases I have actually tried out and to show listings that I know will work. I have purposely made each operation *very* elementary to make it easy to experiment with various combinations of transformations. Most reasonable graphics systems use something like this, so it shouldn't be too hard for you to translate my examples into your own language.

Instructions for rendering a scene take the form of a list of commands and their parameters. These will be written here in TYPEWRITER type. All commands will have four or fewer letters. (The number 4 is used because of its ancient numerological significance.) Parameters will be separated by commas, not blanks. (Old-time FORTRAN programmers don't even see blanks, let alone use them as delimiters.) Don't complain, just be glad I'm not using O-Language (maybe I'll tell you about *that* sometime).

Basic Command Set

These commands modify **C** and pass primitives through it. Each modification command premultiplies some simple matrix into **C**. No other action is taken. The command descriptions below will explicitly show the matrices used.

Translation

```
TRAN x, y, z
```

premultiplies **C** by an elementary translation matrix.

$$\mathbf{C} \leftarrow \begin{bmatrix} 1 & 0 & 0 & 0 \\ 0 & 1 & 0 & 0 \\ 0 & 0 & 1 & 0 \\ x & y & z & 1 \end{bmatrix} \mathbf{C}$$

Scaling

```
SCAL sx, sy, sz
```

premultiplies **C** by an elementary scaling matrix.

$$\mathbf{C} \leftarrow \begin{bmatrix} sx & 0 & 0 & 0 \\ 0 & sy & 0 & 0 \\ 0 & 0 & sz & 0 \\ 0 & 0 & 0 & 1 \end{bmatrix} \mathbf{C}$$

Rotation

```
ROT θ, j
```

The j parameter is an integer from 1 to 3 specifying the coordinate axis (x, y, or z). The positive rotation direction is given via the Right-Hand Rule (if you are using a left-handed coordinate system) or the Left-Hand Rule (if you are using a right-handed coordinate system). This may sound strange, but it's how it's given in Newman and Sproull.[1] It makes *positive* rotation go *clockwise* when viewing in the direction of a coordinate axis. For each matrix below, we precalculate

---

1 William M. Newman and Robert F. Sproull, *Principles of Interactive Computer Graphics* (New York: McGraw-Hill, 1979).

$$s = \sin \theta$$
$$c = \cos \theta$$

The matrices are then

$j = 1$ (x axis)

$$\mathbf{C} \leftarrow \begin{bmatrix} 1 & 0 & 0 & 0 \\ 0 & c & -s & 0 \\ 0 & s & c & 0 \\ 0 & 0 & 0 & 1 \end{bmatrix} \mathbf{C}$$

$j = 2$ (y axis)

$$\mathbf{C} \leftarrow \begin{bmatrix} c & 0 & s & 0 \\ 0 & 1 & 0 & 0 \\ -s & 0 & c & 0 \\ 0 & 0 & 0 & 1 \end{bmatrix} \mathbf{C}$$

$j = 3$ (z axis)

$$\mathbf{C} \leftarrow \begin{bmatrix} c & -s & 0 & 0 \\ s & c & 0 & 0 \\ 0 & 0 & 1 & 0 \\ 0 & 0 & 0 & 1 \end{bmatrix} \mathbf{C}$$

Perspective

PERS α, z_n, z_f

This transformation combines a perspective distortion with a depth (z) transformation. The perspective assumes the eye is at the origin, looking down the $+z$ axis. The field of view is given by the angle α.

The depth transformation is specified by two values—z_n (the location of the *near* clipping plane) and z_f (the location of the *far* clipping plane). The matrix transforms z_n to $+0$, and z_f to $+1$. I know that the traditional names for these planes are *hither* and *yon*, but for some reason I always get these words mixed up, so I call them *near* and *far*.

Precalculate the following quantities (note that far clipping can be effectively disabled by setting $z_f = \infty$, which makes $Q = s$).

$$s = \sin(\alpha/2)$$
$$c = \cos(\alpha/2)$$
$$Q = \frac{s}{1 - z_n / z_f}$$

The matrix is then

$$\mathbf{C} \leftarrow \begin{bmatrix} c & 0 & 0 & 0 \\ 0 & c & 0 & 0 \\ 0 & 0 & Q & s \\ 0 & 0 & -Qz_n & 0 \end{bmatrix} \mathbf{C}$$

Orientation

ORIE a, b, c, d, e, f, p, q, r

Sometimes it's useful to specify the rotation (orientation) portion of the transformation explicitly. There is nothing, though, to enforce it being a pure rotation, so it can be used for skew transformations.

$$\mathbf{C} \leftarrow \begin{bmatrix} a & d & p & 0 \\ b & e & q & 0 \\ c & f & r & 0 \\ 0 & 0 & 0 & 1 \end{bmatrix} \mathbf{C}$$

Transformation Stack

PUSH
POP

These two commands push and pop **C** on/off the stack.

Primitives

DRAW name

A primitive could be a list of vector endpoints, points-and-polygons, implicit surfaces, cubic patches, blobbies, etc. This command means "pass the elements in primitive *name* (however it's defined) through **C** and onto the screen."

Advanced Commands

The simple commands above can be implemented in about two pages of code. The enhancements below are a little more elaborate. The following constructions make sense only in the "editor" mode of operation.

Parameters

Any numeric parameter can be given a symbolic name. A symbol table will be maintained and the current numeric value of the symbol used when the instruction is executed. For example, our cube scene could be

```
PERS FOV, ZN, ZF
TRAN XSCR, YSCR, ZSCR
ROT BACK, 1
ROT SPIN, 3
SCAL 1, 1, -1
DRAW GPLANE
PUSH
TRAN X1, Y1, Z1
ROT ANG, 3
DRAW CUBE
POP
PUSH
SCAL .3, .4, .5
TRAN -5, -3.8, Z1
DRAW CUBE
POP
```

By setting the variables

```
FOV = 45      ZN = 6.2       ZF = 11.8
XSCR = 0      YSCR = -1.41   ZSCR = 9
BACK = -80    SPIN = 48
X1 = 0        Y1 = 0         Z1 = 1
ANG = 20
```

and executing the command list, the same results would be generated. The same symbol can appear in more than one place, allowing a certain amount of constraint satisfaction.

Abbreviations

Each time a subobject is positioned relative to a containing object, the instructions usually look something like

```
PUSH
   :
   :
various TRAN, ROT, SCAL commands
   :
   :
```

```
DRAW primitive
POP
```

While explicit, the above notation is sometimes a bit spread out and hard to follow. This sort of thing happens so often that it's helpful to define an abbreviation for it. We do so by following the DRAW command (on the same line) by the list of transformation commands, separated by commas. An implied PUSH and POP encloses the transformation list and DRAW. Our cube scene now looks like

```
PERS FOV, ZN, ZF
TRAN XSCR, YSCR, ZSCR
ROT BACK, 1
ROT SPIN, 3
SCAL 1, 1, -1
DRAW GPLANE
DRAW CUBE, TRAN,X1,Y1,Z1, ROT,ANG,3
DRAW CUBE, SCAL,.3,.4,.5, TRAN,-5,-3.8,Z1
```

Subassembly Definitions

These are essentially subroutines. A subassembly is declared and named by bracketing its contents by the commands

```
DEF name
    :

any commands
    :
----
```

Once defined, a subassembly can be thought of as just another primitive. In fact, the "designer" of a list of commands should not know or care if the thing they are drawing is a primitive or a subassembly, so a subassembly is "called" by the same command as a primitive.

```
DRAW assy_name
```

The subassembly calling and return process is completely independent of the matrix stack PUSH and POP process. Interpretation of commands begins at the built-in name WORLD.

I typically organize my definitions so that WORLD contains only the *viewing transformation*, i.e., its rotations and transformations tell where the "camera" is and in which direction it is looking. My favorite all-purpose viewing transform is

```
DEF WORLD
PERS FOV, ZN, ZF
TRAN XSCR, YSCR, ZSCR
ROT BACK, 1
ROT SPIN, 3
ROT TILT, 1
TRAN -XLOOK, -YLOOK, -ZLOOK
SCAL 1, 1, -1
DRAW SCENE
----
```

The variables XLOOK, YLOOK, and ZLOOK determine the "look-at" point. BACK, SPIN, and TILT tumble the scene about this point. Then XSCR, YSCR, and ZSCR position the "look-at" point on the screen. XSCR and YSCR might very well be zero, but ZSCR needs to be some positive distance to move the scene away from the eye.

The assembly SCENE contains the contents of the scene and can be designed independently of how it is being viewed. Our cube scene again:

```
DEF SCENE
DRAW GPLANE
DRAW CUBE, TRAN,X1,Y1,Z1, ROT,ANG,3
DRAW CUBE, SCAL,.3,.4,.5, TRAN,-5,-3.8,Z1
----
```

Index